CONFRONTING CRIME

CONFRONTING CRIME

AN AMERICAN CHALLENGE

ELLIOTT CURRIE

PANTHEON BOOKS

New York

All rights reserved under International and Pan-American Copyright Conventions. Published in the United States by Pantheon Books, a division of Random House, Inc., New York, and simultaneously in Canada by Random House of Canada Limited, Toronto.

Library of Congress Cataloging-in-Publication Data
Currie, Elliott.
  Confronting crime.
  Includes bibliographical notes and index.
  1. Crimes and criminals—United States.
2. Criminal justice, Administration of—United States.
3. Violent crimes—United States—Prevention. I. Title.
HV6789.C87 1985 364'.973 85-6300
ISBN 0-394-53219-8

Manufactured in the United States of America

Designed by Robert Bull

First Edition

CONTENTS

Acknowledgments   vii

1   RETHINKING CRIMINAL VIOLENCE   3

2   THE CONSERVATIVE MODEL   21

3   THE LIMITS OF IMPRISONMENT   51

4   UNDERSTANDING CRIME:
    WORK AND WELFARE   103

5   UNDERSTANDING CRIME:
    INEQUALITY AND COMMUNITY   143

6   UNDERSTANDING CRIME:
    FAMILIES AND CHILDREN   181

7   NEW DIRECTIONS   223

    Notes   279

    Index   317

ACKNOWLEDGMENTS

Most books about social questions are, to a much greater extent than is usually recognized, the products of collective effort. This one is no exception. I've been especially fortunate in the amount of encouragement, advice, and good-natured criticism I've received from the start; here, unfortunately, I can only begin to list those whose contributions have been most important.

This book grew out of a two-part series of articles written for *Working Papers* magazine in 1982. Robert Kuttner, then the magazine's editor, gave his strongest encouragement from the beginning, meanwhile helping immeasurably to strengthen the arguments with a firm but supportive editorial hand. To him—and to *Working Papers* itself, a much-missed forum for serious writing on social policy—I owe a great debt. These articles were partly supported by a grant from the Democracy Project, for which I thank the project and its director, Mark Green.

I can't possibly mention all of those whose timely encouragement emboldened me to take on the much more formidable job of turning two brief articles into a book; but special thanks to some whose support, in various ways and various times, was especially crucial: John Brockman, Lynn Curtis, Fred DuBow, Dave Fogarty, Diana Gordon, Katinka Matson, Ilene Philipson, and Tom Wicker. The manuscript itself received unusually thoughtful comments from Paul Chevigny, Robert Dunn, Diana Gordon, Terry Kandal, and Jerome H. Skolnick. I deeply appreciate their counsel and suggestions, even where I've recklessly disregarded them.

Much of this book, and the articles that preceded it, took shape when I was a Visiting Scholar at the Center for Study of

Law and Society at the University of California, Berkeley. My thanks to the center's then-director, Jerome H. Skolnick, and administrator, Rod Watanabe, for their assistance and support.

Readers rarely appreciate the extent to which the book they hold in their hands doesn't simply spring forth from the brow of its author—but is the product of a rich collaboration between author and editors. Again, I've been particularly fortunate. This book has benefited enormously from the careful, committed, and spirited editorial attention of Sara Bershtel at Pantheon Books, who turned what can be a grueling experience of rethinking and rewriting into a challenging and downright enjoyable experience. Special thanks, too, to others at Pantheon—including David Frederickson and David Sternbach—whose efforts have helped make this a better book.

And thanks, most of all, to Rachael Peltz and Susannah Currie, for putting up with my author's preoccupation and for making my life infinitely richer in spite of it.

—E.C.

CONFRONTING CRIME

1

RETHINKING CRIMINAL VIOLENCE

This book is about why there is so much crime in America and what we can do about it. No one living in a major American city needs much convincing that despite more than a decade of ever-"tougher" policies against crime, the United States remains wracked by violence and fear. Criminal violence is woven deeply into our social fabric—a brutal and appalling affront to any reasonable conception of civilized social life.

In recent months, these incidents took place in the United States: In Illinois, armed marauders attacked travelers on an interstate highway, robbing the occupants of two cars and killing a twelve-year-old boy. In Florida, a passing motorist's intervention barely saved a young woman from attack by a crowd of nearly a hundred men. In New York, gangs of youths robbed and beat participants in a charity walkathon in Central Park. In Fort Lauderdale, Florida, a bandit held up an entire church congregation during an evening service. Not far away, near Pompano Beach, two intrepid men broke *into* a prison and robbed two inmates. A United States senator and his companion, on their way to dinner with the mayor of New York, were mugged by two men just down the street from the mayor's mansion. In Los Angeles, eleven people died in a single weekend in episodes of youth-gang violence, while the home of the chief of the Los Angeles Police Department was burglarized—twice.

The public response to criminal violence has become correspondingly bitter and even desperate. Three-fifths of the American public expressed their support for a self-styled vigilante who shot down four young black men after they asked him for five dollars in a New York subway; respected commentators urge people living in cities to "adopt the tough attitudes of an embattled population."

To live in the urban United States in the 1980s is to feel that the elementary bonds of society are badly frayed. The sense of social disintegration is so pervasive that it is easy to forget that things are not the same elsewhere. Violence on the American level comes to seem like a fact of life, an inevitable feature of modern society. It is not. Most of us are aware that we are worse off, in this respect, than other advanced industrial countries. How *much* worse, however, is truly startling.

Criminal statistics are notoriously tricky, and comparisons of one country's statistics with another's even more so. But the differences in national crime rates—at least for serious crimes of violence, which we rightly fear the most—are large enough to transcend the limitations of the data. In recent years, Americans have faced roughly seven to ten times the risk of death by homicide as the residents of most European countries and Japan. Our closest European competitor in homicide rates is Finland, and we murder one another at more than three times the rate the Finns do.

These differences are sometimes explained as the result of America's "frontier" ethos or its abundance of firearms. Both of these are important, but neither even begins to explain the dimensions of these international differences. With similar frontier traditions, Australia and Canada have murder rates that are, respectively, less than a fourth and less than a third of ours. Though their numbers are roughly the same, Californians are murdered almost six times as often as Canadians. Nor does this simply reflect the relative ease with which Americans can obtain handguns: more Californians are killed with knives alone than Canadians are by *all* means put together. And Canada ranks fairly high, internationally, in homicide rates.

What holds for homicide also holds for other serious crimes of violence. Here the comparisons are more chancy, because of greater problems of definition and measurement. But careful research reveals that Americans are more than three times as likely to be raped than West Germans, and six times as likely to be robbed. These rates were derived from police statistics, which are known to be subject to strong biases. But similar results come from "victimization" studies, which calculate crime rates by asking people whether, and how often, they have been the victims of crime.

In the first English study of this kind, the British Home Office (using a sample of eleven thousand respondents) estimated that the British robbery rate in 1981 was about twenty for every ten thousand people over age sixteen in 1981. In the same year, a comparable American survey by the Bureau of Justice Statistics estimated a robbery rate nearly four times higher. The British study turned up not one rape and only a single attempted rape: the American survey estimated an overall rape rate of about ten per ten thousand (three completed, seven attempted). And Britain is by no means one of the most tranquil of European countries: rates of serious criminal violence in Denmark, Norway, Switzerland, and the Netherlands are lower still.

In the severity of its crime rates, the United States more closely resembles some of the most volatile countries of the Third World than other developed Western societies; and we won't begin to understand the problem of criminal violence in the United States without taking that stark difference as our point of departure. Its consequences are enormous. If we were blessed with the moderately low homicide rate of Sweden, we would suffer well under three thousand homicide deaths a year, thereby saving close to sixteen thousand American lives—nearly three times as many as were lost in battle annually, on average, during the height of the Vietnam War.

The magnitude of the contrast between the United States and most other developed societies is often ignored as we scrutinize the fluctuations in our own crime rates from year to year. We watch the state of the public safety, like that of the economy, with a kind of desperate hopefulness. Just as the economy has "recovered" several times in recent years, so we have periodically "turned the corner on crime." And indeed, by the mid-1980s, the level of violent crime had fallen off from the disastrous peak it had reached at the start of the decade. That respite was certainly welcome; but it should not obscure the more troubling general upward trend since the sixties. From 1969 through 1983, the rate of violent crime—as measured by police reports—rose nationwide by 61 percent. Rape went up 82 percent, robbery 44 percent, and homicide 14 percent (the first two figures are almost certainly inflated because of changes in reporting, the third probably not). Measured this way, the more recent declines have only returned us to the already horrendous levels of the late 1970s, just before we suffered one of the sharpest *increases* in criminal violence in American history. Still more disturbingly, reported rapes and aggravated assaults *rose* again in 1984—at the fastest pace since 1980. Criminal victimization surveys offer a somewhat different but scarcely more encouraging picture, indicating virtually no change in crimes of violence for the past decade, with a slight decline in many violent crimes in 1983—but a slight *rise* in others in 1984.

The recent dip in crime, moreover, has been ominously uneven. Between 1982 and 1983, the murder rate in the economically depressed states of Illinois and Michigan rose by 10 percent; reported rapes shot up by 20 percent in Michigan and 27 percent in Wisconsin. Detroit's murder rate jumped 17 percent from 1981 to 1983; that of East St. Louis, Illinois, by an astonishing 96 percent. Drug-related gang wars helped boost the homicide rate in Oakland, California, by 17 percent between 1983 and 1984. The national crime rate, in short, may have improved—but the situation in some of America's inner cities was worsening.

What makes all this so troubling is that our high crime rates have resisted the most extraordinary efforts to reduce them. Since 1973, we have more than doubled the national incarceration rate—the proportion of the population locked up in state and federal prisons and in local jails. By 1983, the prison inmates alone would have filled a city the size of Atlanta, Georgia; including the inmates of local jails (a number that jumped by more than a *third* between 1978 and 1982 alone) would have swollen the "city" to the size of Washington, D.C. And this number doesn't include those confined in juvenile detention facilities, military prisons, and psychiatric facilities for the criminally insane.

Nor is this all. We have not only put a record number of offenders behind bars; we have also drastically changed our daily behavior and escalated the level of social resources we devote to defending ourselves against crime. In 1969, the National Commission on the Causes and Prevention of Violence made a gloomy prediction of what urban life would be like if America did not take immediate and fundamental measures to attack the root causes of crime. Central business districts would be surrounded by zones of "accelerated deterioration," largely deserted at night except for police patrols. The affluent would huddle together in what the commission called "fortified cells," high-rise apartment houses and residential compounds protected by increasingly elaborate security devices and private guards. Homes would be "fortified by an array of devices from window grilles to electronic surveillance equipment," and the affluent would speed from these fortified homes to their fortified offices along heavily patrolled expressways that the commission, in a revealingly military euphemism, called "sanitized corridors." People with business in the central cities would require access to indoor garages or valet parking; schools and other public facilities would be patrolled by armed guards. The ghetto slums would be "places of terror" that might be out of police control altogether after dark.

The commission, writing in a more hopeful time, found this prospect of a society in which the haves were forced to defend themselves ever more vigilantly against the have-nots foreign to the American experience and abhorrent to American values. Yet what is striking is that, in the eighties, much of the commission's indignant vision seems almost old-hat. Most of the changes they feared have taken place, and though their scenario doesn't accurately describe *every* American city, it does describe many. Virtually every big-city police department now possesses a sophisticated armory—from the ubiquitous police helicopter to the armored personnel carrier recently acquired by the Los Angeles police. More generally, we have changed the way we live and go about our daily business in ways that would have seemed appalling and unacceptable in the sunnier sixties. In 1984, a New York Appellate Court justice, speaking for an association of judges calling for still more severe prison sentences in that state, declared that the climate of fear suffusing New York "would have been unthinkable" a generation before. "If then someone had said that in 1984 hundreds of thousands of apartment windows in New York City would be covered with metal gates," said Justice Francis T. Murphy, Jr., "and that private security guards would patrol the lobbies, hallways, and rooftops of apartment buildings, we would have thought him insane." Like the unprecedented increase in incarceration, this new defensiveness might have been expected to do something substantial about the crime rate. With the possible exception of declines in burglary resulting from more elaborate "hardware," it did not.

Our devastating levels of criminal violence, moreover, have also proved to be remarkably resistant to the effects of a benign demographic change. The frightening rise in violent crime in the late 1970s and early 1980s came just when the most volatile segment of the population—young adult and teenaged men—was growing smaller relative to the population as a whole. Between 1975 and 1982, the proportion of young men aged fourteen to twenty-one in the population fell by 10 percent. Other things being equal, as many criminologists argued, this should have brought down the crime rate. But other things weren't equal, for though the decline in the youth population may have kept the crime rate lower than it would have been otherwise, other forces were clearly keeping it up.

What progress we've made against our uniquely high crime rate seems disturbingly small given our massive attempts to control it. The disparity between effort and results tells us that something is clearly wrong with the way we have approached the problem of violent crime in America, and few are happy with the results. But there is no consensus on how we might do better.

To be sure, there is no lack of prescriptions, ranging from the merely silly to the bizarre and the brutal. Within the last few years, some established scholars have solemnly proposed that we "restore" regular corporal punishment in the schools and home; others, that we revive the practice of sending criminals to penal colonies, perhaps on distant islands. Some have urged that we devise elaborate physiological tests to weed out those children who, on the basis of irregular encephalograms or insufficiently sweaty palms, seem likely to be the robbers and killers of the future. Others wistfully hope for a revival of the movements of temperance and "moral uplift" of the nineteenth century. Many of these proposals seem barely serious; some are a little frightening. All of them reflect a sense of social and intellectual desperation.

More often, our social policies toward crime and punishment have simply lost a sense of direction or definable vision. In a 1981 cover story, *Newsweek* deplored what it described as an "epidemic" of violent crime, but also declared that we were apparently helpless to deal with it. We had lost, the magazine lamented, "the old optimism proclaiming that we know what the problems are and that we have the solutions at hand." For the indefinite future, we would have to learn not to "expect too much." In the same year, the Reagan administration's Task Force on Violent Crime, departing sharply from a long line of more ambitious commissions, refused even to take on the task of investigating the causes of crime in America, on the ground that intervention at that level wasn't the government's job. "We are not convinced," they wrote, "that a government, by the invention of new programs or the management of existing institutions, can by itself recreate those familial and neighborhood conditions, those social opportunities, and those personal values that in all likelihood are the prerequisites of tranquil communities." The passivity that began to infect scholarly thinking about crime during the seventies had become enshrined as a fundamental principle of government policy.

How did we arrive at this impasse?

As with many other issues of social policy in the eighties, there is a pervasive sense that older ways of thinking about crime have lost their usefulness and credibility; but no convincing alternatives have come forward to take their place. It is painfully apparent that the decade-long conservative experiment in crime control has failed to live up to its promises. That experiment, launched with high hopes and much self-righteous certainty, was based on the alluringly simple premise that crime was pervasive in the United States because we were too lenient with criminals; in the economic jargon fashionable during the seventies, the "costs" of crime had fallen too low. The reverse side of the argument was that other ways of dealing with crime—through "rehabilitating" offenders or improving social conditions—at best didn't work and at worst had made the streets more dangerous. But the policies that resulted from these premises have left us with both the world's highest rate of incarceration for "street" crimes *and* the highest levels of criminal violence outside of some developing countries. We have created an overstuffed and volatile penal system of overwhelming barbarity, yet we endure levels of violence significantly higher than in the more "permissive" sixties.

To be sure, it is likely that some part of the recent dip in the crime rate is a result of the huge increases in incarceration in the past several years; after all, it would be remarkable if they had had *no* effect on crime. But the hard fact is that violent crime is worse in America today than before the "prison boom" of the seventies and eighties began, and indeed was highest just when our rate of incarceration was increasing the fastest. At best, very little has been accomplished, at great social cost. To borrow a medical analogy, it's plausible to argue that a series of drastic and unpleasant treatments has relieved some of the symptoms of the disease; it is not plausible to argue that the patient is well, or even demonstrably recovering. And as we shall see, there is little ground for hope that the same strategies can accomplish much more in the future, short of draconian measures on a scale that would transform our criminal-justice system—and American society as a whole—beyond recognition.

It could, of course, be argued that this strategy *would* have worked, if it had only gone far enough—but that it was undermined by the leniency and obstinacy of officials and the public, especially the unwillingness of legislators to vote for more prisons. If the streets are still unsafe despite the swelling of the prisons, blame it on the failure to build enough new prison cells and the consequent vacillation of judges hesitant to pack still more criminals into the time-bombs that our prisons have mainly become. In 1984, for example, the Federation of New York Judges declared that the streets had become "lawless marches of robbers, rapists, and felons of every kind," and called for more prisons, on the ground that "swift and severe punishment is the only defense against predators." Appellate Justice Murphy even went so far as to argue that without a greater investment in punishment "we will live in the sickly twilight of a soulless people too weak to drive predators out of their own house." Justice Murphy and his colleagues were apparently unfazed by the fact that criminals had "taken the city" despite the doubling of New York's incarceration rate during the previous decade.

So proponents of this "get-even-tougher" approach are confronted with a formidable job of persuasion. It is difficult to think of any social experiment in recent years whose central ideas have been so thoroughly and consistently carried out. The number of people we have put behind bars, for ever-longer terms, is unprecedented in American history. And unlike most such experiments, which are usually undertaken with minimal funding and on a limited scale, this one has been both massively financed and carried out on a grand scale in nearly every state of the union. If it has failed to work in the way its promoters expected, they have fewer excuses than most applied social theorists.

We have become a country in which it is possible to be sentenced to a year behind bars for stealing six dollars' worth of meat from a supermarket, but we are still by far the most dangerous society in the developed world. That paradox has deeply undercut the credibility of the conservative strategy of crime control in the eighties. No one today seriously disagrees that we need a strong and effective criminal-justice system; that is no longer a matter for real debate. But that is a far cry from believing that we can rely on the prisons to solve the crime problem. Clearly, we need more creative approaches to crime—and we need them urgently.

But I do not think that the earlier perspective, which for want of a more precise term I will call "liberal criminology," can, by itself, offer a sufficiently compelling alternative. It is risky to generalize about that perspective, because it included several diverse—and not always compatible—lines of thought and practice. But there were common themes. Most liberal criminology linked crime to the pressures of social and economic inequality and deprivation, and assumed that a combination of rehabilitation for offenders, better opportunities for the disadvantaged, and a more humane, less intrusive criminal-justice system would reduce crime, if not end it. By the end of the sixties, that vision was a shambles, undermined by the apparent "paradox" of rising crime rates in the face of the Great Society's social programs, the general improvement in the American standard of living, and the reduction of unemployment. Conservatives made much of the fact that American society seemed to be becoming more dangerous just when it was also becoming both more affluent and more committed to action against poverty, inequality, and racial subordination.

That "paradox," as I'll argue in some detail in a later chapter, was highly exaggerated. And indeed, the vision of the liberal criminology of the sixties has been unfairly maligned and often misunderstood. Much of what it had to say about the roots of crime and about the potentials of the criminal-justice system remains both remarkably fresh and, more important, correct. It rested on several crucial perceptions that have stood up well under the test of time and experience. One was that crime could not be dealt with through the criminal-justice system alone, and that the system is likely to crack if we load it with that burden. Another was that if we wanted to deal with crime in America in other than marginal ways, we would have to move beyond the level of merely patching up, punishing, or quarantining individuals who had gone wrong to confront a range of deep and longstanding social and economic problems. Both of these principles fell out of fashion during the seventies, but both were right—and both must be a part of any credible analysis of crime in the future.

But the liberalism of the sixties had important limitations as well. At times, it seemed to say that crime wasn't really as much of a problem as the public naïvely thought it was—a position that won few friends outside the relatively tranquil preserves of the academic world. Most other Americans were afraid of crime, or enraged by it, and they had good reason to be. It didn't help to imply, as some liberal and radical criminologists did, that worrying overmuch about being mugged or raped was a sign of incipient racism or an authoritarian character. Likewise, it didn't help when liberals, pressed for answers to the problem of violent street crime, responded by insisting that the crimes of white-collar people and corporate executives were *also* costly and vicious. That was certainly true, but it simply sidestepped the question at hand.

More generally, liberals were often reluctant to acknowledge the depth and seriousness of the human damage that violent crime both caused and reflected. The brutality of some youth crime, for example, suggested that something was deeply wrong with the way some children were being brought up in America. But liberal criminologists sometimes argued that any concern with the family life of delinquents was an expression of middle-class bias. The ferocity of urban crime likewise underscored the need for more intensive approaches to the problems of violent offenders than the minimal efforts typically offered as "rehabilitation." But some liberal criminologists instead adopted an extreme posture of "nonintervention": the less we did with criminals, the better.

There were good reasons for this position. A great deal of abusive and inhumane treatment had been meted out under the guise of rehabilitation, much of it cloaked in high-sounding language and humane intentions. And most students of crime believed—rightly, as I'll show in Chapter 3—that the experience of being processed through the courts and prisons, even if it was done in the name of rehabilitation, often made criminals worse rather than better, particularly if they were young and relatively unspoiled when they first encountered the criminal-justice system.

The noninterventionist approach led to many overdue reforms designed to get less dangerous offenders out of the justice system, and especially out of closed penal institutions. But noninterventionists sometimes went too far. In particular, they were often vague about what should be done about serious crimes of violence and the more hardened or disturbed people who committed them. A hands-off attitude was justifiable when applied to juvenile runaways or marijuana smokers, but less than adequate as an approach to armed robbers or repeat rapists.

At the same time, other liberals adopted the quite different view that crime, like many other social problems, could best be attacked through the twin mechanisms of big money and high technology. There is nothing wrong with spending money to solve social problems, and I think it is naïve to believe that we can affect crime very much without spending any. But some liberal criminologists simply opted for throwing money at the criminal-justice system on the one hand and at the inner cities on the other, in a kind of scattershot approach that sometimes substituted for hard thinking.

Thus, in 1969, the National Commission on the Causes and Prevention of Violence proposed that we "double our investment" in the criminal-justice system, but it was remarkably un-specific about what the money would be spent for, and equally unclear about how that proposal fit with its several hundred pages of analysis of the roots of violence in America. For nothing in that analysis really supported the idea that the problem existed because the justice system was starved for money.

This was one illustration of a bigger problem. The liberal criminology of the sixties was often long on ameliorative rhetoric but short on more concrete ideas for social action—especially ones that were clearly linked with its theoretical understanding of the causes of crime. The President's Commission on Law Enforcement and the Administration of Justice set the rhetorical tone of the Great Society's anticrime efforts in 1967 when it declared, in a much-quoted passage, that "warring on poverty and inadequate housing" was "warring on crime," that money for schools was money against crime, that "every effort to improve life in America's inner cities is an effort against crime." Although this was a worthy sentiment and not a bad starting-place for social policy, it was also quite vague. Would *every* effort to improve life in the inner cities be equally helpful in reducing crime? And which of the many possible measures we might use to "war" on the inner city's problems—higher welfare benefits, community economic development, summer jobs for kids—would bring the biggest payoff in the fight against crime? Like much liberal urban policy at the time, the commission's approach put most of its stock in fiscal solutions to the cities' problems. But was there really much evidence that money for public housing would by itself reduce crime? And were we so certain that the *main* prob-lem with the urban schools was sheer lack of money—or that we knew exactly what we would spend the money *for*?

The failure of liberal criminology to follow through on some of its most important perceptions gave it an oddly disjointed character, for its programs were frequently at odds with its the-ory. A fundamental liberal theme, for example, was that eco-nomic inequality and stunted opportunities were fertile breeding grounds for serious crime. Yet with few exceptions, most liberal anticrime programs did not directly address those problems. In-stead, they tried to equip individuals to make better use of the limited opportunities already available to them. They were designed to increase what economists call the "human capital" of high-risk people, through job training, vocational counseling, and remedial education. These programs were often worthwhile; but they fit uneasily with theories whose central point was that there were not enough jobs for all of the poor at respectable wages. Confronting the problem of creating jobs, of course, is much more difficult than funding another program to increase the "employability" of ghetto teenagers. But by avoiding that issue, liberal anticrime programs often got the not entirely undeserved reputation of being token responses to tough problems that cried out for deeper intervention.

The same confusion undermined the liberal commitment to the "rehabilitation" of offenders. That commitment was, for the most part, principled and humane, and it originated in a sense of social responsibility that was far more civilized than the glorification of punishment for its own sake that has dominated public policy in more recent years. But liberal practice failed to carry its understanding of crime to its logical conclusions—and, in the process, helped undercut the credibility of the idea of rehabilitation itself. If, as most liberal criminologists believed, crime was ultimately a *social* problem rooted in economic and racial disadvantage and the erosion of communal and familial institutions, the rehabilitation of individual offenders, even if it was successful in the short term, was sure to be overwhelmed if they were simply returned to the deprived and shattered communities from which they had come. But instead of insisting that rehabilitation couldn't work well unless it was firmly linked to larger social interventions, many liberals simply adopted the staple conservative platitude that rehabilitation didn't work. This default encouraged the sense that there were no practical alternatives to simply warehousing offenders in the prisons, and helped speed the demise of both the rehabilitative impulse and the social vision that lay behind it.

If we are to build a society that is less dangerous, less fearful, and less torn by violence, we will have to move beyond *both* perspectives—liberal and conservative. Can we do so? I think we can, and in this book I hope to show how that might be done.

The chapters that follow fall roughly into two parts. The first examines the theory and practice of the anticrime strategy we have been haplessly pursuing for a decade and more, and argues that its disappointing results are due to the most basic of reasons: its premises have been wrong from the start. The second part takes on a tougher and more complicated question: whether, given the failure of our current strategy, there are credible alternatives. I think there are, and in those chapters I will offer my evidence for that optimistic position.

Let me note here, however, what I will *not* try to do. First of all, this book is not a comprehensive treatise on the causes of crime in general or the workings of the criminal-justice system. I won't have much to say about white-collar crime, for example: for despite its importance, it is sufficiently different from the problem of ordinary criminal violence to require separate treatment. Nor will I address equally important reforms designed to make the police or courts fairer or more efficient, unless they clearly possess the potential for reducing crime. Finally, this book is about *serious* crime, and especially serious criminal violence. Much that is illegal isn't very serious; though various kinds of juvenile misbehavior and minor drug use, for example, raise important social issues in their own right, they are not problems on the level of robbery, rape, and murder. Nor is there convincing evidence that the two levels of lawbreaking are rooted in the same social conditions or would respond to the same remedies.

My approach in this book is bound to disappoint both those who believe that nothing much can be done about serious crime and those who hunger for immediate solutions. Both views are deeply embedded in the public culture in America; but both are terribly misleading. We will not eliminate criminal violence from American life overnight; but there is much we can do to reduce it. Doing so, however, will require hard choices and a serious commitment of social and economic resources. In a society traditionally drawn to the quick fix, many people, at all points on the political spectrum, want to know what will stop crime next month, and are impatient with the idea that we are in for a long haul. But the hard truth is that there are no magic buttons to push, no program waiting just around the corner to reform the courts or strengthen the police or organize the neighborhood that will make criminal violence disappear tomorrow. There are, however, steps we can take now that can begin to make a difference in the safety of our streets and homes—and to reverse the tragic waste of lives that criminal violence involves.

Many of those steps are based on evidence that has been available for years. It was often said during the seventies that we knew very little about the causes of crime. That was not true then, and it is even less true now, after several more years of research and experience. We do not know as much as we would like, but we are not groping in the dark, either. To agree that more research needs to be done is not the same as saying that we don't know enough to start.

If we know as much about crime as I think we do, why haven't we already acted on that knowledge more consistently and more constructively? Part of the answer has to do with the relative obscurity of much of the best and most serious research and writing in criminology. It is scattered through several social science disciplines whose practitioners sometimes have trouble communicating with each other, let alone with a wider audience; it is frequently buried in specialized journals and, especially in the last several years, often couched in numbing jargon and a forbiddingly arcane and mathematical style. It isn't often that anyone tries to make this material accessible or understandable beyond limited academic and professional circles. The result is that policies toward crime are often created in a near-vacuum.

Another reason for inaction is the tendency to compartmentalize social problems along bureaucratic lines. We take it for granted that it is the business of the criminal-justice system to deal with crime, but someone else's to deal with the social, economic, or familial problems that foster it. As a result, the more important causes of crime are nearly always regarded as someone else's problem. Policy-makers rarely consider how their decisions may increase the risks of criminal violence, whether the decisions involve shutting down a factory, tightening the money supply to slow the economy, eliminating jobs through technological change, or cutting off funds for family planning. All of these actions may affect the crime rate; but it is nevertheless unthinkingly assumed that crime should be exclusively the province of police, lawyers, and judges, who are rarely in a position to influence those decisions. The failure to make these necessary connections between causes and consequences stifles the development of intelligent policies to prevent criminal violence, and burdens the criminal-justice system with the impossible job of picking up the pieces after broader social policies have done their damage.

But there is another, still more important reason for our failure to come to grips with criminal violence. It is not lack of knowledge or technical prowess that keeps us from launching an honest and serious fight against crime; the obstacles are much more often ideological and political. What seem on the surface to be technical arguments about what we can and cannot do about crime often turn out, on closer inspection, to be moral or political arguments about what we should or should not do; and these in turn are rooted in larger disagreements about what sort of society we want for ourselves and our children. If we are serious about rethinking the problem of crime, we need to engage the issues on that higher level of moral and political values. It is always easier, as R. H. Tawney once observed, to "set up a new department, and appoint new officials, and invent a new name to express their resolution" to do things differently. "But unless they will take the pains," Tawney cautioned, "not only to act, but to reflect, they end by effecting nothing."

All societies suffer from predatory and brutal behavior. But not many of them—and no other advanced industrial societies (except perhaps South Africa, a revealing but not inspiring example)—suffer it to the extent we do in America. This tells us that the unusual dangerousness of American life is not simply the result of fate or of human nature, but of forces which, within broad limits, are subject to social action and control. We have the level of criminal violence we do because we have arranged our social and economic life in certain ways rather than others. The brutality and violence of American life are a signal—and a particularly compelling one—that there are profound social costs to maintaining those arrangements. But by the same token, altering them also has a price; and if we continue to tolerate the conditions that have made us the most violent of industrial societies, it is not because the problem is overwhelmingly mysterious or because we do not know what to do, but because we have decided that the benefits of changing those conditions aren't worth the costs.

Not all of those changes will be easy. To be sure, some of them are much less difficult than we have lately been led to believe. But others involve reversing institutional patterns whose origins lie far back in our history. I am not suggesting that this could be a simple task, but I hope to show that it is within our means to build a society that is less brutal, less fearful, and more cohesive. Whether we do so is up to us.

2

THE CONSERVATIVE MODEL

To understand why we've arrived at our present impasse in dealing with crime, we must first reconsider the assumptions that have guided the dominant policies on crime in America throughout the past decade. This means taking a hard look at the conservative argument about the causes of crime.

--------------- i ---------------

At first blush, that may seem a contradiction in terms: during the seventies, conservatives often ridiculed the very idea of searching for the causes of crime. James Q. Wilson took this stance to its most adamant extreme in his influential book, *Thinking About Crime.* To those who contended that crime could be dealt with only by attacking its root causes, Wilson said, he "was sometimes inclined, when in a testy mood, to rejoin: stupidity can only be dealt with by attacking its root causes. I have yet to see a root cause," he continued,

> or to encounter a government program that has successfully attacked it, at least with respect to those social problems that arise out of human volition rather than technological malfunction. But more importantly, the demand for causal solutions is, whether intended or not, a way of deferring any action and criticizing any policy. It is a cast of mind that inevitably detracts attention from those few things that government can do reasonably well and draws attention toward those many things it cannot do at all.

On closer inspection, however, it's clear that Wilson's statement confuses two quite different arguments. The first is that it makes no sense to talk about the social or "root" causes of crime at all, either because such causes do not exist or because no one knows what they are or how to find them. The second is an essentially political, rather than conceptual, argument—that government either cannot or should not intervene in the conditions that many criminologists had held to be root causes of crime. The first argument is difficult to take seriously (Professor Wilson, indeed, has recently abandoned it himself); after all, it is hardly possible to say anything very compelling about crime —or any other social problem—without working from some assumptions about why the problem exists. And, in fact, beneath their rhetoric about the futility of looking for the causes of crime, conservatives have offered at least the elements of a causal theory of their own.

That theory has never been carefully articulated, and it changes form with the writer. But it is always some variant of the idea that crime is caused by inadequate "control," that we have a great deal of crime because we have insufficient curbs on the appetites or impulses that naturally impel individuals toward criminal activity. Most conservative writers regard these lurking appetites as a fundamental part of "human nature." As Wilson put it in *Thinking About Crime*, a "sober" or "unflattering view of man" tells us that "wicked people exist" and that "nothing avails but to set them apart from innocent people." Several years later, President Ronald Reagan, in a similar vein, told a convention of police chiefs that "some men are prone to evil, and society has a right to be protected from them."

The difficulty with this as an explanation for crime is not exactly that it is untrue—but that, at this sweepingly general level, it is unhelpful. No one would deny that wicked people exist or that human beings have destructive and predatory impulses against which others must be protected. But such generalizations cannot help us understand why crime is so much worse at some times or places than others. Why are people in St. Louis so much more "prone to crime" than those in Stockholm or, for that matter, Milwaukee? Why are people in Houston not only far more likely to kill each other than people in London or Zurich, but also much more likely to do so today than they were twenty-five years ago?

Faced with these questions, the criminological Right has countered with a number of intellectual ploys. One is simply to ignore or deny the difference between our crime rates and those of other industrial societies. Thus, in *Thinking About Crime*, Wilson scorned the idea that crime was, as he put it, "an expression of the political rage of the dispossessed, rebelling under the iron heel of capitalist tyranny"; that this view was thoroughly misguided, he asserted, was proven in part by the fact that "virtually every nation in the world, capitalist, socialist, and communist, has experienced in recent years rapidly increasing crime rates."

One problem with this assertion is that, stated so flatly, it was simply untrue. Several capitalist countries, most notably Japan and Switzerland, did *not* experience rapidly rising crime rates in the sixties and seventies; and there was at least one socialist developing country, Cuba, whose rates of criminal violence fell rather dramatically. Moreover, although many other developed societies did suffer rising levels of crime in the sixties and seventies, the rises were primarily in property and drug offenses, not in violent crimes like homicide.* In the midseventies—just as Wilson was portraying *every* country as wracked by rapidly rising crime—it was still possible for two respected Scandinavian criminologists to conclude that the risks of victimization by criminal violence remained quite low in Denmark and Norway; indeed, the Danish and Norwegian homicide rates had been "fairly constant" for forty or fifty years.

An even more important difficulty with the Wilson argument is that the industrial countries whose rates of criminal violence did rise in the sixties and seventies usually began—and ended—at such low levels that to emphasize the similarities between those countries and the United States obscured the much more compelling and dramatic point—the scale of the differ-ences. After what Wilson and others described as nearly two

---

* Throughout this book, I will observe the standard American practice of defining homicide, forcible rape, robbery (theft with at least the threat of force), and assault as *violent* crimes. *Property* crimes include burglary and other forms of theft *not* involving force.

decades of unremitting increases in crime "throughout the world," by the late seventies (in per capita terms) about ten American men died by criminal violence for every Japanese, Austrian, West German, or Swedish man; about fifteen American men died for every Swiss or Englishman; and over twenty for every Dane. During the sixties and seventies, murder rates increased in some of those countries and didn't in others—but in none of them, when Wilson wrote, did they begin to approach those of the United States; nor do they today; nor are they likely to in the foreseeable future.

Obviously this stubborn reality causes tough problems for an argument that blames crime on a vaguely defined and immutable "human nature." Consider Wilson's remarks on the prospects for reducing robbery rates. "A sober view of man," he wrote in 1975, "requires a modest definition of progress. A 20 percent reduction in robbery would still leave us with the highest robbery rate of almost any Western nation but would prevent about sixty thousand robberies." The internal contradiction in Wilson's reasoning is painfully clear. The wide cross-national variations in crime to which he alludes completely undercut the explanatory power of a "sober view of man"—for "man" is presumably no worse in the United States than in Denmark or Switzerland. But the differences in robbery rates between these places are staggering.

In his more recent work, Wilson acknowledges that several factors—the effects of "real and imagined" racism, the "sharpening of consumer instincts through the mass media," the increased availability of handguns, and the abandonment of the inner city by "persons with a stake in impulse control," among others—may have a special impact on crime in America. Nevertheless, Wilson continues to insist on the curious argument that since the recent increase in crime "is not a peculiarly American phenomenon, but a feature of virtually every industrialized society," a "true understanding of crime depends on what these nations have in common, not what differentiates them." This remarkable conclusion allows Wilson to retain intact what turns out to be his central premise: that an "ethos of self-expression" common to most modern societies is the fundamental cause of the industrial world's crime problem. In the process, the uniqueness of the American situation simply drops out of sight.

. . .

The argument from human nature, then, is really too general to be of much help. A similarly unhelpful abstraction lies at the heart of the most systematic conservative theory of the causes of crime—what is called, I think misleadingly, the *economic model* of crime. There could, of course, be as many economic models of crime as there are economic theories, but in fact the conservative model is based on just one: the brand of neoclassical economics developed by the "Chicago School." In this model, whether a potential offender commits a crime or not is determined by calculated choice based on a rational weighing of the relative costs and benefits (or *utilities*) of committing the crime versus not doing so. In an early and often-quoted formulation, the University of Chicago economist Gary Becker argued that someone commits a crime

> if the expected utility to him exceeds the utility he could get by using his time and other resources at other activities. Some persons become "criminals," therefore, not because their basic motivation differs from that of other persons, but because their benefits and costs differ.

Similarly, the conservative economist Gordon Tullock wrote some years later, "If you increase the cost of committing a crime, there will be fewer crimes." Still more recently, the philosopher Ernest van den Haag put the same argument in terms of the "comparative net advantage" of crime over other activities. "The number of persons engaged in any activity, lawful or not," van den Haag writes, "depends on the comparative net advantage they expect."

> Thus, the number of practicing dentists, grocers, drug dealers, or burglars depends on the net advantage which these practitioners expect their occupations to yield compared to other occupations available to them.

Human behavior, criminal or otherwise, is assumed to be like any other exchange in the marketplace. Armed with this conveniently simplified view of human motivation, conservatives have generally blamed the crime rate on the lack of punishment—

crime is common because it's "cheap"—although they could just as plausibly argue that where crime rates are especially high, the "comparative net advantage" of lawful behavior must be particularly low. In practice, conservative criminology has concentrated on increasing the "cost" of crime; increasing the relative "benefits" of lawful activity has taken a distinctly subordinate place. To van den Haag, for example,

> our only hope for reducing the burgeoning crime rate lies in decreasing the expected net advantage of committing crimes (compared to lawful activities) by increasing the cost through increasing the expected severity of punishments and the probability of suffering them.

Van den Haag's emphatic rejection of the other side of the "cost-benefit" equation is hardly unique. As a group of researchers from New York's Vera Institute of Justice have pointed out in a careful review of the economic literature on crime and punishment, "one important cost—deterrence through the application of formal criminal sanctions (arrest, conviction, and punishment)—is emphasized by economists to the virtual exclusion of the role of other factors, such as incentives derived from improved employment opportunity." Given the practical difficulty of increasing arrest and conviction rates, partisans of the economic model have in effect placed most of their bets on increasing *punishment*—especially through longer and more frequent prison sentences.

This choice of strategy rests, in part, on a set of arguments about the inability of social policy to do much to boost the "benefit" side of the ledger. I'll come back to those arguments in later chapters. For the moment, though, we can focus on the merits of the "cost" argument itself. On the most abstract level, it certainly isn't unreasonable to believe that perceptions of "cost" have some weight in determining the course of individuals' behavior. But to make the basic argument stick as an explanation of *variations* in crime rates—why a particular country or period has more crime than others—it is necessary to go further: to show that the "costs" of crime are, in those instances, actually lower than in other times or places with less crime. To the extent that the criminological Right offers an explanation of American crime patterns vis-à-vis those of other countries (or other periods in our own history), it is that the costs of crime are peculiarly low here and, at least by implication, lower than in the past.

A recent *Wall Street Journal* editorial, for example, explained the rising crime rates of the late 1970s and early 1980s this way:

> The sharp increase of crime in many states has undoubtedly resulted from the absence of punishment. . . . As the certainty of punishment rises, prison populations will rise. But so will the cost of crime. If states stay on their present course, it is reasonable to expect that the present surge in prison populations will cease. There will be less crime and fewer people going to jail. If so, it will be worth the cost of correcting those years of neglect.

This view of the roots of America's crime problem would doubtless bring ready assent from most conservatives. But how well does the claim of an "absence of punishment" in recent years —and of a penal system crippled by "years of neglect"—fit the reality?

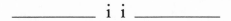

i i

There is a fundamental difficulty for the conservative argument: It is hard to maintain that our high rates of crime are caused by insufficient punishment when our penal system is one of the most punitive in the developed world. We lock up offenders at a far greater rate than any other advanced society (except the Soviet Union and South Africa—where the comparison is not wholly appropriate, since many prisoners are political offenders, not "street" criminals). At the beginning of the eighties, the incarceration rate in the United States was about 217 per 100,000.* At the opposite extreme, the Dutch rate was about 21 per 100,000. In between lay most of the rest of the world's industrial societies, many clustered toward the lower end of the scale: Japan's rate was 44 per 100,000, Norway's 45, Sweden's 55, West Germany's 60,

---

* The rate is higher now, but I'll use the earlier figure to make comparison with other countries possible.

Denmark's 63, France's 67, Great Britain's a relatively high 80 per 100,000.

In part, these low rates reflect some countries' use of prison as only a last resort, for the most dangerous offenders; in part they reflect a common practice of incarcerating criminals for relatively short periods. The latter is especially true in Holland, where the average time served in the late 1970s was an astonishing 1.3 months, versus about 5 months in Britain and about 16 in the United States. The shorter sentences are not simply a reflection of the less serious range of offenses in Holland; average sentences handed down for a given *class* of offenses also differ greatly. Thus the average maximum sentence for robbery was 150 months in the U.S. federal prisons and 68 months in the state prisons; in the Dutch prisons, it was 19 months.

Moreover, many Western European countries deliberately decreased their use of imprisonment during the sixties and seventies, while beginning in the seventies we moved relentlessly in the other direction. The average Dutch robbery sentence fell to 19 months in 1981 from 32 months in 1950; between 1951 and 1975, the Dutch prison population as a whole dropped by *half*.

Given these huge and growing disparities between our rates of imprisonment and those of otherwise comparable societies, how can anyone argue that our crime rate (as the *Wall Street Journal*'s editors put it) "has undoubtedly resulted from the absence of punishment"? One attempt to maintain the argument is to turn it on its head, and claim that given the severity of the American crime problem, we make relatively limited use of incarceration—so that the likelihood of punishment for convicted offenders is actually smaller here. Wilson, for example, draws an analogy with medical care; to claim that we "overimprison" people in the United States, he writes, "is like disproving the need for hospitals by saying that the United States already hospitalizes a larger fraction of its population than any other nation," for it "implies that we are sending people to prison without any regard to the number of crimes committed (or sending them to hospitals without regard to whether they are sick)." The "proper question," Wilson insists, is "whether we imprison a higher fraction of those arrested, prosecuted, and convicted than do other nations." His answer is that we do not.

There are two things wrong with Wilson's argument. To begin with, it is not at all clear why this is the "proper question." For if it is offered as an explanation of high crime rates in America, the argument is perilously close to circular, since it does not tell us why so many crimes are committed here in the first place. A closer look at the medical analogy reveals the logical problem. If one country already possesses more hospitals per capita than any other, but still produces more sickness, it is implausible to blame its comparative ill health on the relative lack of hospitals. To be sure, a country with a lot of illness will "need" many hospitals, just as a country with a lot of crime will "need" many prisons. But if we want to understand either why so many people are ill to begin with or how we could prevent these excessive levels of illness in the future, we will need to look at other aspects of the country—sanitation, nutrition, environmental hazards, perhaps even cultural values—or we will be fruitlessly building hospitals forever to accommodate the ever-increasing flow of the sick. The same logic ought to apply in the case of criminal justice. If we already imprison people at a higher rate than other countries, we cannot blame our own uniquely high crime rate on the underuse of imprisonment, without reasoning in a circle. If we want to understand why so many people here have become criminals, we will need to look at other factors that distinguish us from more fortunate countries.

But there is an even more immediate difficulty with Wilson's argument—its facts are wrong. Wilson's only source of evidence for his contention that the United States is relatively sparing in its use of prison is a 1978 study by the Yale economist Kenneth I. Wolpin. This analysis showed that in the 1960s—when American incarceration rates were much lower than they are today—the chance of imprisonment for convicted robbers was higher in England than in the United States (although the American sentences were more severe): between 1961 and 1967, a convicted robber's chance of going behind bars was 48 percent in England and 31 percent in the United States (for an average sentence of 2.9 years in England, 3.5 years in America).

On the surface, these figures lent some credence to the notion that the British might be "tougher" on robbers, if only in the sense of greater consistency, not severity, of punishment. The trouble is that Wolpin's analysis—as he pointed out himself in a later study—neglected to include in its estimates of incarceration rates the great numbers of convicted offenders sent to local *jails* in the United States—a crucial omission indeed, since including them in the calculations completely reversed the outcome.

Wolpin's later, more inclusive, study compared robbery in the United States (specifically California), England, and Japan. This time he found that convicted robbers were considerably *more* likely to go to prison or jail in the United States than in either England or Japan. Wolpin's study covered the years from 1955 to 1971—well before the prison "boom" of the seventies that doubled the American incarceration rate. But even then, a convicted robber had a 63 percent chance of going behind bars in California, versus 48 percent in England and 46 percent in Japan. English robbers, furthermore, spent only about half as much time behind bars as either Japanese or Californians. Meanwhile, according to official statistics, California's robbery rate averaged over seventeen times the British rate and over twenty-eight times the Japanese. Developments over time are also revealing. In all three countries, as Wolpin's later study showed, convicted robbers were *less* likely to go to prison at the end of the period than at the beginning. But this consistent decline in the "costs" of robbery had completely contradictory effects on robbery rates in the different countries: robbery increased in California and still more in England, but declined rather dramatically in Japan.

In short, contrary to Wilson's claims, we do indeed incarcerate more of those arrested and convicted than the British and Japanese—who, in turn, use incarceration more readily than, for example, the Swiss or the Dutch. Wolpin's studies do bring up an important distinction: the Japanese and the British *catch* criminals more often than we do, and generally convict them more frequently once caught. Why this should be so is a difficult and unresolved question, which I will take up again in the next chapter. Suffice it to say here that the difficulty in apprehending criminals has little to do with the *leniency* of American justice; and while the difficulty in convicting them once caught may have some relation to American court practices, the evidence indicates that any effects of this on the crime rate are quite small. The fundamental point at issue here remains: the United States is indeed the most punitive of advanced Western industrial societies toward those offenders brought to the stage of sentencing.

Moreover, we have become dramatically more punitive over time. If there ever were "years of neglect" in the punishment of criminals in America, they are long past. In the 1960s, those who believed that the "softness" of American justice was responsible for our crime rate had a more plausible case. In some places at least, we made less use of imprisonment than we had some years before. Our incarceration rates fell for several years, and didn't rise even as the crime rate began to in the sixties. In that context it was at least possible to argue that crime might be rising because criminals had it easier than before. But we have been steadily and massively increasing the "costs" of crime for many years.

The simplest measure of these changes is the national incarceration rate. In 1970 there were fewer than 200,000 inmates of state and federal prisons in the United States; by mid-1984, more than 450,000. Because the country's population grew during the same years, the change in the *rate* of incarceration is slightly smaller, but not much: about 96 of every 100,000 Americans were in a state or federal prison in 1970; in 1984, about 195 of every 100,000. (Note that these figures do not include the rising population in local jails. And in some states, the rise was even more rapid—South Carolina went from 105 per 100,000 in 1970 to 268 in 1982.)

It might be argued that these huge increases only reflected a desperate race to keep up with the crime rate—or to cope with a much more serious mix of criminals coming before the courts. But this is not the case. The rate of imprisonment was rising much faster than the crime rate; yet not only did the crime rate refuse to fall in some reasonably corresponding fashion, but at the end of the seventies it surged sharply—and by the logic of the conservative model, incomprehensibly—upward.

Let's focus on the experience of one state. In 1982, the Correctional Association of New York released a grim and devastating analysis of the results of that state's harsh penal policies of the seventies. The prison population had increased by 107 percent between 1971 and 1981—for prisoners convicted of felonies, by 121 percent. These increases did not simply reflect equally rapid increases in the crime rate; though serious crime did rise in the state, "the rate of increase was substantially lower than the corresponding growth in prison population." Nor did the growth in prison population reflect more vigorous law enforcement; arrest rates didn't change markedly.

Instead, the increases in the prison population represented a greater proportion of convicted felons going to prison—and staying longer when they went. In 1970, 35 percent of offenders convicted of felonies went to the state's prisons; by 1975, 50 percent did, and the proportion stayed at least at that level throughout the decade. The big increases came in robbery (from 49 percent in 1971 to 75 percent in 1979), rape (60 to 82 percent), drug offenses (24 to 50 percent), burglary (32 to 45 percent), and felonious assault (33 to 47 percent). Meanwhile, the proportion of newly sentenced prisoners with maximum sentences of more than five years doubled for burglary between 1974 and 1980, and increased by 28 percent for manslaughter, 26 percent for robbery, and 44 percent for assault. There were even bigger increases in *minimum* sentences: the proportion of inmates with minimum sentences of at least thirty-one months rose from 4 percent in 1970 to *31 percent* in 1980. (Remember the less-than-two-month average sentence in Holland?) This represented an especially severe crackdown on youthful criminals; in 1971, only 1 percent of offenders aged 16 to 20 received minimum sentences of thirty-one months or more; by 1980, 21 percent did—an increase of 2,000 percent.

Finally, as the Correctional Association pointed out, once imprisoned, New York's felony offenders were less likely to be released on parole. In 1972, the state granted parole to 69 percent of all inmates eligible for release; by 1981, the release rate had plummeted to just 42 percent.

What these increasingly harsh policies did to the state's prisons—in terms of severe overcrowding, diminished services, and heightened potential for violence—is graphically spelled out in the association's report. "The state's new policies," they concluded, "have been staggeringly expensive, have threatened a crisis of safety and manageability in the prison system, and have failed to reduce the rate of crime or even stop its increase." After almost ten years of "getting tough," the report concluded, "the citizens of New York are more likely to be victims of crime today than in 1971." Moreover, the largest rise in crime came at the end of the decade, during 1980–81, well *after* the introduction of more severe sentencing policies.

New York's experience is not unique. Most states sharply increased their use of imprisonment—thus boosting the "costs" of crime for those offenders they managed to apprehend—during the seventies and early eighties; meanwhile, their rates of serious crime went up, sometimes dramatically.

Consider Texas, always known for a tough penal policy, which raised the costs for convicted criminals with a vengeance during the seventies. In 1970, Texas already boasted the second-largest prison population of any state (after California). In 1981, having raised it from 14,000 to more than 31,000, Texas had won the dubious distinction of having the largest number of inmates of any state in the country. (At this writing, California has once more moved into the lead.) Meanwhile, depressingly, Texas's homicide rate rose by 41 percent. In Houston, hardly a model of weak law enforcement, the murder rate jumped by two-thirds between 1970 and 1982, giving the city one of the highest metropolitan homicide rates in the United States.

The same story could be repeated many times over in other states. But the point should be clear. It isn't credible to argue that the unprecedented crime rates of the late seventies and early eighties were caused by excessive leniency. Our criminal-justice system was not particularly lenient to begin with, and became markedly less so throughout the decade. To be sure, some criminals still get off more lightly than they should. Everyone has stories to tell of dangerous criminals who have slipped through the cracks of the justice system, sometimes with tragic consequences. These problems are real ones—and we are right to be concerned about them. But that concern should not obscure the comparative severity of American criminal justice as a whole or the dramatic increases in that severity in recent years.

———————— i i i ————————

Some conservatives, indeed, have come to recognize the limits of a strategy of increasing "costs," especially given the depressing results of a decade of getting "tough" with criminals. Yet this experience has not generally altered the underlying premises of the conservative argument—only shifted its ground. For most conservative writers, crime still represents a weakening of controls over what is solemnly regarded as an obdurate and fundamentally wicked human nature. The finger of blame points more often, these days, to a range of institutions outside the criminal-justice system—the schools, the family, and American culture as a whole, along with a wide gamut of liberal social policies and the malignant influence of "government." The central theme is still that our society is insufficiently punitive and controlling, especially of children and youth; that we allow too much easy gratification of the darker impulses and actively encourage a destructive "self-expression," instead of the virtues of sobriety, self-restraint, and the curbing of appetites. The institutions that ought to keep wayward impulses in line—and, according to this argument, once did—have lost much of their influence. This is usually blamed either on long-term shifts in the norms and values common to modern societies or on the naïveté (or malevolence) of the liberal shapers of contemporary opinion.

The evolution of James Q. Wilson's views reflects this change of emphasis. His *Thinking About Crime* was a fairly straightforward mid-seventies statement of the economic model of crime. We had "trifled with the wicked," Wilson thundered, and "encouraged the calculators." Even then, Wilson—unlike some of his less restrained colleagues—did not argue that we could expect *great* reductions in crime through increasing its "costs," but that was still the main policy recommendation in what was generally an admonition that we would have to "learn to live with crime." In his recent revision of the book, Wilson still insists that "deterrence works," but he has moved further away from believing that *much* can be accomplished by increasing penalties—and even less by improving "benefits." The deeper, more intractable sources of crime, Wilson now tells us, are the effects of "discordant homes, secularized churches, intimidated schools, and an ethos of self-expression." What has ultimately corroded social life in the United States during the twentieth century is the triumph of "self-expression over self-control as a core human value"; we have learned to "exalt rights over duties, spontaneity over loyalty, tolerance over conformity, and authenticity over convention."

This theme of insidious moral decline is familiar; it has been invoked to explain not just crime and delinquency but nearly everything the contemporary conservative finds wrong with American society—from the divorce rate and the decline in the growth of productivity to the much-lamented weakening of America's will to impose military solutions on a recalcitrant world. What should we make of it as an explanation for American crime rates?

Not much. The links between these broad cultural shifts and crime—particularly serious, violent street crime—are not at all evident, even if we accept Wilson's assessment of our recent moral decline. For one thing, as he himself makes clear, the moral and cultural changes that he says explain America's *current* crime problem began decades before our recent rises in crime; further-more, they don't correlate even remotely with the trends of seri-ous criminality in American history. Wilson's valiant attempt to maintain his position in the face of this disparity gives us one of the more tortuous discussions in recent criminological writing.

For Wilson, America's moral downfall can be traced back to the 1920s, when "we see the educated classes repudiating moral uplift as it had been practiced for the preceding century." A pervasive and, Wilson believes, largely effective nineteenth-cen-tury effort to control "self-indulgent impulses" was increasingly derided by the "educated elite" as narrow-minded, fundamental-ist, and provincial, and replaced by the "self-expression ethic." This transformation was facilitated by an imposing, if unusual, array of villains, including Freudian psychology, cultural an-thropology, and the women's magazines. Popular versions of Freudian theory proclaimed that "repressing one's instincts was bad, not good." Cultural anthropology further undermined the moral order of American society by promoting the view that "this culture was wrong, or at the very least no better than several competing cultural forms." Margaret Mead comes in for a special drubbing for having claimed that "the greater happiness of Sa-moans arose from their being granted greater sexual freedom and from being raised in more nurturant, less repressive families."

Granted, these changes are real, and Wilson is entitled to his jaundiced view of them. But what do they have to do with crime?

Wilson himself vacillates between acknowledging that he isn't sure they have anything at all to do with it, and speculating that these cultural and intellectual shifts somehow created a moral climate that must be held responsible, albeit forty years later, for the crime rates of the late sixties. One way they could have influenced crime, he suggests, is by prompting changes in child-rearing, which might "alter the behavior of the young by making them more daring and more impatient of restraints." Possibly; but as Wilson admits, "it is quite difficult to say much about the changes in child-rearing that occurred, and it is almost impossible to say anything about how these changes might have affected the behavior of the young." Then why should we continue this unpromising line of investigation? Because, Wilson insists, despite the lack of evidence, we can still say "something about" how elites *advised* mothers to bring up their children; and since the advice appeared in popular magazines, it reached a wide audience, whether in fact it influenced anyone or not. This advice shifted the aims of child-rearing away from the nineteenth-century emphasis on guarding the child from "evil within and evil without" —that is, from a view of the child as "endowed by nature with dangerous impulses that must be curbed"—to one in which the child was seen as equipped with "harmless instincts that ought to be developed."

Wilson's description of this literature is something of a caricature; in fact, it is hard to find child-rearing literature in this period that totally ignores discipline and supervision in the name of developing "harmless instincts." More crucially, it is difficult to detect any convincing chronological relationship between the cultural changes that did take place in the 1920s and the course of serious crime over the next sixty years. Wilson does not claim that the rise of an ethos of "self-expression" had any observable, direct connection with crime rates. Indeed, he concedes that "it is not clear that this shift in the dominant ethos of the social and intellectual elites had immediate and important practical consequences." After all, in the twenties and early thirties, criminal violence was high (a phenomenon often considered an unfortunate side effect of Prohibition, a program of "moral uplift" that Wilson apparently admires), but it was lower thereafter until its rise during the sixties. How then can we argue that the two are strongly and closely related—or explain why the new ethos skipped a generation before causing the crime of the sixties and seventies?

Wilson's answer has two parts. First, the deadly suffusion of the ethos of self-expression was "cut short" by the Great Depression. Youths in particular were forced by grim economic reality into hard work and "traditional" attitudes, and the crime rate went down. Though this is a vastly oversimplified rendering of what the evidence says about crime in the Depression (as I'll document in a later chapter), it isn't altogether far-fetched. But it wasn't grim economic reality that kept the crime rates low in the prosperous postwar period—precisely the years that witnessed both the emergence of the "youth culture" Wilson deplores and the spread of the child-centered approaches to upbringing whose pernicious impact he singles out for blame. An "explanation" contending that both good times and bad had similar restraining effects on the movement toward "self-expression" is not easily grasped; indeed, Wilson barely tries to make its logic clear to us.

The second half of the explanation for the delay of more than four decades between the onset of the disease of self-expression and the sudden, explosive manifestation of its symptom of criminal violence is that—as Wilson puts it—in the early years these cultural shifts affected only "elite," rather than "mass," attitudes. The hint here, never fully articulated, is that at some point, by some mechanism, destructive ideas about authenticity and self-expression filtered down from the avant-garde to a wider audience. In the sixties, apparently, this resulted from a "celebration of the youth culture in the marketplace, in the churches, and among adults." This "institutionalization in all parts of society of the natural desire of youth for greater freedom," Wilson suggests, "may well have given legitimacy to all forms of self-expression— including, alas, those forms that involve crime and violence."

Once again, this line of argument combines a blend of truisms with dizzying leaps of inference that, on close inspection, lack support. Wilson merges a common critique of the shenanigans of the sixties youth culture with another matter altogether: the serious criminality that wracked the United States in the late sixties and seventies. Certainly some of what went on in the name of self-expression and liberation was at best silly and at worst destructive and inhumane. No doubt there was a connection between these attitudes and a wide range of youthful behavior that violated the law, especially with regard to drugs and sex. But that isn't the issue. The crucial question is whether the ethos of "rights, not duties," a preference for "spontaneity over loyalty, conscience over honor, tolerance over conformity, self-expression over self-restraint," which animated the salons of the twenties and the campuses of the sixties, also accounts for the brutal violence in the streets and homes of the sixties, seventies, and eighties. And here the argument collapses.

It collapses partly because it makes the wrong prediction about where serious criminal violence takes place. "Elite" and intellectual communities are not where violent crime is common; in fact, they are usually remarkably free of it. Places like Madison or Ann Arbor, which led the campus counterculture in the sixties, maintained the low rates of serious crime that we rightly associate with communities of fairly affluent young people and professionals. The same is true of the urban and suburban concentrations of that "new class" that Wilson holds responsible for many of the social problems of the past twenty years. Wilson would probably counter that the real problem isn't that "elite" values lead to violence among the elite themselves, but that, in a wonderful parallel with supply-side economics, they "trickle down" to the lower orders, who promptly go out and put guns to people's heads.

I am not suggesting that cultural changes had nothing to do with the rising crime rate of the sixties. One such change in particular—the weakening of long-standing social norms justifying racial inequality—probably had an important influence. Although we have no hard quantitative measures, many careful observers at the time were convinced that this momentous change helped turn minority anger fueled by decades of injustice and deprivation outward against whites and their institutions. Some of that anger was expressed in formal protest, some in rebellion, and some in street crime—which may help explain the rising incidence of interracial robbery and of "stranger-to-stranger" crime generally in the sixties. But this is not the same as the vague argument that the values of "tolerance" and "authenticity" were what motivated the youth of the New Orleans or Detroit ghettos to inaugurate the rising curve of urban violence in the late sixties.

In fact, everything we know from social research about the values usually found in the social strata that produce most severely violent criminals tells us something very different. There, tolerance and individual expression, especially in child-rearing practices, are not encouraged, but more often, their opposite—conformity, constraint, and unquestioning obedience, sometimes enforced by violence. Obviously, parents' efforts to instill these values often fail. But that is very different from saying that young people from the ghettos and barrios of America's inner cities go astray because their parents have taught them bohemian values learned, at some distant remove, from the writings of elite, liberal intellectuals.*

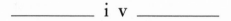

i v

In order to argue that the roots of our high crime rate lie in creeping attitudes of permissiveness, tolerance, and self-expression, conservatives must also be prepared to show that these

---

*Since this chapter was written—and unfortunately too late for an extended discussion here—Professor Wilson and the psychologist Richard Herrnstein have published a new book, on *Crime and Human Nature* (New York: Simon & Schuster, 1985). On the whole, the new work does not contain much that would change the assessment of Wilson's views I've drawn here. What makes this book different from most of Wilson's earlier writing is the prominent place it gives to "constitutional" factors in explaining crime. Wilson and Herrnstein are more restrained than some other commentators in their claims for the importance of genetic and biological factors in explaining the crime rate; but they are prepared to argue that "distributions of crime within and across societies may, to some extent, reflect underlying distributions of constitutional factors" (p. 88). We are not offered evidence for that suggestion—nor even an argument, however speculative, about why those concentrations of constitutional predispositions to crime should turn up when and where they do. Instead, that assertion—coupled with their continuing skepticism about the possibilities of reducing crime through intervention in the labor market or the larger community—seems invoked mainly to support the curiously passive stance toward the possibilities of concerted social action against the roots of crime that has characterized Wilson's work from the beginning. Indeed, Wilson and Herrnstein appear in this book to come close to abandoning the search for workable policies against criminal violence altogether; after more than 450 pages of analysis of research on the causes of crime, they are able to conclude only that their argument is not one "from which many (possibly any) clear policy recommendations can be deduced" (p. 460).

attitudes are more widespread here than in other countries. But there is no evidence to support this assumption—and much to contradict it.

It hardly seems likely that Americans take these attitudes farther than they have been taken in nations with much less serious crime—that, for instance, Dallas is a more "tolerant" city than Amsterdam, or that the values of conscience and self-actualization are more pervasive in Cleveland than in Copenhagen. What formal research we have, moreover, points clearly in the opposite direction. One recent study of cross-national differences in attitudes toward deviance and nonconformity found that American students valued "external conformity" more than English students did, and were also more likely to support punishment of social deviance. Compared to us, the Dutch, too, are generally tolerant of social deviance and hold decidedly "soft" views on crime and punishment. Support for the death penalty, a revealing gauge of social values, is far greater in the United States than in Europe; as David Bruck points out, we are "the only country among all the Western industrial democracies which still executes its own citizens."

A similar punitiveness marks American attitudes toward child-rearing. In a recent article on crime and family policy, the sociologist Travis Hirschi blames something he calls the "metaphysic of the age"—distinguished by its "tolerance for natural tendencies"—for leading to permissiveness in child-rearing and parental failure to punish children consistently. This failure, in turn, presumably leads to delinquency. But as Hirschi concedes, this "metaphysic" has been with us for quite some time. He does not say exactly when we began "preaching tolerance for natural tendencies," but he implies that it has been going on at least for several decades and perhaps since Rousseau. But if that is the case, it isn't clear what this tolerant metaphysic has to do with the much more specific and time-bound problem of the recent growth of crime in America. Like Wilson's argument about "self-expression," Hirschi's invocation of the "metaphysic of the age" fails to explain why, since every Western industrial society has been infected with the "metaphysic" for decades, ours should be the one with the worst problem of criminal violence.

Cross-national evidence on attitudes and practices regarding children supports a very different interpretation. American attitudes about punishment in child-rearing are more severe—less "tolerant" of "natural tendencies"—than those of many other countries. Our support for corporal punishment, for example, is much greater than Scandinavia's. Sweden outlawed corporal punishment in its secondary schools in the 1920s, while our Supreme Court affirmed the schools' right to beat children in 1977. According to opinion polls, about three-quarters of Americans believe that the physical punishment of children is acceptable, "normal" behavior; in Sweden, the proportion is closer to one-fourth. Yet in Sweden, where corporal punishment was outlawed in 1979, even when inflicted by parents, rates of serious violent crime are much lower than in Finland, where corporal punishment is more widely accepted. But the Finns are less violent than we Americans, whose support for punishment is among the highest in the industrial world. Even higher rates of criminal violence are found in some Caribbean countries, where corporal punishment—especially in low-income families—is applied on a scale and with a severity that might shock even Americans.

The problem is not that the conservatives are asking the wrong questions, but that their answers strain credulity in what often becomes a single-minded, virtually obsessive search for signs of "permissiveness" or "weak control." This quest for excessive "leniency" or "tolerance" survives not only the absence of evidence to support it, but even the most straightforward evidence to the contrary.

Consider an article by Edward A. Wynne, professor of education at the University of Illinois, ominously titled, "What Are the Courts Doing to Our Children?" Wynne offers alarming statistics on the rising rates of homicide among American youth, as well as of suicide and illegitimate birth. These are troubling problems, of course, but how, exactly, are they connected with the *courts*? Because, Wynne argues, recent Supreme Court decisions giving students more rights of due process in the schools, along with other educational policies that he regards as increasingly permissive, have undermined adults' authority over children.

Such a conclusion isn't unreasonable, if there is concrete

evidence to back it up. Yet Wynne points out, with rather disarming candor, that his own data show unmistakably that the rise in "self-and-other destruction" among young people began well *before* the liberalizing court decisions and the other "permissive" shifts in school policy of the late sixties and early seventies. Wynne's response to this discrepancy is to insist that although the changes in law and policy didn't *cause* the increase, they didn't *stop* it either—true, but hardly surprising, and slender support for his line of reasoning. Wynne nevertheless persists in concluding that destructive youthful behavior has grown more widespread because there are "too few reins" on the young; they need "more intense protection, scrutiny, and restraint." Now surely this cannot be entirely wrong; some youth doubtless do need these things. But Wynne provides no evidence that the lack of "protection, scrutiny, and restraint" can be laid at the door of the Supreme Court, much less that the Court's actions can be held responsible for the rise in youth crime.

Wynne's ability to extract evidence of excessive permissiveness from the most stubborn material, virtually excluding other possible explanations, is remarkable, but not unique among conservative thinkers. On the strength of data from surveys of school violence, sociologist Jackson Toby describes school crime as a massive problem caused mainly by the lack of sufficient discipline. For Toby, the specific culprits are (again) the atmosphere created by rising concern for the rights of youth in general and students in particular, and also the criticism of authoritarianism in the schools launched by critics like John Holt and Jonathan Kozol in the sixties and seventies. Toby believes that the emphasis on "due process" for young people in the schools and the juvenile court has hamstrung the capacity of authorities to isolate and punish troublesome youth, and that the school-reform writers undermined the authority of teachers and administrators by calling them racist and authoritarian. Like Wilson, Toby possesses an almost mystical belief in the ability of liberal intellectuals to demoralize the inner-city masses; Toby acknowledges that few inner-city residents probably ever read the books in question, but insists nevertheless that the "anti-establishment" message "percolated" down to them, with disastrous and far-reaching consequences.

"What makes violence likely," Toby insists, "is weak control"; if we want to reduce school violence, we must make it easier for schools to expel the "handful" of troublemakers and to back that up with the threat of locking them up in youth prisons. Toby acknowledges that these solutions are rather drastic, but he declares that "society must be permitted to give up on students who are threatening the educational opportunities of their classmates."

Toby's superficially tough-minded approach fits well with the attitude—increasingly common in the eighties—that society should indeed "give up" on people who, for one reason or another, are particularly troublesome. His view has caught on—not surprising in a conservative political climate that favors simplistic, authoritarian responses to the complex problems of the schools. A little "old-fashioned discipline," as Ronald Reagan suggested in 1984, should do wonders, turning beleaguered urban schools into paragons of academic decorum and efficiency. All of this soothes conservative sensibilities, but does it fit the facts?

Once again, as with Edward Wynne's argument about the courts and youthful destructiveness, the most damaging rebuttal comes from Toby's own data. These show that it is precisely in the big-city schools where violence is highest that tough discipline and control are *already* most consistently practiced. All punishments other than "paddling" (which even Toby apparently doesn't advocate) were employed during the seventies, according to the survey he cites, much more often in the violence-ridden urban schools than in rural schools, where there was far less violence. These disciplinary measures, difficult to describe as weak, ranged from mandatory ID cards and hall passes to suspension, expulsion, and transfer to special disciplinary schools or mental-health facilities for particularly disruptive students.

The fact that violence is highest in the schools that are most heavily controlled, of course, doesn't necessarily mean that harsh discipline *causes* school violence. More likely, these schools use extreme discipline as a response—obviously not a very effective one—to high levels of violence that are primarily influenced by conditions outside the schools. (Much research on school violence indicates that the youths who are violent in school are usually violent outside—and, unsurprisingly, that the schools most plagued by violence are located in communities which are them-selves torn by violence.) But all the available evidence about the effects of school climate and organization on the level of school crime and violence suggests that following Toby's prescriptions would be apt to make matters worse, not better. The British psychiatrist Michael Rutter and his colleagues, in one of the most careful analyses of the effect of high-school practices on students' behavior, found that the responsiveness and encouragement of teachers and staff and the "ample use of rewards, praise and appreciation," along with a "focus on good behavior rather than disruptive acts," were characteristic of schools with fewer delin-quents (and better academic performance), while the "total amount of punishment" was not a major factor. In the United States, Richard A. Kulka and his coworkers, studying high schools in the Detroit area, found in certain schools what they called a "vicious, self-fueling cycle of alienation and deviance," in which "engaging in aggressive or deviant behavior results in negative sanctioning from school authorities, which leads to neg-ative perceptions of school staff, reduced involvement in school, and negative school attitudes," ultimately leading back to "fur-ther involvement in deviant and rebellious behavior."

This implies that the law-and-order approach to the schools favored by Toby and other conservatives may well be not only ineffective—something Toby's data already suggest—but coun-terproductive, as likely to encourage violence as to reduce it. This is especially true because harsh treatment of violence in school is bound to have repercussions in the community as a whole. As Joan McDermott points out, cracking down on trouble inside the schools by expelling or suspending troublemakers wholesale "puts them on the streets with nothing to do"—shifting the bur-den of dealing with them from the school to the community.

———————— V ————————

The overemphasis on control to the exclusion of other issues appears even in some more thoughtful writers who have moved beyond this simplistic reliance on "permissiveness" as an explanation of America's unusually high crime rates. Consider the work of David Bayley on crime in Japan, which squarely takes on the question of what might account for Japan's relatively stable (and at some points declining) crime rate in recent years —a phenomenon all the more remarkable because the Japanese have generally minimized the use of formal criminal-justice sanctions in fighting crime. Bayley argues that Japan's low crime rate mainly reflects strong controls over misbehavior exerted by family and neighborhood. Bayley's analysis is unobjectionable, as far as it goes; but it stops short of addressing a number of crucial elements—most importantly the ways in which Japanese society is more *supportive* than ours, not simply more "controlling." Nothing is said about the far narrower spread of income inequality in Japan or the relative absence of a severely deprived and marginal "underclass," which in turn partly reflects a conscious and generally effective (if sometimes overstated) full-employment policy and a range of deliberate efforts to integrate Japanese workers into a stable, enduring connection with a workplace. Bayley's stress on family and neighborhood "controls" is so detached from any sense of their larger social and economic context that we have no way of understanding *why* those controls have remained stronger than in many other industrial societies. Lacking an account of how these communal strengths have been maintained by economic and social policies, the analysis focuses, by default, on just those selected aspects of a presumably immutable Japanese culture that are most compatible with the stock conservative emphasis on crime as a reflection of insufficient "control."

As the anthropologist Robert J. Smith argues, the invocation of a "reified culture" to explain the successes of postwar Japanese social policy is misleading. What the Japanese experience most clearly tells us is that there are "alternative ways in which a mass society can be constructed"—and that crime, in particular, is not an "inevitable consequence of urbanization and industrialization," but is "susceptible to control through social engineering." The notion of human and social perfectability, Smith suggests, provides the cultural underpinnings of Japan's social and economic successes. Conservatives should find it sobering that one of the societies that has been most effective in controlling crime subscribes to a view of "human nature" dramatically opposed to their own.

But Bayley's analysis prompts him to a fashionably pessimistic conclusion:

> The levels of criminal behavior that Americans find so disturbing may be the inevitable consequence of aspects of national life that Americans prize—individualism, mobility, privacy, autonomy, suspicion of authority, and separation between public and private roles, between government and community. The United States may have relatively high levels of criminality because it is inhabited by Americans.

This argument does point to something important about the American experience—but in this form, it obscures more than it illuminates. By shifting the explanation of the causes of crime onto an amorphous, ill-defined realm of culture or values detached from the social and economic context that nourishes or undermines them, such reasoning conveys a vague sense—more a mood than an argument—that the roots of crime are beyond human control, thus encouraging inaction and passivity. If we have a lot of crime in America *because* we're Americans, there isn't much we can do about it. But the argument fits uneasily with the facts. If "individualism" and a cultural penchant for "autonomy" are indeed the problem, why do the notoriously individualistic Yankees of New Hampshire ("Live Free or Die") or the ruggedly individualistic Scandinavians of Minnesota have rates of serious criminal violence that compare well with those of Western Europe—or of Japan? Why do black Americans, who presumably do not value "individualism" any more than white Americans (or Hispanic Americans, who may value it less), have rates that are so much higher?

It is important to acknowledge that even with all its rhetorical excesses, the conservative argument about the links between crime and culture raises important questions that liberal criminology has sometimes sidestepped. The criminology of the sixties too often focused on the simpler malfunctions of what was viewed as an otherwise smoothly functioning social and moral order; it implied that a little income support here, a summer-job program there, would, by themselves, stop crime. The conservative argument at its most suggestive points beyond, to what Peter Steinfels, in *The Neoconservatives*, aptly calls the "murkier and more trying questions of culture and spirit"—and, I would add, of family and community. These issues are difficult to grasp and especially hard to frame in the manageable terms of quantitative social science, but I do not think we will really understand crime without paying them respectful attention.

In the hands of conservative writers, however, these issues have usually been raised in terms so mired in ideology and so beholden to political agendas as to obscure the questions they suggest. Conservative analysis has steadfastly shied away from confronting—or even naming—the underlying forces that shape cultural, communal, and family life. As Steinfels has also noted, this stance fixes our attention on a "realm of ideas and ethos" that seems to float free of its moorings in the economic and social changes that have transformed American society, and as a result obscures the interconnection between them.

Conservative writing on crime, for example, has often focused on the spread of an ethos of "immediate gratification," a concern voiced even in the pages of the report of the Reagan administration's Task Force on Violent Crime. There is reason for this concern; some kinds of crime are almost by definition the expression of a search for immediate gratification. Yet—aside from the incessant references to the noxious influence of liberal permissiveness—conservative writers don't identify the forces that might foster such an "ethos." This is surely a remarkable omission in the society where, more than in any other, an ethos of ever-increasing consumption for the sake of impulse gratification has become indispensable to our economy and has penetrated almost every corner of our life; where the world's most sophisticated advertising industry devotes itself, day in, day out, to promoting just that ethos; and where, in contrast to many other advanced industrial societies, the search for the highest and fastest short-term profit at the expense of longer-term economic stability —the corporate version of instant gratification—is enshrined as the overarching principle of economic life.

I've argued that from an international perspective, America

cannot plausibly be considered a "tolerant" or "lenient" society; it is, however, an acquisitive and materialistic one. These cultural attitudes surely have some relationship to the severity of our crime problem. But we must also understand that they are indissolubly linked to an economy dependent on the incessant stimulation of mass consumption. As Daniel Bell writes in *The Cultural Contradictions of Capitalism*, "The one thing that would utterly destroy the 'new capitalism' is the serious practice of 'deferred gratification.' " If we have become a more grasping, less cooperative culture in recent years—and I believe we have—we must look, as Bell does, to the social and economic forces that have brought about this shift.

In the absence of that sort of analysis, the conservative emphasis on culture, values, and tradition degenerates—as we'll see—into sheer passivity and wistful nostalgia or, worse, into a self-righteous, punitive demand for more corporal punishment, harsher discipline in the family and the schools, and the indiscriminate use of the prisons as holding pens for an urban underclass we have decided to "give up on."

The conservative model, then, turns out to be shot through with contradictions. In a world of dramatic national variations in criminal violence, it blames crime on an invariant human nature. In a society that ranks among the most punitive in the developed world, it blames crime on the leniency of the justice system. In a country noted for its harsh response to social deviation, it blames crime on attitudes of tolerance run wild. If we want to understand the American experience of criminal violence, we must look elsewhere for the elements of an explanation, particularly to those features of our social life that distinguish us—in fact rather than in fantasy—from more fortunate societies.

But this gets us a little ahead of the story. First, we must look more closely at the prospects for the social policies that have, in practice, flowed from conservative theories of crime. I've shown that we cannot credibly explain America's extraordinary crime rate as a result of the failure to punish criminals. But that is a different question from the more specific and more technical one of *why* such a heavy investment in punishment has produced so little effect—and whether doing more of the same might have a greater one. These questions will be our focus in the following chapter.

3

THE LIMITS OF
IMPRISONMENT

Can we bring down the crime rate by putting more people in prison?

Perhaps; but not by much.

It is still widely believed that lowering crime by increasing its "costs" ought to be a simple matter, like cutting taxes or voting more money for defense. But research increasingly shows that things aren't so simple. Indeed, outside the abstract world of the more extreme proponents of an "economic" view of crime, most criminologists today—whether Left, Right, or Center—generally acknowledge that only a fraction of serious crime can be prevented by increased incarceration.

They disagree, to be sure, over just how large that fraction is and what it would take to attain it. Criminologists of a conservative bent argue that the potential fraction is fairly large and that only wrongheadedness and weakness of purpose keep us from achieving it. I think, on the evidence, that the fraction is disturbingly small—more because of inherent limitations in the criminal-justice system's capacity to prevent crime than because of a failure of toughness or moral purpose. I am not suggesting that imprisonment has *no* effect (for reasons that will become clear, I think it does have an effect); and it is likely that the huge increases in imprisonment since the early 1970s have kept the crime rate slightly lower than it would otherwise have been. But the experience of the past decade leads to the inescapable conclusion that the impact is small, relative to the investment it requires; that although imprisonment is all too often an unavoidable necessity, it is not an effective way to prevent crime.

This is hardly a new argument; it was one of the fundamentals of what I've called liberal criminology, and unlike some of its other guiding themes, it has withstood the test of time and experience well. To understand why, we must look more closely at how putting people in prison is said to reduce crime. Traditionally, criminologists have distinguished two ways this can happen—ways that are easier to separate in theory than in practice. One is *deterrence*—that the experience of going to prison may deter offenders from committing more crimes when they get out *(special deterrence)*, and that the threat of going to prison may deter others from becoming criminals *(general deterrence)*. The second is *incapacitation*—meaning that the number of crimes offenders might otherwise commit will be reduced simply by getting them off the streets. Both mechanisms are plausible; both are often viscerally accepted by legislators and the public. But each, for a variety of reasons, is limited in its capacity to reduce crime. Some of the reasons involve the nature and distribution of the criminal population, others the fundamental obstacles within the criminal-justice system, and still others the nature of crime itself.

i

The extent to which punishment deters crime is one of the oldest and least settled questions in criminology. On the surface, the issue seems simple enough. What is sometimes rather grandiosely called the *deterrence doctrine* holds that—other things being equal—people will be less inclined to break the law if they think they are likely to be punished for it. On that very general level, the argument isn't really controversial; but neither is it very helpful. For it is a long way from this relatively innocuous "doctrine" to the more specific argument that we can deter much crime by sending more criminals to prison.

If we wish to make reasonable judgments about the role of punishment in an intelligent strategy against crime, we need to know more. To begin with, we must specify what kind of punishment—or *sanction*—we mean. Do we mean spanking, fines, prison, losing a hand? The anger of one's parents, the loss of a job, the electric chair? Without some specifics, the general idea that punishment deters is useless for guiding social policy, since depending on which kinds of punishments work best, we will be moved toward drastically different approaches to crime prevention.

Then there is the related issue of who does the punishing, and where. Most of the sanctions a society imposes to influence behavior are administered informally—at home, on the job, among peers. Indeed, only comparatively recently did *formal* punishments—particularly imprisonment—take on the major role they now play. (The penitentiary itself is a creation of the late eighteenth and early nineteenth centuries.)

Even within the sphere of formal punishments, we must answer more questions before we can begin to think in practical terms about the uses of the criminal-justice system in deterring crime in the real world. For example, do more severe punishments, say longer prison sentences, deter any better than less severe ones? Or is it the consistent application of punishment—its "certainty"—that is most important? Each emphasis requires a different strategy. And even if we have settled, at least theoretically, the question of what kind and level of punishment deters crime most effectively, there remains the equally important practical question of how—or whether—the criminal-justice system can actually provide it. And there is still another complication: formal punishment may deter some people but not others; it may even make some offenders worse than before.

A final question, related but distinct and especially crucial for translating the general idea of deterrence into sensible social policy, looms in the background. If punishing criminals does indeed "work," how *well* does it work? And "well" compared to what? After all, many things besides punishment may also deter crime, ranging from steady work to religious conviction, from moral exhortation to marriage. Social policy is necessarily made up of choices among alternatives; hence, even in the barest cost-benefit terms, it is important to have evidence not just that formal punishment has *some* deterrent effect, but that it has a *superior* deterrent effect.

Recent American social policy has been based, at least tacitly, on a set of choices about each of these questions. It has emphasized formal punishment administered through the criminal-justice system, and imprisonment as the punishment of choice. And in practice, it has relied mainly on increasing the severity of punishment rather than its certainty. In part, these policies are a response to the widespread belief that other approaches to crime prevention—social programs, rehabilitation—had failed, a view that was part of a broader conservative critique of the more activist public policy of the sixties. The then-dominant liberal criminology was decidedly lukewarm, if not hostile, to the idea that the threat of formal punishment (especially imprisonment) could do much to deter serious crimes. Liberal criminologists did not necessarily deny that some deterrent effect existed, but they granted it only a secondary status. (The term *deterrence*, for example, does not even appear in the index of the 1967 Report of the President's Commission on Law Enforcement and Administration of Justice.)

The liberal argument had several levels, both theoretical and empirical. At the most general level, many criminologists felt that the deterrence model was based on a severely limited conception of the mainsprings of human behavior and motivation. Most liberal criminologists took their bearings from sociological and social-psychological theories that held that people behaved as they did because of a complex interplay of values and norms learned in their cultural and institutional settings, from family to workplace. The idea that criminals (or anyone else) could be understood as simply atomized, rational calculators of costs and benefits, carefully weighing the gains of crime against the risks of punishment, seemed grossly inadequate. It might fit some criminals, under certain conditions; but as a model of criminal behavior in general, it strained the imagination. Criminologists were well aware that many crimes took place in the heat of passion (including many homicides and assaults between family members) or under the influence of alcohol or drugs. Others, like much youth-gang violence, reflected a quest for "manhood," status, or street level "glory"—which, given the values prevalent on the street, might even be enhanced by a stint behind bars. These points remain valid. We don't have much research on what goes on the minds of criminals before they commit crimes, but what we do have suggests that rational planning is the exception rather than the rule, even for crimes involving material gain. The enormous role of drugs and alcohol in serious crimes has likewise been reaffirmed in recent Department of Justice findings.

This emphasis on the psychological and social context of crime led many criminologists to believe that, if a general deterrent effect of punishment existed at all, it was much more likely to come from "informal" sanctions than from the fear of formal punishment. The desire for the respect of society and the local community, the need for the esteem of family and peers, the power of religious or other institutions to include individuals within the pale or to exclude them, were felt to be far more influential deterrents than the threat of punishment by a formal and distant justice system. Once again, recent research bears this out.

In 1972, the sociologists Charles Tittle and Charles Logan, reviewing the research on deterrence, concluded that it was impossible to say anything stronger about general deterrence than that "sanctions apparently have some deterrent effect under some circumstances." In 1978, after intensive research, the National Academy of Sciences reviewed the accumulating evidence and concluded that it was "woefully inadequate for providing a good estimate of the magnitude of whatever effect may exist." Three years later, another noted specialist on deterrence, the sociologist Jack P. Gibbs, declared that "only incorrigible partisans regard the evidence as compelling one way or the other."

Virtually all this research affirms that if a general deterrent effect of punishment exists, it is produced primarily by informal communal institutions. By implication, when these sources of informal sanctioning are badly disrupted and the task of deterrence falls by default to the formal justice system, the task is likely to be accomplished poorly, if at all. As Charles Tittle concluded in a 1980 study, the ability of communities to exercise "social control" is apparently "rooted almost entirely in how people perceive the potential for negative reactions from interpersonal acquaintances"; formal sanctions are "largely irrelevant." A more recent series of studies by Raymond Paternoster, Linda Saltzman, Gordon Waldo, and Theodore Chiricos similarly concludes that "extra-legal influences"—especially the fear that their parents, best friends, or lovers might disapprove of them—are a particularly strong deterrent against theft and drug use among the students they surveyed, while perception of the risks of formal punishment "plays virtually no role."

To whatever extent formal punishment deters crime, it may be largely because it has an *indirect* effect on these more personal, informal relationships. Tittle discovered, for example, that among his subjects "any apparent general deterrent effect" of formal sanctions "seems to be a function of the person's perception of interpersonal respect loss"—that is, potential offenders feared the criminal-justice system mainly because arrest might provoke the disrespect of family and peers. Similarly, in a six-year study of drug dealers, Sheldon Ekland-Olson and his coworkers at the University of Texas found that the risks of arrest and imprisonment deterred the dealers' activities mainly by disrupting or threatening to disrupt their relations with family, friends, and other dealers.

Another kind of evidence for the central importance of informal sanctions comes from the few studies that shed light on why most people who get involved in crime at some point in their lives *stop.* Most young Americans do things in the course of growing up that could land them in court, but most don't go on to a deepening criminal "career": if they did, American society would be altogether uninhabitable. But why don't they? The evidence suggests that most youths desist from crime less because they are afraid of being caught and locked up than because the rewards of becoming valued and productive members of a community and earning the approval of family and peers begin to outstrip the lures of delinquency. In a long-term study in Racine, Wisconsin, Lyle Shannon found that most of the young men he interviewed reported having committed crimes serious enough to merit arrest, but that most of them had stopped by the age of 18. Why? Fewer than 8 percent said they had quit because they were afraid of being caught and punished. Most had reappraised their behavior on their own in the light of the trouble it caused them with families, friends, or school and of the effect it would have on their future in the community.

The importance of informal sanctions has vital—though unduly neglected—implications for social policy. It suggests that the best deterrent to crime is the creation and maintenance of stable communities in which people may reasonably expect that good behavior will lead to esteemed and rewarding social roles.

In the abstract, even many conservative criminologists would probably agree, but they would counter with two related arguments. The first is that conscious social action cannot do much to build and maintain such communities—a central theme in the conservative attitude toward crime. The second is that, even if formal punishments don't work as well as informal sanctions in deterring crime, that doesn't mean they don't work at all; hence, in the absence of strong communal bulwarks against crime, we have little choice but to invoke harsher or more frequent prison sentences.

Yet the evidence that increasing imprisonment can markedly deter serious crime is murky at best. The lack of interest in deterrence among liberal criminologists in the 1950s and 1960s was based in part on their awareness that in the United States an extraordinarily high crime rate had historically gone along with a notoriously punitive penal system. (Indeed, those places with the most punitive penal systems—notably parts of the South—also tended to have the worst rates of criminal violence.) This constituted a substantial prima facie case that if indeed imprisonment "worked" in some marginal sense, it didn't work very well.

More recently, criminologists have studied the question from a variety of angles, but none have offered strong or consistent support for the general deterrent effect of imprisonment. To begin with, although we would expect increases in incarceration rates to be followed by declines in crime (and lower rates, by increases) that isn't what the evidence shows. Consider the recent American experience again: though imprisonment rates have risen *faster* than crime rates since the early seventies, the latter have stubbornly failed to oblige by falling in reasonable proportion. This crude, but fundamental, observation is supported by more elaborate studies using what statisticians call a *time-series analysis*, which allows a much more precise calculation of any possible relationships, over time, between levels of imprisonment and levels of crime.

In one such study, the American criminologist Lee Bowker charted crime and imprisonment in the United States between 1941 and 1978. He found that the rates for crime and for imprisonment were negatively related—crime went down when imprisonment went up, and rose when imprisonment fell—for *part* of the period he studied, but not for all of it. Indeed, increases in the imprisonment rate were associated with *increases* in the crime rate during some of the earlier years studied. Bowker concluded that the widely varying relationships between imprisonment and crime rates probably meant that the connection between them is tenuous—and that therefore (as liberal criminologists had long argued) it was "impossible to construct policies about the use of imprisonment as a social sanction based on its presumed relationship with the crime rate."

The Australian criminologist David Biles confirmed Bowker's conclusion in a study comparing crime and imprisonment rates in England and in Australia from 1960 to 1979. Disconcertingly, the trends in crime were very similar in the two countries, while the trends in imprisonment were almost exactly opposite. In both countries, reported crime went up during the sixties and seventies—by 177 percent in England and Wales and by a remarkably similar 180 percent in Australia. But during the same years, the British were greatly increasing their incarceration rate, while the Australians were slightly decreasing theirs. On the whole, Biles discovered, the Australian incarceration rate tended to go down when the crime rate rose; but this decrease in imprisonment had no effect on the crime rate in ensuing years. Biles concluded that a rising number of offenders in custody has "no measurable effect on the level of public safety."

On the other hand, several studies since the early seventies—mostly by economists trained in the Chicago school of neoclassical economics—have compared crime rates in states with stricter versus more lenient penal policies and have come up with at least moderate support for the supposition of a deterrent effect of imprisonment (mainly, it should be noted, for the certainty but not necessarily the severity of sentences). But such findings must be taken with a heavy dose of skepticism.

For one thing, there are at least equally convincing findings in the opposite direction. In a study of the United States, Canada, and Australia, David Biles found that the relationships between crime rates and levels of imprisonment were *positive*—that is, other things being equal, the more imprisonment, the more crime. This distressing result didn't necessarily mean that imprisonment *caused* crime; more likely it meant that, although rising imprisonment was a predictable *response* to rising crime, it had little effect of its own on crime rates.

A second reason for skepticism is that these cross-sectional studies are beset with such formidable methodological problems that it is difficult to know what to make of them. One problem is that a host of factors other than a state's penal policy influence its crime rate, and they are very difficult to isolate—to "control" statistically—while estimating the effect of punishment itself. Suppose we discover that state x has a lower robbery rate than state y, and that x also puts robbers in prison more often than y. Does this mean that greater use of imprisonment reduces the robbery rate? Maybe; but it may also mean that some other aspect of life in state y produces more robbers—or more energetic ones. It may be an economic factor (like higher unemployment among youth), a demographic one (like a bigger proportion of youth in the state's population), or a social one (like a greater degree of residential mobility). Or it may be that y is a richer state and therefore that more is stolen simply because there is more to steal. Since all these factors, and a great many more, have been held to influence robbery rates, we must control for the potential effects of all of them in order to be sure that any apparent effect of putting more robbers in prison isn't an illusion. But without knowing all these other relevant factors, and fitting them into our equations, we cannot eliminate their potentially biasing influence, no matter how mathematically sophisticated those equations are.

This problem bedevils even the most technically sophisticated cross-sectional research. Over and over, the only really consistent finding has been that whether or not increased imprisonment (or other variations in criminal-justice policy, such as increased spending on police) shows a deterrent effect depends almost entirely on what assumptions are made about these other potentially relevant variables—as the language of econometrics puts it, on *how the model is specified.*

Another source of uncertainty in this kind of deterrence research comes from the nature of the criminal-justice system itself. The deterrence argument is based on the assumption that what happens in the criminal-justice system influences the crime rate; but it usually ignores the less obvious fact that the influence runs both ways. Suppose, once again, that state x puts many robbers in prison and has a low robbery rate, while state y puts proportionately fewer robbers behind bars and has a higher rate. Does this mean that the lower risk of imprisonment in y is responsible for its higher robbery rate? Perhaps; but it could also mean that the high robbery rate in y makes it hard to apprehend and convict robbers in the first place, and also makes it less feasible to send them, once convicted, to already overcrowded and volatile prisons. So the crime rate isn't simply a response to criminal-justice policies; to an important extent, the crime rate itself influences the effectiveness of the system. And since these occur simultaneously, it is difficult to isolate and measure the effect of either one by itself.

The research, in short, shows at best only an uncertain deterrent effect of increases in imprisonment. A similar uncertainty surrounds studies of the deterrent impact of specific efforts to "get tough" on criminals in the courts—for example, mandatory prison sentences. Traditionally applied to "habitual" offenders or to crimes accompanied by special circumstances, like gun use, mandatory sentences have been increasingly established for lesser offenses as well. By 1983, only two states in the Union had no mandatory minimum sentences at all. Such penalties are often easy to legislate and popular with the public, because they promise that by reducing the discretion of the courts they will increase the certainty and severity of punishment and thereby lower the crime rate. But is this what happens in practice?

Apparently not—at least not consistently. Several careful studies of the effects of mandatory sentencing have been made, and though there is debate about how to interpret the results, they can't be described as encouraging. These studies do not disprove the abstract notion that more certain punishment deters crime. But they do show that accomplishing this, within the limitations of the justice system, is harder in practice than in theory—a point so important that it is worth considering in some detail.

One of the best-known recent experiments in self-consciously "tough" mandatory sentencing was New York State's drug law of 1973, often known as the "Rockefeller drug law" and widely billed as the "nation's toughest" drug legislation. This law mandated draconian penalties for many drug offenses, on the untested theory that cracking down on drug use and sales would indirectly cut drug-related crime. The minimum sentence for possessing two ounces of heroin, for example, was fifteen to twenty-five years; the maximum, life. A repeat conviction for possessing any stimulant or hallucinogen "with intent to sell" carried a mandatory minimum of one to eight and a half years, a maximum of life imprisonment. Probation and other alternatives to prison were prohibited under most circumstances, as was plea bargaining to lesser charges. Though it took a while, in the end the drug law did substantially increase the number of drug offenders in the prisons of New York and lengthen their sentences.

The law accordingly became one source of the state's serious prison overcrowding. The proportion of convicted drug felons sentenced to prison more than doubled between 1972 and 1975; the proportion given maximum sentences of more than five years shot from 57 percent in 1974 to 91 percent in 1975.

That increase was costly, economically and otherwise. New York poured tens of millions of dollars into the court system to handle the added load; nevertheless the courts quickly became clogged—in part because defendants responded to the threat of harsher penalties by demanding more trials. The average time between arrest and disposition in drug cases doubled from 173 days in 1973 to 340 in 1976—an outcome hardly encouraging to those who thought mandatory sentences would increase the swiftness as well as the certainty and severity of punishment.

Yet, for all this, the drug law's impact on crime (or, for that matter, on drug use) is unclear. Certainly it did not hold back the big increases in burglary and robbery, frequently drug-related crimes, that hit New York in the late seventies. According to an analysis by Kenneth Carlson, the proportion of people charged with felonies who were identifiable drug users did decrease slightly just after the drug law was passed; but it had already been dropping before that. On careful inspection, the proportional decrease turned out to be the result of a *growing* number of non-drug-users in the arrested population, not a shrinking number of drug users. It wasn't clear that the law had much impact even on drug sales and use, much less the hoped-for impact on other serious crimes. (Recognizing all this, the state legislature moved, in the late seventies, to modify some of the law's mandatory imprisonment provisions).

The drug law's unanticipated effect of overloading the courts with demands for formal trials had parallels in Massachusetts. There, a 1974 law mandated a one-year minimum prison term, without possibility of parole, for anyone caught illegally carrying a gun. Although the aim was to increase the certainty as well as the severity of penalties for the illegal possession of guns, in practice the law probably *reduced* certainty, while increasing severity for those ultimately convicted. The tougher mandatory penalty apparently spurred defendants to go to trial to seek acquittal (rather than accepting a lighter penalty in exchange for a guilty plea). Accordingly, there were more verdicts of not guilty, more dismissals, more appeals, and more new trials. As Kenneth Carlson concludes, "For most defendants at most stages of the process the effect was to increase the chance of outcomes favorable to the defendant." As a result, before the law was passed, about half of gun-violation defendants were released without conviction, but two years afterward, *four-fifths* got off free.

Once again, the results in terms of crime prevention were ambiguous. Homicides in Boston fell after the law was passed, but the rates were falling well beforehand. Assaults with guns also dropped, but they followed a pattern that is difficult to interpret. Gun assaults had risen sharply in the early seventies, reaching a peak in 1974. They declined over the following two years, but not enough to bring them down to their level before that sudden rise. It's impossible to tell, therefore, whether the drop was connected with the gun law or whether, for unknown and unrelated reasons, the rates were merely once again approaching their usual level.

Similar ambiguities appear in an evaluation of a 1977 Michigan statute, the "Felony Firearm" law, which mandated an extra two years in prison for criminals using guns while committing felonies, besides the sentence for the original crime. The statute was popular with the state legislature, which passed it overwhelmingly, and with the public. In Detroit, the county prosecutor was an avid supporter and mounted a vigorous, highly visible campaign—complete with bumper stickers and billboards warning potential gun-wielders that "one with a gun gets you two"—to let it be known that the law would be enforced. He also prohibited plea-bargaining in the Detroit courts. All things considered, it was a tough law, seriously pursued. Did it deter gun-related felonies?

According to an analysis by Colin Loftin, David McDowall, and Milton Heuman, it did not. Some gun-related crimes decreased in Detroit shortly after the passage of the gun law, but not, apparently, because of it. The drop in crime began well before the passage of the statute; moreover, the rate of *non*-gun felonies dropped as much as that of felonies with guns—all to the good, of course, but making it unlikely that the drop in crime resulted from a law aimed solely at the use of firearms. Armed robberies fell, but so did unarmed robberies. Gun homicides fell —but not just killings during planned robberies and other murders that might reasonably be prevented by the threat of an added two-year sentence; unplanned murders (as in lovers' quarrels) fell as well. Serious crime, furthermore, increased sharply in the city a few years later. Whatever caused Detroit's happy (though, as it turned out, short-lived) slump in crime, it apparently wasn't the Felony Firearm law.

Why? The first hypothesis that comes to mind is that the law wasn't really enforced. Not surprisingly, the courts in Detroit did not act exactly as the law prescribed (courts rarely do); they didn't uniformly impose the two-year sentence in all possible cases. Sometimes, apparently, with serious offenders who would probably have received tough sentences anyway, the courts "absorbed" the mandatory sentence by reducing the original sentence, thus arriving at a relatively steady "going rate" for specific kinds of crimes. In less serious cases, some judges and prosecutors may have felt uncomfortable with long prison sentences for, say, first offenders, and gotten around the gun law by charging the original cases as misdemeanors, not felonies.

But the researchers argued that none of these maneuvers really altered the law's genuine toughness or—perhaps more importantly—the way it was perceived in the community and by potential felons. "This was a tough law," they write.

There were no major loopholes in its formulation and the Wayne County prosecutor was aggressive in his policy of charging the law and resisting attempts to circumvent it. Our interviews indicate that, in spite of some cynicism about the impact of the law, many defendants were concerned that they might get caught in its rigid flat time provisions. A strong message was sent to the community that gun offenders would be dealt with sternly.

To believe that potential gun-wielding robbers would have figured out that, by means of complex and subtle mechanisms barely teased out by these experienced researchers, they might excape the clutches of the gun law requires us to grant the average street criminal some very sophisticated analytical abilities indeed. It's more plausible, Loftin and his colleagues argue, that the law's deterrent impact on crime was intrinsically limited, largely because it realistically affected only a narrow range of offenders. For robbers planning serious crimes where they were likely to meet armed resistance, the inducement to carry guns was likely to be too strong to be much influenced by mere two-year additions to what were already sure to be stiff potential sentences. The law was therefore likely to have a strong impact only on those robbers who had no compelling reason to use a gun in the first place but *might* have used one if there were no law—and that can't be a very substantial group.

The apparent inability of the Michigan statute to deter gun crime doesn't mean there aren't other arguments—moral and philosophical—for inflicting special punishment on people who use guns while committing crimes. It *does* suggest, however, that we have no strong reason to believe that such laws will markedly reduce gun-related crime.

More generally, it affirms that we are unlikely to gain much more deterrence through the simple expedient of restricting the discretion of the courts, for the crucial reason that the courts' "discretion" is not the main part of the problem—usually not even a very significant part.

Those who believe that we could cut crime dramatically if only we would "get tough" with criminals in the courts often quote dramatic figures on how few crimes, proportionately, result in prison sentences. The figures are real enough. But what they show is that most of the "slippage" between crime and punishment—between the commission of a crime and the realistic "costs"—takes place at the "front end" of the criminal-justice process: in the difficulty of catching and, to a lesser degree, of convicting criminals, not in the leniency of the courts once they've been convicted. According to the Rand Corporation's survey of repeat felons in the California prisons, for example, almost nine out of ten of those arrested for robbery were convicted; of these almost nine out of ten were imprisoned.

To be sure, criminal cases do get "lost" between arrest and conviction. But despite widespread belief in the pernicious effects of laws protecting the civil liberties of criminals, a growing body of evidence shows that not many serious criminals, especially violent criminals, go free because the courts are "handcuffed" by rules that favor criminals over the welfare of the public at large. Probably the most criticized of the constraints on the justice system is the *exclusionary rule*, which requires courts to disregard evidence in criminal cases that is illegally acquired by the police. Critics argue that the rules circumscribing the ways police may conduct searches or seize evidence cause the "loss" of vast numbers of criminal cases, drastically lower the conviction rate, and therefore undercut the deterrent effect of the criminal-justice system. Periodically there has been a great outcry, recently taken up by the Reagan administration, to modify (if not eliminate) the exclusionary rule. But careful studies of the exclusionary rule's real effects do not support this rather apocalyptic view. The United States General Accounting Office concluded in the late seventies that in the federal courts, less than eight felony arrests in a thousand were "lost"—either screened out by prosecutors or dismissed by the court—because of the exclusionary rule. A similar study of urban courts by the Institute for Law and Social Research found that less than 1 percent of felony arrests were rejected because of illegal searches. In 1982, a National Institute of Justice study in California claimed to have found more substantial effects of the rule in causing prosecutors to reject felony cases; but on closer inspection, the results mainly confirm those of earlier research. Less than 5 percent of all felony cases in California rejected by prosecutors involved the exclusionary rule; therefore less than 1 percent of *all* felony arrests were rejected because of violations of the rule and something over 2 percent of felony cases were lost at *any* stage of the court process because of illegal searches. Even these minor effects were concentrated in one kind of crime—felony drug offenses—and were still smaller in the most serious crimes of violence.

Several recent studies give a more complex view of what usually happens as criminal cases wend their way through the courts. Researchers at the Vera Institute of Justice found that two factors in particular—the relationships between offenders and victims, and the offenders' prior records—explained a substantial proportion of variation in the risks of conviction and incarceration in New York City courts. If victims and offenders knew each other, the cases were often dismissed because the victims didn't press charges, either because they had become reconciled with the offender or because they were afraid of retaliation. Cases involving strangers much more often resulted in conviction and incarceration. Moreover, 84 percent of convicted felony defendants with criminal records (versus just 22 percent of those without them) were given prison sentences. Another recent study similarly finds that prosecutors' decisions about which cases to try and which to dismiss or plead downward to lesser charges are usually governed by "rational and consistent" guidelines. Thus the cases prosecutors are willing to take to trial on the most serious charges are, predictably, those in which the evidence is strong, the offense is grave, and the perpetrator has a prior criminal history.

To be sure, none of this research tells us that the courts are uniformly efficient at putting serious offenders away. No one can deny that some awful people are let off with a slap on the wrist or that the process of justice can be arbitrary, chaotic, and frustrating. Specialists can fruitfully debate the precise consequences of particular rules and regulations—such as the exclusionary rule or the frequent practice of discouraging the use of juvenile-court records in adult-court proceedings—on the courts' effectiveness. We should certainly continue to do whatever we can to increase the courts' efficiency. But no one has demonstrated that their inefficiency can be blamed for America's uniquely high rate of criminal violence, or that we can achieve significantly more deterrence by making the courts work better between arrest and conviction.

There are exceptions to this general point, of which the most important is the courts' ambiguous and often lenient treatment of domestic violence (I will return to this issue in the concluding chapter). Another is drunken driving, taken much more seriously as a potentially violent offense in some countries—Sweden, for example—that are otherwise far less harsh in their penal policies than the United States. (Close to a third of Sweden's relatively small prison population consists of inmates convicted of drunken driving.) Indeed, some of the strongest evidence for a general deterrent effect of punishment comes from studies of "crackdowns" on drunken driving—but this exception helps prove the rule, for drunken driving so rarely meets with serious sanctions that crackdowns by courts and police represent a dramatic change in the risks of punishment. If the courts were likewise routinely lenient with murderers and robbers, a better argument might be made that getting "tougher" would dramatically deter murder and robbery. But that simply isn't what the evidence shows. As the Vera Institute of Justice concluded in their study of the processing of felony arrests in New York, "Where crimes are serious, evidence is strong, and victims are willing to prosecute, felons with previous criminal histories ended up with relatively heavy sentences." If criminals are indeed "getting away with it," they argued, "they may be getting away with it more on the streets than in the courtrooms."

They *are* often "getting away with it" on the streets. The same Rand Corporation survey showing that nine out of ten convicted robbers were incarcerated in California also noted that the chances of their being arrested in the first place for any given robbery were only a shade over one in ten. The risks of arrest were slightly less for a burglary and just one in twenty-five for an auto theft. Even for armed robberies, the Rand researchers estimated that the chance of being caught for any particular crime was about one in eight.

As these facts suggest, the best place to improve the certainty of punishment is at the stage of apprehension. Apprehending criminals, of course, is mainly a function of the police, and whether we can improve their ability to carry it out remains an unsettled question. It's all too easy to blame the police for the frustratingly low proportion of crimes that result in solid arrests, easy to wax indignant over their inefficiency or their oversensitivity to the rights of offenders. But to argue that changes in police behavior or attitudes would markedly increase the certainty of punishment requires us to show that the police are now, *in general*, markedly inefficient in ways we know how to improve. The evidence for that position is scanty at best. The little we know about what factors affect the ability of police to "clear" crimes suggests that the most important of them is one that cannot be affected by changes in policy: the nature of the crimes committed. Some crimes are simply easier to "clear" than others. A murder in the family or a robbery with witnesses produces reasonably identifiable suspects; "stranger" crimes, especially if there are no witnesses, much more rarely result in arrests that hold up in court. Whether there are ways to improve the ability of the police to make inroads on stranger crimes is a complicated (and unresolved) question, one I'll come back to in the final chapter. The essential point here is that increases in general deterrence, if we can achieve them at all, will come primarily through our increased capacity to catch offenders in the first place, not by adopting an even harsher approach to those who have arrived at the stage of sentencing.

i i

General deterrence, then, turns out to be far more difficult to achieve (or even to measure) in practice than in theory. What about special deterrence? Does going to prison frighten offenders into going straight thereafter? The basic principle is simple and, in the abstract, plausible. But in reality the case for special deterrence is ambiguous. Even in the best interpretation, the evidence is only vaguely positive: at least for some offenders, going to prison may well slow down, even if it doesn't stop, their criminal "careers." But that mildly optimistic interpretation is countered by the increasing evidence that imprisonment makes other offenders *worse*.

Like that for general deterrence, the case for special deterrence confronts a formidable obstacle at the start. The problem for general deterrence, as we have seen, is the absence of consistent relations between crime and imprisonment rates. What haunts the idea of special deterrence is the high rate of *recidivism* — the undeniable fact that many offenders who do go to prison continue to commit serious crimes when they get out. High recidivism rates are a troubling, stubborn prima facie case that if imprisonment deters individual criminals at all, it clearly doesn't do so reliably or consistently.

Given the dreadful nature of imprisonment, the number of people who are willing (or driven) to risk it again—often over and over again—is astonishing. The statistics on recidivism are legion; a few will suffice. About a third of prison inmates generally, according to recent Department of Justice data, go back to prison after release. For some offenders, the rates are even higher. Among a cohort of youthful serious offenders who did time in California Youth Authority facilities in the sixties, two-thirds were reincarcerated in a state or federal prison, 70 percent within two years after release. Over half were rearrested for at least one "violent-aggressive" offense—murder, rape, or assault. In a study of heroin-addicted offenders in Baltimore, John C. Ball and his coworkers discovered that the average of three stints behind bars they had endured had "little noticeable effect" on their astonishingly active criminal careers. Between 1952 and 1971, Ball estimated, the 243 addicts had accumulated over 473,000 crimes among them; those who were *more* often incarcerated, in fact, committed crimes at a higher rate.

Even more discouraging implications can be drawn, if indirectly, from a series of recent Rand Corporation studies of prisoners in California, Michigan, and Texas. These studies were not explicitly designed to test deterrence, but rather to devise ways of predicting which criminals were most likely to become chronic or *high-rate* offenders, who commit far more crimes than even the typical prison inmate. (I'll return to these studies later in this chapter.) The findings, however, inspire little confidence in the deterrent effect of imprisonment. One of the most powerful predictors of which inmates would become what Jan and Marcia Chaiken called "violent predators"—repeat criminals who specialized in a cluster of offenses including robbery, assault, and hard-drug dealing—was that they had "spent a lot of time in juvenile institutions and/or prison in the recent past." Likewise, two of the seven criteria used by Peter Greenwood and Allan Abrahamse to predict which inmates would become high-rate offenders were having been incarcerated for more than half of the two-year period immediately before their most recent arrest, and having been committed at some point to a state or federal juvenile facility. Incarceration, then, as a youth or an adult, turns out to be one of the most reliable signals we have that an offender will go on to further serious, repetitive criminality.

It could, of course, be argued that the problem isn't that prison is intrinsically ineffective as a deterrent, but that prison sentences simply aren't severe enough to do the job. Yet the fact that American prison sentences are typically far longer than those in most of the rest of the developed world renders this line of reasoning implausible from the start. That common-sense observation is reinforced by the absence of evidence that long sentences deter crime any better than short ones. As far back as the end of the sixties, the National Commission on the Causes and Prevention of Violence reviewed the evidence on the relationship between sentence length and recidivism; had their conclusions been heeded, we might have been spared some of the human and social cost of the "prison boom" of the following decade. The commission found that longer sentences did not consistently reduce recidivism rates—and sometimes seemed to increase them. In the late seventies, the economist Samuel Myers found that with several potentially complicating factors controlled—seriousness of offense, prior incarceration, age, race, and others—longer sentences still resulted in higher rates of recidivism, especially for blacks. In the early 1980s, John Berecochea and Dorothy Jaman of the California Department of Corrections assigned carefully matched inmates to either an experimental or a control group, differing only in that the experimental group served an average of about six months less than the controls. The shorter sentences made no difference in the frequency of reconvictions.

Neither the brute fact of recidivism nor the failure of long sentences to deter crime better than shorter ones rules out the possibility that imprisonment may be a special deterrent for *some* offenders. Not all former prisoners return to crime. And though the threat of going back to prison may not be enough to keep most offenders from repeating altogether, it may be enough to slow them down.

This is the central argument of one of the few studies that claim to find a substantial special-deterrent effect of imprisonment. In the mid-1970s, the Illinois Department of Children and Youth Services and the Illinois Law Enforcement Commission created a project for youthful offenders called Unified Delinquency Intervention Services (UDIS), whose guiding principle was to use the "least drastic alternative" in the treatment of serious delinquents. It offered a wide range of alternatives to imprisonment for youths whose delinquency was so chronic or so severe that they would normally have been sent to one of the state's youth prisons. Even some of the most serious delinquents were to be placed in community-based programs that allowed them to stay in their own homes; where that wasn't feasible, they would be given more intensive services that—while necessarily taking them away from their families and neighborhoods—would at least keep them out of the youth institutions.

The "least drastic" level of placement included a variety of services for youths who continued to live at home—psychological counseling, vocational training, remedial education, and advocacy with welfare, housing, and other social agencies. One step up were residential group homes, mainly providing counseling and education or training programs. Wilderness-experience programs were a third alternative; rural camps offering a mix of work experience, education, and recreation were a fourth. The fifth, "most drastic" alternative was what the program defined as "intensive care": treatment either in a conventional psychiatric hospital or in a small residential program that mainly offered intensive group counseling. Finally, those who failed in UDIS could always be sent to the conventional youth prisons.

In the late seventies, Charles A. Murray and Louis A. Cox of the American Institutes for Research published an evaluation of the UDIS program that created a considerable stir. They claimed, first, that *all* the different levels of treatment seemed to have "worked": that is, all reduced the frequency of later arrests among the youth who went through them. The "less drastic" alternatives, however, were also the least effective, while the "tougher" ones, including commitment to a conventional prison, reduced delinquency the most. Murray and Cox interpreted these findings to mean that—contrary to what many assumed (and contrary to the assumptions that underlay the UDIS program itself)—institutionalization was probably the most effective way to deal with young offenders after all. (However, the study also confirmed that longer prison sentences were no more effective than short ones.) This conclusion was widely regarded as "a blow for the 'get-tough' side," as one review of the study put it; and it helped speed the demise of UDIS, which shortly thereafter fell to the budgetary axe. But is this what Murray and Cox's results really showed?

I don't think so. Though the study raised important questions, Murray and Cox overstated the case that it established a clear-cut deterrent effect of imprisonment on delinquents. Even more importantly, their study did not really demonstrate what they claimed to be its most significant result: that imprisonment worked better than its less conventional alternatives.

To arrive at the conclusion that all of the UDIS programs *and* the youth prisons reduced delinquency, Murray and Cox departed from the usual approach to measuring recidivism. Instead of asking whether the delinquent did or did not commit any crimes after release, they chose to measure what they called a *suppression effect*—the difference in the number of arrests a delinquent accumulated before and after treatment. By this measure, only one of the UDIS alternatives—the wilderness programs—failed to cut delinquency rates by at least half, and even they reduced it nearly that much. And while imprisonment in a Department of Corrections institution "suppressed" delinquency by more than two-thirds, both the out-of-town camps and "intensive care" had even greater effects.

As critics quickly pointed out, moreover, the impressive results of this simple "before and after" comparison may well be more apparent than real. The existence of a suppression effect was based on the fact that these youths typically demonstrated a sharp *rise* in delinquency just before they were sentenced to prison or to UDIS. But those apparently rising rates probably reflected the courts' tendency to lower the boom on delinquents precisely when they have been arrested for several offenses in fairly short order. To produce this pattern, therefore, the delinquents needn't have actually increased their overall rates of offending—they need only have been caught during one of perhaps many periods in which they had committed a number of offenses in succession. Since the appearance of a sharp rise in criminality before arrest, then, is probably misleading, the apparent correspondingly sharp decline after treatment probably is, too.

This criticism makes good sense. After all, the Murray-Cox conclusions require us to believe that minor interventions in the lives of extremely tough young men mysteriously accomplished dramatic changes, for reasons that are neither clear nor justified by any discernible theoretical explanation. Why should, say, three months of counseling at a community center cause a long-time, repeat offender to cut his crime rate in half?

However one reads these complex methodological issues, the more important point is that Murray and Cox's data do not show that incarceration is superior to its alternatives—even for the most seriously delinquent youth. (Few, of course, would disagree that it's a necessary alternative for some of them.) The largest suppression effects were found among youth sent to out-of-town camps and to intensive treatment in psychiatric hospitals or group residential treatment centers. But even the "at-home" placements, although they required time to take effect, astonishingly began to show suppression effects as large as those produced by incarceration within two years after the youths' discharge. Furthermore, the data revealed an important finding that Murray and Cox passed over so quickly that it was easy to miss altogether. Many of the delinquents sent to at-home placements remained in them for *three months* or less; but receiving these at-home services for a year or more brought the suppression effect of the "least" and the "most" drastic alternatives so close together that it is difficult to grant much significance to the remaining differences (the year-long at-home placements "suppressed" future arrests by 61 percent, imprisonment by 68 percent). These findings, indeed, generally *affirm* the underlying logic behind UDIS and similar programs: not that every serious delinquent can be handled equally well with less drastic forms of treatment, but that a range of carefully designed placements can be an effective—as well as humane and fiscally appealing—alternative to conventional youth prisons.

Whether the Murray-Cox study demonstrates a significant special-deterrent effect of imprisonment, then, is not clear; but what *is* clear is that it confirms the suspicion that if the experience of prison deters future criminality at all, it does so no more effectively and probably less effectively than intensive rehabilitation programs—a finding with important implications that I'll take up in the final chapter.

But there is yet another, even more important point. The shaky and limited support for special deterrence in current research must be balanced against the steadily growing evidence that the experience of prison, at least for some offenders, has the opposite effect. It makes them worse.

The belief that imprisonment made some offenders more dangerous was widespread among criminologists until the 1970s. To be sure, it was agreed, incarceration might frighten some criminals into mending their ways. But it might also make others more alienated or "hardened" and teach them criminal skills they didn't possess before. And it would surely hurt their chances of competing successfully for a decent livelihood outside prison walls. Though there was not really solid quantitative evidence that the prisons had these unfortunate effects, that didn't mean there was *no* evidence. In fact, there was a great deal.

Sociologists who had studied the prison as a functioning social institution, rather than regarding it abstractly as one factor in the potential criminal's calculation of costs and benefits, often discovered that in practice it worked in ways that undermined the possibility of either deterrence or rehabilitation. For one thing, the prisons fostered inmate "subcultures," which in turn encouraged values and forms of behavior that conflicted with the stated aims of the institution. What prisoners learned in "the joint," if they learned anything at all, was how to "make it" within the peculiar status hierarchy and value system that prevailed inside—

not how to function productively and cooperatively outside. From these studies, too, as well as from a steady stream of autobiographical and journalistic accounts, a picture of imprisonment as a brutally alienating experience emerged that took hold within much of the scholarly community, and informed liberal opinion generally. No one who had experienced an American prison of the fifties or sixties from the inside, or who had worked closely with those who had, could fail to be impressed by the prisons' capacity to induce bitterness, to close off legitimate opportunities for inmates on release, and generally to cripple their ability to cope with the demands of the larger world. The President's Crime Commission summed up this near-consensus in 1967:

> Life in many institutions is at best barren and futile, at worst unspeakably brutal and degrading. To be sure, the offenders in such institutions are incapacitated from committing further crimes while serving their sentences, but the conditions in which they live are the poorest possible preparation for their successful reentry into society, and often merely reinforce in them a pattern of manipulation or destructiveness.

These perceptions convinced many criminologists that the advocates of ever-harsher prison sentences were both glib and uninformed about the institutional and social-psychological realities they were invoking. But with the rise of a more punitive attitude toward offenders in the 1970s, the idea that they might be damaged by the prison experience was easily dismissed as the mushy rhetoric of the incorrigibly softhearted, the predictable response of those with emotional or ideological aversions to a strong criminal-justice system. And it's true that the argument was somewhat oversold in the fifties and sixties. It was virtually an article of faith among some criminologists that the often-observed escalation from youthful troubles to serious adult crime was the result of progressively more alienating and stigmatizing encounters with a repressive and inequitable criminal-justice system. At the extreme, some partisans of this view came close to arguing that young delinquents were not much more than passive pawns in a game set in motion by the official agencies of social control; that they were channeled inexorably into a downward spiral of progressively restricted opportunities for normal life. All this produced a backlash during the seventies, and any lingering concern for the effects of prisons on offenders was swamped in the general rush to put more criminals behind bars.

But recent evidence from several sources, including three of the most important studies of youthful delinquency in the past decade, offers considerable vindication for the liberal argument and forces a renewed skepticism about the place of formal sanctions in a strategy against crime. Indeed, the finding that formal punishment is often associated with an *increase* in crime is one of the most consistent in recent criminological research. "What we found," writes Lyle Shannon in his study of youth crime in Wisconsin, "in a variety of analyses and with considerable regularity, was an increase in the frequency and seriousness of misbehavior in the periods following those in which sanctions were administered." Shannon wasn't able to determine whether these youths got into trouble *because* of something that happened to them in the justice system, or whether they would have gotten worse anyway. "But the data," he concluded, "made one wonder."

This disturbing positive association between punishment and delinquency had already appeared in one of the earliest and best-known long-range studies of delinquency, a study of youth crime in Philadelphia carried out by Marvin Wolfgang, Robert Figlio, and Thorsten Sellin at the University of Pennsylvania and published in the early seventies. They found that, contrary to the common belief that juvenile criminals were routinely let off with a slap on the wrist, the city's juvenile-justice system had done a fairly good job of isolating and punishing hard-core youthful offenders. But "unfortunately the product of this encounter with sanctioning authorities is far from desirable." For "not only do a greater number of those who receive punitive treatment . . . continue to violate the law, but they also commit more serious crimes with greater rapidity than those who experience a less constraining contact with the judicial and correctional system." Again, with the data at hand, it was impossible to tell whether this simply meant that the delinquents most likely to commit more (and more serious) crimes got the most punitive treatment in the first place, thus making the criminal-justice system look worse than it really was. Wolfgang and his colleagues were forced to conclude, however, that "at best" the system had *no* effect on the criminal careers of Philadelphia's delinquent youth and at worst a "deleterious" one. The more recent studies offer firmer evidence for the second of these possibilities. In a study of youth crime in Columbus, Ohio, John Conrad, Simon Dinitz, and their coworkers at Ohio State University found that "committment to a state facility or other formal control agency will increase the speed with which individuals return to serious delinquency." In this case, the "return to serious delinquency" was measured by what Dinitz and Conrad call the *velocity* of the delinquent's criminal career—that is, the amount of "street" time between the arrest that sent the youth to prison (or to some other disposition) and the first arrest after release. The average street time between arrests for the entire group was about 9.3 months. But among those who had been in a state youth prison, this interval was *reduced*, on average, by over half—to 4.8 months. Being sent to a county jail also reduced the street time between arrests, though only by about 1.2 months. Formal court supervision reduced it by 0.8 month; and what the Ohio researchers called the "least intrusive alternatives"—various kinds of informal supervision outside the courts—*added* 2.7 months of street time, on average, before the youth was arrested again.

It could be argued that this is nothing more than the natural result of the more serious delinquents being selected for imprisonment, rather than for less intrusive alternatives, in the first place. If the toughest cases were the ones who most often went to the youth prisons, it isn't surprising (though still not encouraging) that they came out worse than lesser risks sentenced to less severe treatment; after all, they went *in* worse. But the Columbus researchers took this possibility into account, controlling for a number of potentially influential factors, including type of offense, age, sex, race, and socioeconomic status—and the finding didn't change. "With all else controlled," they concluded, "there is a moderate to high inverse relationship between the severity of the sanction for the first in every pair of crimes and the time elapsed until the arrest for the second in the pair."

How do we square these results with Murray and Cox's claims for the more positive effects of imprisonment? One possibility is that the two different measures of recidivism used in the two studies may have affected the results. Accordingly, Dinitz and two colleagues restudied their Columbus data using a measure of the "suppression" of delinquency similar to the one adopted by Murray and Cox. But again their results were strikingly different from those of the UDIS study. To be sure, a substantial proportion of the delinquents desisted from crime after release from prison; in addition, about 30 percent showed evidence of a suppression effect: they were arrested after release from prison, but less often than before. But the rest—over a third —had *higher* arrest rates after release than before they entered prison.

That some delinquents do seem to be made worse by institutionalization, as Dinitz and his colleagues point out, doesn't rule out the possibility that "some of the young may respond favorably" to it. But since we don't yet know which youths fall into which category—or why—the Ohio researchers' conclusion is hard to avoid: "The indiscriminate use of institutionalization" could generate "as many crimes as it prevents."

None of these studies tell us *why* putting people in prison often produces worse results than less severe sanctions, but there are a number of possible explanations. One, of course, is that the results don't really mean what they appear to on the surface. Even careful efforts to account for confounding factors (like differences in offenders' backgrounds or in the severity of their crimes) don't exhaust all the possible ways in which one group of offenders may differ from another. It may be, as Dinitz and Conrad point out, that judges "intuitively" select the most troublesome cases for imprisonment, using criteria too subtle to be captured by the relatively crude nets provided by the standard legal, social, and demographic variables so far used in this kind of research. Another possibility is that the type of treatment meted out to different offenders doesn't affect their actual criminality once released as much as it does the intensity with which they are scrutinized by the police, courts, schools, and other agencies of social control. Therefore, since ex-inmates may well face greater risks of being arrested for whatever crimes they do commit, the official arrest statistics may overrepresent their criminality as compared with that of offenders who have not been in prison. That possibility can't be discounted; but neither can the more direct explanation:

that in one way or another, the experience of incarceration itself often leads to a faster or more frequent relapse into crime.

This likelihood is further strengthened by the results of a twenty-year study of delinquency by the British criminologist Donald West and his colleagues at Cambridge University. The study followed more than four hundred youths, born in the early 1950s in a working-class London neighborhood, from age eight to age twenty-five. One question it addressed was whether being convicted in a criminal court helped to restrain delinquents from further crimes, or whether—as critics had long charged—it "amplified" whatever delinquent tendencies they already possessed. "The general trend," West concludes, "was toward a worsening of behavior following the first finding of guilt." Fifty-three boys who were formally convicted between age fourteen and age eighteen were compared with fifty-three others who had reported the *same* levels of delinquency in interviews at fourteen but had not been convicted in the interim. Among the convicted youths, delinquency increased by 16 percent between the two interviews; among the others, delinquency *fell* by about 14 percent.

The finding that conviction led to worse delinquency was "contrary to expectations," and the researchers accordingly "tried hard to discern an alternative explanation for the findings, but found none." They took considerable pains to eliminate all potential sources of bias that might have influenced their results. For example, they rematched the fifty-three convicted youths with another group carefully chosen for their similarity in a number of background characteristics and in assessments by teachers and peers of their "troublesomeness" at younger ages. But "the outcome was the same, the improvement of the unconvicted youths was just as striking and the contrast with the worsening of the convicted group just as large." Moreover, these researchers used both official arrest data and "self-reports" by delinquents on their rates of criminality—which made it highly unlikely that the higher rates after conviction simply reflected the increased scrutiny of convicted delinquents by the police. The conclusion that conviction tends to produce higher rates of delinquency was unavoidable.

Like the American research in the same sphere, the Cambridge study doesn't tell us why, exactly, this should be so. But the interviews did reveal two significant changes in the convicted delinquents' outlooks that offer some partial clues: they became more hostile to the police, and they developed generally more aggressive feelings toward the world at large. As Dinitz and Conrad put it, "What the boy didn't know or feel before incarceration, he soon learns in the training school." Liberal criminologists had long suspected still another explanation: that conviction in general and imprisonment in particular may cut the offender off from the normal social contacts that generate jobs, new friends, and the possibility of putting together a stable family life, while simultaneously adding the powerful stigma of imprisonment to the myriad other disabilities that the typical ex-inmate brings to the labor market and the larger community. No one has yet succeeded in untangling all of these possible explanations for the recurrent finding that the more severe the sanction, the less positive the result—much less the even more difficult question of which offenders are likely to be affected in which ways by incarceration. But these cautions don't negate the importance of the findings—which are recurrent, pervasive, and remarkably resistant to every effort to explain them away.

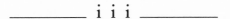

i i i

The case for the second mechanism by which imprisonment may reduce crime—incapacitation—is stronger than the one for deterrence. Common sense suggests that, all else being equal, taking criminals off the streets will at least keep them from committing more street crimes for as long as they stay behind bars. It isn't true, of course, that locking up criminals will keep them from committing crimes *inside* the prisons, a fact frequently ignored in most discussions of the crime-reducing effects of incapacitation. This is no minor issue, for an extraordinary amount of serious crime takes place in prisons; the fact that its victims are often (through by no means always) other inmates doesn't make it any less criminal. Still, if the issue at hand is the reduction of crime on the street, the prima facie evidence for some incapacitation effect is strong. How *large* an effect it may be, however—

and what it takes to achieve it—is another question, and not an easy one to answer.

The problem is that estimates of the amount of crime that can be prevented through incapacitation depend on several "important, and as yet untested, assumptions," as a panel of the National Academy of Sciences put it in a review of this issue in 1978. To calculate how much crime is prevented by putting a given number of known criminals in prisons, we need to know how much of the total crime in the community is now being committed by these particular offenders, and also whether, upon their removal from the street, other criminally inclined people simply take their place.

Consider the second problem first. Curiously, the idea that incapacitation is doomed to be relatively ineffective because other, equally vicious people will spring up to take the place of imprisoned offenders has recently been argued most forcefully, not by liberal critics of the prisons, but by staunch conservatives adhering to a strict version of the "economic" model of crime. Their reasoning rests on the assumption that the crime rate at any given time is determined mainly by what Ernest van den Haag calls the "comparative net advantage" of criminal activities as opposed to legitimate ones. "Thus," van den Haag tells us, "the number of practicing dentists, grocers, drug dealers, or burglars depends on the net advantage which these practitioners expect their occupations to yield compared to other occupations available to them." That number will not change, therefore, unless the "net advantage" does; "the rate at which dental or criminal acts will be committed remains unchanged, unless the net advantage of committing them changes." It is possible to lower the crime rate (or the dentistry rate) by increasing the costs of criminal (or dental) behavior. (Hence, for van den Haag, this becomes an argument for general deterrence.) Not much, however, can be gained by locking up individuals.

Shorn of its pervasive silliness (van den Haag is given to saying things like "I do not see any relevant difference between dentistry and prostitution or car theft, except that the latter activities do not require a license") and of its unhelpfully abstract "economic" imagery, this argument surely has some truth, although just how much is anybody's guess. Certainly, for those crimes that involve illicit markets—say, hard-drug dealing—plucking one offender out of circulation may well mean that some other enterprising type steps in to take over the territory. The argument also touches on a much larger issue that indeed bedevils any strategy of incapacitation: to the extent that serious crime reflects the existence of social pathologies outside the reach of the criminal-justice system, and that those conditions do not change, there is bound to be some "replacement effect" that partly offsets the effect of removing individual offenders from the social settings that produced them in the first place. Finally, as Franklin Zimring and others have pointed out, much serious crime—especially youth crime—is committed in groups, not by isolated individuals acting alone. Removing one, even several, members of a large inner-city youth gang from the street, for example, will not necessarily diminish the gang's collective crime rate.

An even more important limitation on the incapacitation effect has to do with the distribution of criminal behavior within the population. Consider two extreme models. In the first, virtually all serious crime is committed by a handful of very active criminals. Assuming that they can be caught and convicted (most improbable, as I've argued above), incapacitation will "work" very well. Taking even one of this wicked handful off the streets will make a noticeable dent in the crime rate, while taking *most* of them out of circulation will cut crime dramatically. But now suppose, at the other extreme, that crime is evenly distributed throughout the population. Nearly everyone commits some crime, but no one commits much more crime than anyone else. In this case the "payoff" in crime prevention for locking up any single offender will clearly be much less, and even locking up several will have a discouragingly small effect on the crime rate. Imprisoning *enough* of the population to have a major effect on the crime rate, on the other hand, would have large and troubling social repercussions, since cutting crime by, say, a quarter would mean locking up a quarter of the population.

The first model is obviously comforting. It implies that crime may be managed without much investment of social resources or substantial efforts to deal with the larger related social conditions —like a disease that, although serious, is infrequent and therefore easily controlled by quarantining the few hapless victims. So it isn't surprising that something like the first model has generally guided public policy in the past decade—but does that model fit reality?

Only partly. That a disproportionate amount of crime is committed by a *relatively* small fraction of the population is supported by a good deal of research—but not as strongly as is often claimed. Consider again the study of delinquency among Philadelphia youths by Marvin Wolfgang and his colleagues.

Of about ten thousand Philadelphia boys born in 1945, roughly 35 percent had been arrested at least once by age eighteen for something other than a traffic offense—a startlingly high percentage, and one that surprised the researchers themselves, who had expected a rate closer to 10 percent. This evidence of widespread delinquency in the city's population, however, was overshadowed by another finding that seemed to lead to opposite conclusions. Though more than a third of the boys had been arrested at least once, most did *not* go on to become what the researchers called *chronic* offenders—those who had accumulated at least five arrests before their eighteenth birthdays. And the few who did become "chronics"—about 6 percent of the boys in the 1945 "cohort" under study—apparently accounted for a strikingly high share of the cohort's total crimes (at least as measured by official statistics), including more than half of all offenses, three-fifths of the aggravated assaults, and three-fourths of the rapes.

This finding was widely cited in support of the conventional belief that a small core of delinquent youth was responsible for most of the crime problem. (And sometimes even mis-cited in an excess of zeal; it wasn't uncommon to hear that 6 percent of all *offenders*, rather than 6 percent of all *boys*, committed most of the serious crime in Philadelphia—implying an even smaller "hard core.") Since then, similar results have turned up in other research. A second study of Philadelphia boys by Wolfgang and his coworkers—this time of youths born in 1958—found that chronic delinquents made up 7.5 percent of the young men in the cohort —and were responsible for 69 percent of the serious crimes committed by the entire group. Similarly, in Lyle Shannon's study of Wisconsin youths born in the forties and fifties, between 5 and 7 percent of each cohort accounted for over half of all contacts with the police.

These findings are indeed important, and they do show that serious youth crime is concentrated within a fraction of the young population. But what we make of this for purposes of social policy is less clear. One problem is that although the supposedly "tiny" hard-core delinquent group is indeed only a fraction of the population, it is hardly tiny, as becomes evident when the fraction is translated into absolute numbers. Consider Wolfgang's 1958 cohort again. About 7.5 percent of *all* boys born in Philadelphia in that year became chronic recidivist delinquents. In other words, about one boy out of every thirteen became a juvenile delinquent of such persistent and repetitive criminality that he racked up at least five *arrests* (not to mention the many other crimes he surely committed) before his eighteenth birthday. In absolute numbers, this meant that Philadelphia's parents were providing over 1000 *new, chronically delinquent* boys to scourge that beleaguered city's streets each year. Adding the smaller group of chronically delinquent *girls* brings the total up to nearly 1200. Extrapolating to the roughly 2.1 million live male births in the United States in 1958 would give us nearly 160,000 new additions to the ranks of chronically delinquent boys and more than 20,000 chronically delinquent girls each year. Six years of this would suffice to put well over a million active delinquents on the streets. If we take the period of most active criminality to lie between the mid-teens and the early thirties, we begin to get some sense of just how large the well-known "tiny hard core" may be.

The numbers become even more alarming if we use only slightly less restrictive measures of repeat criminality. Thus, although 7.5 percent of boys were arrested five times or more by age eighteen, *19* percent had been arrested two to four times, enough to get themselves classified as "recidivists" in Wolfgang's study. That a fifth of big-city American youth born in the late fifties would turn out to be recidivist delinquents is a startling finding, and one that has distressing implications for a policy of crime control through incapacitation. If a fifth of *all* American boys born in 1958 became recidivist delinquents, that means more than 400,000 to contend with in that year's crop alone.

Of course, Philadelphia is a big city with a crime rate more representative of big cities than of the country as a whole. But even if we look at cities with lower crime rates, the proportion of the young who are repeatedly arrested is substantial. In Sacramento, California, where researchers at the California Youth Authority recently published a study patterned on the Philadelphia research, 13 percent of young men and 4 percent of young women born in 1959 were arrested twice or more before age eighteen.

And if looking at big-city statistics tends to overstate the proportion of recidivist delinquents in the population as a whole, the reliance on official arrest statistics surely *understates* it, for (as we've seen above) most crimes never end in an arrest. So the true proportion of the offender population who would be classifiable as recidivists, or even "chronics," is surely considerably higher than the usual figures suggest.

The same points hold for adult offenders. Thus, a recent study by Alfred Blumstein and Elizabeth Graddy began by distinguishing between what they called the *prevalence* versus the *incidence* of crime. Prevalence is the extent of participation in crime within a given population—the proportion of people who commit *some* crime over a given period. Incidence is the rate at which those people commit crimes. If what determines the total amount of crime is its wide *prevalence* in the population, more than its intensive *incidence* among a few offenders with high individual crime rates, they argued, then a successful strategy of incapacitation would "require unacceptably large resource investments and would be inherently ineffective." What they discovered was that *both* prevalence and incidence were remarkably high in large American cities. About a fourth of *all* men—and *half* of all black men—in cities of more than 250,000 could expect to be arrested at least once by age fifty-five for murder, rape, robbery, aggravated assault, burglary, larceny, arson, or auto theft (the crimes assembled in the FBI's Uniform Crime Reports to constitute their "index" of serious crimes). For those once arrested, the chance of being arrested *again* at least once for another "index" offense was between 85 and 90 percent for men of both races. Serious, repetitive criminality, in short, turned out to be remarkably widespread among the male urban population generally and stunningly so among blacks. "Participation this broad," Blumstein and Graddy concluded, "severely limits a general strategy of crime control based on incapacitation." The findings led Blumstein and Graddy to look askance at the whole concept of a small criminal "hard core." "When such involvement is as pervasive as a full quarter of the male population," they argued, "a common perception of a vast law-abiding population and a tiny band of 'criminals' must be reconsidered."

Even disregarding any "replacement effect," then, a strategy of incapacitation runs up against the simple fact that the number of serious criminals in America is enormous. And this problem is compounded by still another limitation. Even if most crime is committed by a relatively small fraction of offenders, we can do little about the crime rate through incapacitating them unless we can catch them. A strategy of incapacitation, in other words, ultimately depends on how likely an offender is to be apprehended. For many crimes, as we've seen, the likelihood is fairly small.

How these two limitations combine to reduce the effectiveness of incapacitation has been shown in Stephan van Dine, Simon Dinitz, and John Conrad's study of serious violent crime in Columbus, Ohio. Tracing the careers of people arrested for murder, robbery, rape, and aggravated assault over the course of a year, van Dine and his coworkers calculated that even a huge increase in imprisonment—achieved by imposing a mandatory five-year sentence on everyone convicted of any felony whatsoever (even less serious ones)—would have prevented as little as 4 percent of Columbus's serious violent crimes during the study year.

Why would even such a major change in sentencing have so little impact on the crime rate? Partly, the researchers found, because the amount of Columbus's violent crime accounted for by repeat offenders (incidence, again) was apparently a surprisingly small part of the total. Over two-thirds of those convicted of serious violent crimes were *first-time* felony offenders; only 11 percent of the entire sample had been previously convicted of a *violent* felony. A surprising proportion of Columbus's violent crime, in other words, was committed by people for whom the crime was their first (known) offense. By definition, a strategy of incapacitating offenders who have been caught and convicted is powerless to do anything to prevent first offenses.

The other part of the problem was that a substantial proportion of violent criminals were not caught. Only about half of the city's crimes of violence were "cleared" by an arrest. Now the strength of the incapacitation effect on the crime rate depends on how many of the crimes that were *not* cleared were the work of the same criminals who were ultimately caught and convicted for other crimes. Obviously, that is difficult, if not impossible, to determine. The van Dine study's low estimate of a 4 percent reduction in crime was based, for purposes of argument, on the assumption that most of the "uncleared" crime was committed by offenders who were still free—an assumption quickly pounced on by critics anxious to defend incapacitation as an effective tool. But the Columbus researchers calculated that even if the opposite assumption were true—that most uncleared violent crime was committed by criminals who were eventually arrested—*and* if the arrests all led to convictions, *and* if all the convictions were followed by mandatory five-year prison sentences (unlikely in the world of real-life criminal justice), the proportion of violent crime prevented would rise to only about 18 percent.

That reduction, to be sure, is not insignificant. But even if we lean toward the higher figure, it is still astonishingly small when we consider the enormous impact such a policy would have on the criminal-justice system. As John Conrad puts it, a mandatory five-year prison sentence for all felony convictions would have "transformed the Ohio prison system beyond recognition." In 1979, Ohio had 13,000 inmates crammed into a prison system with a capacity of 9,000. The five-year sentence would have multiplied the inmate population by five—to 65,000. "What such a draconian law would have done to the rest of Ohio's criminal justice system, and to public attitudes toward the system," Conrad writes, "I must leave to conjecture."

No one seriously doubts that a modicum of crime can be prevented by incapacitating offenders. There are legitimate disagreements about the incidence versus the prevalence of crime, the magnitude of individual crime rates, and the proportion of offenders who elude arrest. But no one has convincingly challenged the fundamental point that emerges over and over again from the growing body of research on incapacitation: the potential reduction in serious crime is disturbingly small, especially when balanced against the social and economic costs of pursuing this strategy strenuously enough to make much difference to public safety.

For those costs are truly staggering. In theory, that ought to be of great concern to conservatives anxious about the fiscal condition of the country and the stability of the social fabric. In practice, much conservative writing relies on the usually unstated assumption that achieving significant reductions in crime through incarceration is virtually costless—leading to the curious argument that, though we may not gain much from increased incarceration, we cannot *lose* either. But that position makes sense only if we accept what might be called the free-lunch model of crime control: the notion that social and economic resources are infinitely available and therefore that pouring them into prison construction and maintenance won't affect our ability to do other things that might equally (or more favorably) affect the crime rate. This view has a familiar ring; it is, in fact, the domestic version of the utopian belief that we can endlessly afford both guns and butter.

In reality, building prisons is extraordinarily expensive, especially if we aim to build prisons that are reasonably humane and secure. And the costs do not end with construction, because the expense of operation is also strikingly high. The figures are often cited, and they rise so rapidly that it's difficult to keep up with them. At this writing, constructing a maximum-security facility costs $75,000 or more per cell; annual operating costs per inmate are conservatively estimated at $15,000 to $20,000. No one is suggesting that we shouldn't provide enough prison space for truly dangerous people. But that is different from the breezy assurance that we can build enough prisons to bring down the crime rate substantially without shortchanging other kinds of social spending.

Consider that by mid-1984, about 454,000 people were being held in state and federal prisons. Tripling that population—in the hope of reducing serious crimes by, say, 20 or 25 percent—would, at current prices, cost perhaps $70 billion for construction alone (ignoring interest costs, and without spending a dime to improve the conditions in existing prisons). To that sum we should add, conservatively, fourteen billion annually in operating costs. We would also need to funnel vastly enlarged sums into state, local, and federal courts to accommodate the increased flow of prison-bound offenders. What this would mean in the real world of budget and resource limitations has been best described in a study of prison capacity done in the late seventies by Joan Mullen and her coworkers for the National Institute of Justice. Such massive investment in prisons, they argued, would bring "a succession of increasingly impossible demands on the budgetary resources of the community"—demands which, contrary to the free-lunch model, would have profound consequences. "For every person who goes to prison," the NIJ study pointed out, "two people don't go to college. For every day a person stays in jail, twenty children eat starch instead of protein."

A few other quick comparisons illustrate the social dimensions of this choice: $70 billion is far more than double the entire 1982 aggregate income deficit of poor families in America—that is, well over twice what it would have taken in that year to lift *every* poor family in the country above the poverty line. The $14 billion a year needed on top of the current operating costs of our penal system could put more than three-quarters of a million people to work at a wage sufficient to support a four-person urban family at the *lower budget level* calculated by the U. S. Department of Labor (about 50 percent above the poverty line). Alternatively, it could provide a million youths with solid jobs at an entry-level wage of $7 an hour.

Realistically, this is roughly the level of spending needed to achieve anything more than a minor reduction in serious crime rates. If this estimate seems extreme or unduly pessimistic, keep in mind that it is based not only on perhaps fallible estimates of social research, but also on the stubborn data of experience. Between the end of 1970 and the middle of 1984, the state and federal prison population increased by 132 percent—with *no* reduction, and indeed some overall increase, in the rates of serious crimes of violence. Remember, too, that although these expenditures would give us an incarceration rate more than twenty times that of some European countries, they would (even assuming that they did accomplish a 25 percent reduction in crimes) still leave us with far and away the highest rates of criminal violence in the developed world.

Nor, of course, are these the only costs involved, or even the most important; they are only those most easily translated into numbers. On a deeper level, the social vision promoted by some of the more extreme advocates of increased incapacitation is downright chilling. The United States already presents the demoralizing spectacle of one of the world's most highly advanced societies confining an unparalleled proportion of its citizens in order to achieve even the most minimal level of public safety. Much greater increases in incarceration would turn the American penal system, already swollen out of all proportion, into a homegrown Gulag of dreadful proportions. This is bad enough in itself; but it would also profoundly disrupt community and family life—which ought to concern any reasonable conservative. The prison already looms as an ugly but pervasive presence in many American communities, especially among disadvantaged minorities. At current rates, every fifth black man in America will spend some time in a state or federal prison, and the proportion is far higher in some communities, especially the inner cities. Further drastic increases in incarceration would decimate these communities beyond recognition and would amount, in practice, to writing off a substantial part of entire generations of minority men. This is what the technical equations of incapacitation research really mean, translated into their potential effects on the lives of real Americans.

i v

Incapacitation, then, certainly has some effect on the crime rate. But this is likely to remain distressingly small, short of extraordinary—and perhaps even counterproductive—investments in prisons. Can we improve on this unhappy trade-off? Perhaps—at least in theory. The effectiveness of incapacitation depends not only on apprehending those who commit crimes, but also on how well we can determine which among the many criminals who come before the courts would go on to become the chronic or *high-rate* offenders who commit much more than their share of a community's crimes. If we can do this better, we may be able to realize a greater incapacitative effect with less *overall* use of incarceration—and, therefore, with lower social and economic costs. The search for more reliable ways to predict criminality is one of the oldest preoccupations of criminology; unfortunately it is also, on the whole, one of the least successful. It's not difficult to predict roughly what *kinds* of people are more likely to become serious offenders (several of those predictors will appear in the next chapters). But it is much harder to predict which *individuals* within these broad categories will be especially violent or will commit offenses at a particularly high rate. In the past few years this eternal quest has been given something of a new lease on life by the concept of *selective incapacitation,* developed mainly by Peter Greenwood and others at the Rand Corporation. The Rand researchers claim to have developed newer and better means to sort out potential high-rate offenders from the rest. Ideally, this should mean that we can achieve a better level of crime prevention by locking up those high-raters for longer periods, without greatly adding to the prison space we already have—since the same prediction techniques theoretically also allow us to pick out less troublesome offenders and sentence them to less stringent terms.

The principle of selective incapacitation has been much criticized on philosophical grounds. Critics argue that imposing widely different sentences for the same crimes in order to prevent crimes that *might* be committed violates the most fundamental standards of fairness. Supporters respond that no criminal-justice system can (or does) entirely ignore the issue of the greater danger some offenders pose to society, and that selective incapacitation merely refines our ability to protect society effectively. And supporters also counter that selective incapacitation would in any case only be applied to offenders who face severe prison sentences anyway. But let's put aside these philosophical issues for the moment. What are the prospects that following a strategy of selective incapacitation would substantially reduce crime?

Like many other panaceas offered over the years, selective incapacitation appeals to that part of the American psyche that is forever on the lookout for the technical breakthrough that will magically resolve tough social problems without tackling their deep roots in American life. But the claims for selective incapacitation have been much exaggerated, and those who have swallowed them whole are doomed to disappointment.

One problem is that selective incapacitation works better for some kinds of crimes than others, and the crimes for which it works best are not necessarily the most serious ones. As the Rand study points out, homicide and sex offenses are "extremely difficult to predict or to reduce through incapacitation, because of the low rate at which they are committed by any one offender"; its analysis, therefore, is concerned mainly with the reduction of burglary and robbery. These are certainly serious and frightening crimes, but not the most serious or the most frightening. (And they are also among those crimes for which alternatives to incarceration are most feasible, a point to which I'll return.)

Another problem is that selective incapacitation works effectively only in those jurisdictions that do not *already* sentence burglars and robbers to very long prison terms. As the Rand researchers note, the "payoff" from longer sentences would be much smaller in Texas than in California, for example, because Texas's sentences for burglary and robbery are *already* so severe. They argue that a 30 percent increase in incarceration achieved by "selective" incapacitation of high-rate robbers in Texas might bring a 10 percent decrease in robberies in that state. To put this in perspective, one recent study indicates that Texas's robbery rate would have to fall about 80 percent to reach the robbery rate of an otherwise comparable West German state.

Further problems have to do with the inherent limits of prediction. The attempt to anticipate the future behavior of offenders is by no means new or unusual. Courts already try to do so at several points; indeed, the criminal-justice system at every stage attempts to estimate which offenders are most likely to be especially dangerous to public safety. From the decision of the police to make a formal arrest and the granting or witholding of bail, through the presentence investigation that guides the judge toward incarceration or probation, to the decision of a parole board to release an inmate or not, these considerations come into play over and over again. Does the delinquent come from a "bad home"? Does the robber have a heroin habit? Does the rapist have a series of prior arrests for crimes of violence? All of these factors now go into the determination of who winds up in prison and how long they stay there. The Rand study concedes that "the predictive factors considered in our analysis, along with many others that have less predictive validity, are currently the normal input for presentence investigation reports and sentencing decisions." Thus the real issue is not *whether* we should "selectively" incapacitate offenders—we do so now—but whether we can devise ways of doing it that are significantly more effective than the ones already in use.

The Rand researchers think we can. On the basis of interviews with inmates in California, Texas, and Michigan, they claim to have discovered seven characteristics that, when combined, powerfully predict high-rate offending among robbers and burglars:

- Incarceration for more than half of the two-year period before their most recent arrest.
- A prior conviction for the type of crime being predicted.
- A juvenile conviction before the age of sixteen.
- Commitment to a state or federal juvenile institution.
- Heroin or barbiturate use in the two years before the current arrest.
- Heroin or barbiturate use as a juvenile.
- Being employed less than half of the two-year period before the current arrest.

These characteristics aren't much different from those most courts now use in sentencing offenders; the Rand researchers themselves point out that the courts in their sample seemed to have done a fairly good job of using these and similar factors to give particularly long sentences to some offenders. Whether, therefore, using this particular "scale" would make much difference could only be discovered prospectively—by predicting offenders' later careers, using these characteristics, before the fact—rather than retrospectively—after the fact.

But prediction is very difficult, as the physicist Hans Bethe is reported to have said, especially when it concerns the future. What's more, although the "predictive" factors do indeed tell us something important about offenders—and something that is likely to be generally true—the information comes too late to be very effective in reducing crime. Once you have assembled a group of offenders who have accumulated, over the years, several of the characteristics that the Rand researchers believe predict high-rate criminality, you can sort out the high-raters from the rest of the offender population with some degree of assurance and with a smaller chance of being wrong. In particular, you will have fewer *false positives*—people whom you've predicted will become high-rate offenders who won't, in fact, turn out that way. But by that time offenders in this group have already committed multiple crimes, have repeatedly been in prison, and, for that matter, are now older and probably beginning to slow down in any case. The knowledge that many of them may be repeaters hasn't helped prevent any of the many crimes they've already committed— indeed, until they've committed multiple crimes, we cannot use this scale to predict what they will do in the future. It *may* help us prevent potential crimes, but these have by now become a shrinking proportion of the crimes they will commit during their careers (surely little consolation to their past victims). In short, this sort of prediction is by no means useless—but it's frustrat- ingly inefficient.

This dilemma shows up clearly in a recent California Youth Authority study on the prospects for "Early Identification of the Chronic Offender." The study focused on the later criminal ca- reers of youths who had spent some time in secure Youth Author- ity institutions in the early 1960s. It discovered that a number of background characteristics could indeed predict later "chron- icity" with substantial accuracy. But this was mainly because so *many* of the youths in their sample—86 percent—wound up as chronic offenders that there was little room for false-positive errors. In other words, you could have flatly predicted that *all* these young men would become repeat offenders and not have been very far wrong. Why? Because most of them were *already* chronic delinquents by the time they wound up in the sample. As the CYA researchers noted, "The high rate of continued offend- ing shown for these youths should come as no surprise," since they represented a select group of youths who were placed in California Youth Authority institutions only after a long process of screening and continued failure on probation, including, for many, prior placements in county camps and/or Youth Authority institutions. These youths, in other words, were accepted for CYA committment largely because of their persistence in criminal activity, thereby comprising a highly select population of the most serious, and chronic, juvenile delinquents.

The fact that the best predictor of future delinquency is *past* delinquency, and the more past delinquency the better—one of the most persistent findings for years in prediction research in criminology—means that much delinquency must take place, and much human damage must be done, before a strategy of selective incapacitation based on offenders' past behavior becomes possible or is even set in motion. We're saying, in effect, nothing more profound—or more useful—than that when a kid has repeatedly committed serious crimes in the face of multiple convictions and even multiple prison stints, if not much has changed in his life, it's a pretty good bet that he'll do it again when he gets the chance. We will probably be on target more often than not. But insofar as this prediction is helpful, it's not very different from what, in general, is already being done with chronic repeat delinquents in California or anywhere else.

There is also another, less sheerly technical, problem with using such a scale of characteristics. Past troubles with the law are not the only predictors of which among the mass of criminals who come before the courts or parole authorities are most likely to go on to repeated later offenses. But when we begin to look at some of the other predictors, more fundamental and more disturbing questions come up. Consider the results of the CYA study again. The general finding was that prediction generally "worked," at least within a group of already very troublesome youth. Those with a particularly high risk of becoming chronic adult criminals could "be identified with sufficient accuracy to be of practical as well as theoretical importance." Other than their prior records, what were the identifying characteristics? The chronic offenders more often came from families of lower socioeconomic status, had more siblings, were more retarded in school (and more negative about school), were younger at first police contact, had longer prior records, expressed more antisocial attitudes, and were behaviorly more hostile, more obtrusive, less responsible and less conforming. . . . youths of Black ethnicity were more often chronic offenders.

Aside from their prior troubles with the law, then, the most important characteristics of the youths who went on to become chronic offenders were a mix of social, educational, and economic disadvantages and early behavioral problems (all doubtless interrelated). As the CYA researchers pointed out, there were "few surprises" in these results; as we'll see in later chapters, they fit the findings of most other research on the characteristics of serious offenders. The important issue is what we *do* with this knowledge. For it simply does not follow from this profile that incapacitation is either the most effective or the most appropriate form of intervention if we want to keep these youths from committing crimes in the future. The CYA researchers correctly noted that the implications of their findings "are not restricted to variations on the currently popular themes of incapacitation and/or harsher punishment." There is, they argued, "no reason to believe that equal or greater consideration should not be given" to programs aimed at early intervention with high-risk youths and intensive rehabilitation; an effective treatment program that reduced these youths' rates of subsequent offending by just 10 percent would have prevented over 2,600 arrests—perhaps 400 of them for crimes of violence.

The point is obvious. If we can predict criminality through characteristics that are amenable to change, then there is no *logical* reason why we should lock up certain individuals on the basis of these characteristics rather than trying to change them. In the Rand analysis, similarly, there are three predictors of high-rate offending (other than prior convictions or imprisonment)—being unemployed for at least half of the two-year period before the current arrest; using heroin or barbiturates during the same period; and using heroin or barbiturates as a juvenile. We have no reason to doubt that all these factors are likely to foreshadow later criminality, and good reason to agree with the Rand researchers that they do. But granted that unemployment and drug use are reasonably good predictors of high individual crime rates, what logic dictates that imprisonment is the best response? Aside from the profoundly disturbing moral and political implications of locking people up because they are out of work—an approach that in the United States has deep racial implications as well—the Rand study presents no compelling *technical* case that incapacitation is the best way to deal with unemployed or drug-dependent offenders. To make their case, the proponents of selective incapacitation would need to show not only that locking these offenders up for long sentences might be expected mathematically to result in a given number of crimes prevented, but also that alternative approaches to the offenders' employment or drug problems would not do just as well—or better. The best that the study can manage, through, is the blanket assertion that "rehabilitation" has not worked so far. This is not in fact true (a point we will explore later); more important, there is no evidence that incapacitation has worked any better. If we can make incapacitation work better by improving our prediction methods, why can't we use the same methods to help us develop better and more carefully targeted rehabilitation programs? (And to do something about the larger communal disadvantages that spawn high rates of joblessness and drug dependency in the first place?) Clearly, the reasons for choosing incapacitation as a strategy for dealing with these problems are political, not technical.

The implications of that choice become troubling indeed when we look again at the predictors of chronic offending isolated in the California study. Young delinquents who went on to become chronic adult offenders were disproportionately black and disproportionately poor. Should we therefore sentence black (or poor) youths to longer terms—for the same crimes—than we do white (or middle-class) youths? The chronics were also more likely to do poorly in school; should we therefore sentence delinquents with low grade-point averages to longer terms than those with higher grades?

This doesn't mean that we should abandon the search for better ways of predicting violent behavior among offenders. The fact that this enterprise hasn't been very successful doesn't mean that it has had no successes at all, or that we wouldn't gain by whatever improvements are possible. At one time some liberal criminologists argued that any attempt to use the resources of social science, psychology, or psychiatry to predict violence was inherently repressive, smacking of efforts to control and regulate social "deviance" in the service of middle-class norms. But as one noted student of violence prediction, John Monahan, has pointed out, the problem with this stance is that it offers no alternatives for dealing with truly dangerous people. "We are not talking," Monahan writes,

> of psychiatry and psychology being manipulated to play an improper role in controlling more or less harmless deviations from social norms. We are talking of murder, rape, robbery, assault, and other forms of violent behavior. There is a widespread social consensus which transcends political, racial, and economic groupings that such activities tear at the already frayed social bonds holding society together. It seems to me that when we lend professional assistance, however marginal, to improve society's control of those who will murder, rape, rob, and assault—provided that we do not let the nature of that assistance be overstated or distorted—we have nothing for which to apologize.

The proviso is crucial. In particular, the line must be drawn at using demographic categories or remediable social disadvantages as criteria for locking offenders up as especially dangerous; as Monahan also remarks, "we must decline to launder for the legal system the social and demographic factors that anticipate future crime." If we fail to heed that boundary, the use of predictive methods in the service of crime control might ultimately lead to preventive detention of the poor, the black, and the youthful unemployed.

Here again, we've come to the heart of the controversy over the uses of imprisonment. As with deterrence, the technical justifications for relying almost exclusively on a strategy of incapacitation are not compelling. We will get much less "payoff" from either mechanism—even in the barest cost-benefit terms—than many people unreflectively assume. After years of investigation, we are not sure that the prisons deter crime to any significant extent, and we *are* sure that they do not deter it effectively. There is a sound case that incapacitation can work to some degree, but the strategy is cumbersome, expensive, and inefficient, requiring extraordinary investments of social resources to accomplish even small results. None of this is to argue that we should shut down the prisons. Nor is it to deny that there is a disturbingly large number of people in America who must be locked up in them, sometimes for a very long time. For that matter, it provides no grounds for opposing judicious investment in new prisons to replace existing facilities that are inhumane or unsafe. But coming to terms with the current role of prisons in American life is not the same as believing that building more of them will markedly reduce crime. The first is a necessary, if sobering, recognition; the second is simply wishful thinking.

The limits of imprisonment as a strategy to reduce crime are understood in principle by most serious criminologists, of whatever ideological stripe. There are differences of interpretation, but among serious students of deterrence and incapacitation they are differences of degree, often quite small ones, rather than differences of kind. The vehemence with which further investments in incarceration are promoted at one end of the political spectrum has more to do with choices about the possibility—or desirability —of *other* ways of dealing with crime than with any demonstrable virtues of incarceration itself. Those who call for still more rigorous efforts at deterrence and incapacitation through harsher sentences and more prison cells base that argument, in part, on the premise that there is little else we can do, by way of changing offenders or their social environments, that will have much effect on crime. Sometimes their reasoning is that many conditions often believed to generate crime are not really very important after all; sometimes, that we do not know how to change them even if they *are* important; and sometimes, that we shouldn't try to change them even if we could.

Meanwhile, those who have correctly pointed out the limits of incarceration have often failed to make a compelling case that there *are* other things we might do—things that are not only less brutal, but also less wasteful and more effective. Unless we can make that case, appeals for more humane alternatives to imprisonment are apt to fall on deaf ears, given the deep—and understandable—current of fear and indignation over criminal violence in America today. Realistically, we are not likely to deflect the movement toward ever-harsher policies unless we can show that there are ways to stop producing so many criminals.

Can we do that? In the following chapters, I will examine the relationships between crime and several social problems whose significance for crime and its prevention has recently been hotly debated: unemployment, inequality, family and community disruption. I will argue that the fashionably pessimistic view is misleading. We know a good deal about the sources of crime in America, and about what it would take to reduce it. The more difficult question is whether we have the political will to take on the job.

4

UNDERSTANDING CRIME: WORK AND WELFARE

Toward the end of the sixteenth century, Richard Hakluyt depicted the ominous consequences of England's widespread
unemployment. "For all the statutes that hitherto can be devised,"
he wrote, "and the sharp execution of the same in punishing idle
and lazy persons for want of sufficient occasion of honest employment," it had proven impossible to

> deliver our Commonwealth from multitudes of loiterers and
> idle vagabonds, which, having no way to be set on work
> . . . often fall to pilfering and thieving and other lewdness,
> whereby all the prisons of the land are daily pestered and
> stuffed full of them, where either they pitifully pine away, or
> else at length are miserably hanged, even twenty at a clap out
> of some one jail.

The same problem worried American observers three centuries later. In 1878, the economist Carroll D. Wright, Massachusetts
Commissioner of Statistics, noted that more than 67 percent of
convicts in that state were recorded as "having had no occupation"; of 220 men sentenced to prison one year, "147 were without a
trade or any regular means of earning a living." Wright warned of
the disquieting implications of this for the "reform" of prisoners:

> Will these men serve their time, and be discharged in their
> present unfit state to battle with the world? They may go out
> into society again resolved to do right; but without a reliable
> means of support they are ill-prepared to meet the adversities
> of hard times, or the temptation to gain by crime what they
> do not know how to obtain by honest labor.

The connection between crime and the lack of any "regular means of earning a living" has changed little since Wright's time, or even Hakluyt's. At the close of the 1970s, nearly 40 percent of state prison inmates and 55 percent of the inmates of local jails had not been working full-time in the months before they went behind bars, while those who did work typically had little to show for it. Only about half of a sample of "habitual felons" in a Rand Corporation survey of the California prisons in the late seventies had gained their usual pre-prison income by working; of those who had, most "had earnings that were not much above a poverty level." Within this generally deprived sample, moreover, those prisoners who had been even slightly more successful in the labor market—those the Rand researchers called the *better employed*— committed crimes, while on the "street," at about one-sixth the rate of the others. This difference is all the more remarkable given the study's extremely generous definition of what it meant to be *better employed*: earning all of $100 a week and working at least 75 percent of their "street" time.

Nor is this all. Later Rand research, as I've noted in chapter 3, suggests that unemployment is one of the most powerful predictors of which inmates among the already "hardened" prison population are most likely to go on to become *high-rate* offenders, responsible for much more than their share of serious crime even in this rather select group.

These findings are no surprise; they fit our commonsense understanding of who goes to prison, and they are compatible with a broad range of theories of crime, including the "economic" approach favored by many conservatives. In a society in which work is the indispensable key to most things—material and otherwise—that our culture considers worth having, it's easy to see why those without work might try other, less legitimate ways to get them. And since work is also one of the most important ways individuals become integrated into a larger community, it isn't surprising that those excluded from the world of work will be held less tightly by the bonds that keep a society together. On the face of it, the appropriate response seems fairly cut-and-dried; if we want to lower the crime rate once and for all, we will have to do a much better job of providing access to work—especially for those groups, like minorities and the young, who have been most excluded from its benefits.

So far, all this seems fairly obvious; and it has been a staple argument of liberal criminology for decades. But as it turns out, the relationship between crime and unemployment is surprisingly controversial. Not everyone agrees that unemployment has much to do with crime; and of those who do, not all agree that there is much we can do about it.

For instance, despite the stark evidence supplied by the work histories of those in prison, James Q. Wilson writes that "contrary to what many people assert, very little research shows a relationship between economic factors and crime." For most conservative writers, it follows that improving the prospects for economic security cannot have much effect on the crime rate. More generally, the argument that unemployment is only minimally related to crime serves to focus attention on more "individual" factors—temperament, family practices, perhaps genetic abnormalities—which are presumably less amenable to social intervention. All this is confusing, to say the least, and it contributes greatly to the paralysis that afflicts our public policies toward crime.

It is also misleading. The relationships between unemployment and crime are real; we won't be able even to begin an attack on crime that is both humane and effective if we do not confront them. But these relationships are more complicated than they might seem at first glance, and they deserve careful analysis.

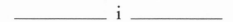

i

One line of argument dismisses the connections between unemployment and crime on the grounds that there is no good evidence that the crime rate responds strongly to economic *fluctuations*. Conservatives point especially to rising crime in the prosperity of the 1960s and its apparent decline in the Depression of the 1930s. And it's true that formal research on crime and economic fluctuations presents a mixed picture.

The connections between crime rates and the ups and downs

of the economy were studied by several noted American scholars in the twenties, and the coming of the Great Depression in the thirties gave the issue new urgency. Many of these early studies were so poorly designed that, as the University of Pennsylvania criminologist Thorsten Sellin concluded in a well-known monograph for the Social Science Research Council in 1937, it was "difficult to arrive at any generalizations" from their results. But two of the most sophisticated efforts in that period—Dorothy S. Thomas's 1927 "Social Aspects of the Business Cycle" and Emma Winslow's study of crime and employment in Massachusetts, commissioned as part of the work of the National Commission on Law Observance and Enforcement in 1931—found strong associations between economic downturns and some kinds of crime, especially what Thomas called "crimes against property with violence"—robbery, housebreaking, and burglary.

Interest in the effect of "hard times" on crime waned in the prosperous postwar era; it was revived only in the gloomier seventies, most notably by the sociologist M. Harvey Brenner of Johns Hopkins University. In a series of studies covering a variety of countries and time periods, Brenner has consistently found chillingly precise correlations between changes in the overall unemployment rate and several measures of crime, including national homicide rates and admissions to state prisons. Thus in 1970, according to Brenner, an increase in the American unemployment rate of one percentage point accounted for nearly 4 percent of that year's homicides, almost 6 percent of its robberies, and close to 9 percent of narcotics arrests. Brenner attributes these tragic effects of unemployment only partly to the pressures of income loss suffered by those out of work; equally important is what Brenner calls the *compound-interest effect* of unemployment on crime rates. Unemployment aggravates two other social pathologies that everyone agrees are closely related to both violent and property crimes: drug and alcohol abuse. Losing a job leads to drug abuse, and drug abuse leads to property crime. Alcohol consumption, Brenner argues, also rises dramatically during economic slumps, and drinking in turn is closely associated with serious violent crime. Moreover, unemployment disrupts family ties by forcing the jobless to migrate in search of work; and this, too, in Brenner's view, leads to higher crime rates.

Brenner has made the strongest recent argument for a clear-cut relationship between national unemployment rates and crime. Other studies in the past two decades have been less confident. On balance, the studies provide what the economist Robert Gillespie, in a 1975 review of the evidence, called "general, if not uniform, support" for the commonsense belief that unemployment rates are related to crime. The kernel of truth in the conservative argument—and it is an important one—is that many careful scholars have found at best what the economists Thomas Orsagh and Ann Dryden Witte call "weak" associations between national-level changes in unemployment rates and crime. Why?

Part of the problem involves technical, methodological difficulties inherent in this kind of research—some of which we've already encountered in considering the results of studies of deterrence: it is very sensitive to the specific assumptions that are made about what other factors might influence crime rates. Depending on how such factors as age distribution or sentencing policies are entered into the equation, researchers of equal honesty and scrupulousness may well come up with strikingly different conclusions.

But the deeper and more crucial issues involve several ambiguities in the relationship between unemployment and crime itself. These do not disprove the importance of the connection between crime and work; indeed, they strengthen it. But they do mean that we have to view that connection through a more refined lens. The ambiguities fall under three general headings:

1. Unemployment itself appears to have *contradictory* effects on crime.
2. The official unemployment rate alone (on which most of this research has been based) is a poor guide to the true significance of the relationships between employment and crime.
3. Those relationships are affected by a number of intervening factors, including public policies and the level of community support, that do not generally show up in quantitative research.

The first complexity is that, while unemployment tends to increase crime in some ways, it may tend to decrease it in others.

In particular, it may restrict the *opportunities* for some kinds of crime, even while increasing the motivation to commit them. Thus, as Lawrence Cohen, Marcus Felson, and Kenneth Land have argued, increases in unemployment may reduce the chances of being robbed by keeping potential victims at home, out of "transit" areas—areas between home and the workplace. By the same token, the fact that unemployed workers spend more time at home restricts opportunities for residential burglary. Looking at rates of robbery, burglary, and auto theft from the late 1940s to the early 1970s, Cohen, Felson, and Land found a "modest" but noticeable association between increases in unemployment and decreases in these crimes. (A somewhat similar argument was made in the late fifties by the sociologists Daniel Glaser and Kent Rice to explain their finding that high levels of unemployment seemed to go hand in hand with increased crime among adults but decreased crime among juveniles. In times of high unemployment, they reasoned, unemployed parents would spend more time at home—and thus give more time and attention to the behavior of their children.) It follows that the same mechanisms probably work in the other direction as well: widespread economic prosperity can increase crimes like robbery and burglary by multiplying the opportunities to commit them.

Another, still more crucial, set of complications arises from the clumsiness of our standard measures of unemployment. At first glance there might seem to be few things simpler than to determine what it means to be unemployed; but in fact, as critics have long pointed out, the conventional definition of unemployment embodied in the official rates obscures more than it reveals. To begin with, it lumps together what are actually widely different experiences among people with very different propensities toward serious crime. In terms of its effects on crime rates, for example, unemployment clearly means one thing in the case of a forty-year-old machinist with three children, a mortgage, and a twenty-year work history who has just lost his job, and another if we're talking about an eighteen-year-old inner-city dropout who has never held a job for more than three months, may never in the future, and knows it. The official rate tells us nothing by itself about the differences between the pain of being out of work for six months and the demoralization of a lifetime with minimal prospects for work. Similarly, because the rate is *national*, it obscures differences at the level of local communities, where, arguably, they count the most. National changes in unemployment may have little effect on the job situation in communities that face persistently high unemployment through good times and bad. When we do focus on specific neighborhoods, the connections between crime and unemployment emerge dramatically. A recent study by Robert Sampson and Thomas Castellano, for example, found that victimization rates were 80 percent higher for crimes of theft and 40 percent higher for crimes of violence in urban neighborhoods with high unemployment than in those with low.

Most important, the strength of the unemployment-crime relationship is obscured by what the official definition of unemployment leaves out. In the first place, it omits great numbers of people who do not have jobs. We count as "unemployed" only those who describe themselves as "looking for work." But if we want to know how the lack of work affects the crime rate, this is misleading. It's logical, after all, that those of the jobless who are still sufficiently hopeful and attached to the world of legitimate work to be actually looking for jobs are *less* likely to be involved in serious crime than those uncounted others who have given up the search for a job—or who have never begun it.

Thus research that has broadened its focus to include people who are both jobless and not in search of work—those who, in economic language, are not "participating in the labor force"— has come up with stronger associations between joblessness and crime than research using the official category of "unemployment" alone. In one of the most careful of these studies, the economists Llad Phillips and Harold Votey of the University of California at Santa Barbara tried to determine how much of the dramatic rise in youth crime in the sixties could be attributed to changes in the labor-market opportunities open to youth. Much had been made (and still is) of the supposed "paradox" of increasing crime in the face of declining *overall* unemployment rates in the sixties. But Phillips and Votey pointed out that despite the *general* improvement in the national unemployment rate, another crucial trend was a simultaneous rise in the unemployment rate for youths—particularly nonwhites—and an even more precipitous drop in their labor-force participation. In 1952, for example, the official unemployment rate for nonwhite men aged eighteen and nineteen was about 10 percent; by 1967 it had reached 20 percent. This took place even though the unemployment rate for the country as a whole was about 3 percent in both years. Measured by their participation in the labor force, the position of youth was even worse; the proportion of nonwhite youths either at work or actively looking for work dropped from nearly 80 percent in 1952 to just 63 percent in 1967. Part of this shift is explainable by the fact that a greater proportion were in school, but not all of it. The harsh fact was that by the late sixties, more youths, especially blacks, were neither working, looking for work, nor pursuing an education. How did that change affect the crime rate?

According to Phillips and Votey, very strongly indeed—so strongly, in fact, that these changes in the labor market were *by themselves* "sufficient to explain increasing crime rates for youths" in the sixties. The most powerful associations between joblessness and youth crime, they found, emerged when they divided their sample into youths who were in the labor force (either working or looking for work) and those who were out of it—those who neither had jobs nor sought them. This distinction was a more accurate predictor of youth crime rates than the more conventional contrast between youths who were working and those who were not. In short, what seemed most closely related to crime among youths was not just being out of work but being so *far* out of work that they had ceased to look for it. To Philips and Votey, this suggested that what principally influenced youth crime was not the *current* state of the economy so much as the long-term experience of fundamentally constricted economic opportunities, an experience that had convinced many urban minority youths that not much was to be gained by looking for a job.

Clearly, then, we need to broaden the focus of investigation beyond the conventional measure of unemployment to include other forms of joblessness. But we need to broaden the terms of our discussion in another way as well; for what the narrow emphasis on the unemployment rate ignores is the larger, ultimately more crucial, issue of how the *quality* of work affects the crime rate. One of the most consistent findings in recent research is that *un*employment is less strongly associated with serious crime than *under*employment—the prospect of working, perhaps forever, in jobs that cannot provide a decent or stable livelihood, a sense of social purpose, or a modicum of self-esteem. As the economist Ann Dryden Witte puts it, "It is not so much individual unemployment per se which causes crime, but rather the failure to find relatively high-wage, satisfying employment." What is at issue, Witte concluded after reviewing the evidence in the late seventies, is "economic viability, rather than just employment per se."

The idea that crime might be linked with the larger problem of inadequate and unstable work, not just the absence of work altogether, is not new. "The kind of labor which requires the most skill on the part of the workman to perform," Carroll D. Wright argued in 1878, "insures the laborer most perfectly against want and crime." Furthermore, he wrote, the benefits of skilled work were passed down across the generations through their elevating effects on family life. "The occupation of the parents has a wonderful effect upon the character and tendencies of their children." The character of work, in other words, shaped the character of individuals in enduring ways; and to Wright, the implication was "so self-evident that it is to my own mind axiomatic in nature." The upgrading of labor—that "elevating process which would make self-supporting citizens out of the unfortunate and criminal classes"—would "conduce to the relief and protection of the community, the alleviation of the condition of the poor and helpless, the judicious punishment of the wicked, and the practical reformation of the vagrant and criminal." "Employers should remember," Wright insisted,

> that if conditions become ameliorated, if life becomes less of a struggle, if leisure be obtained, civilization, as a general rule, grows up. If these conditions be reversed, if the struggle for existence tends to occupy the whole attention of each man, civilization disappears in a measure, communities become dangerous. . . . The undue subjection of the laboring man

must tend to make paupers and criminals, and entail a financial burden upon wealth which it would have been easier to prevent than to endure.

Wright's central point—that an economy that condemns many to "drudgery" as well as to frequent unemployment will be neither just nor safe—still holds true today. It is the condition of being locked into what some economists call the "secondary labor market"—low-level, poorly paying, unstable jobs that cannot support a family and that offer little opportunity for advancement—that is most likely to breed crime. Curiously enough, the same conservatives who continually point to the studies that suggest weaker connections between unemployment and crime rates have not usually gone on to acknowledge that the same research also confirms that *inadequate* employment does matter—and matters a lot.

Some of the most revealing findings come from research at New York's Vera Institute of Justice. In one study, the Vera researchers interviewed a sample of men released from the Riker's Island prison in New York City in the late seventies. These were mainly young, minority men who had been convicted of a variety of misdemeanors, mostly crimes against property, and had usually served time before. Most were also poorly educated: less than a third had a high-school diploma or its equivalent, another third never got past the ninth grade. Some had fairly solid job histories, but most didn't; a few had never worked in their lives. Of those who *had* worked, only about half had ever held a job for more than a year; a third had never kept a job for longer than six months. And even those who had had a reasonably solid connection with the labor market in the past had often lost it well before their current spells in prison. Only 16 percent had been working immediately before the arrest that had put them behind bars.

Not only did these men have a decidedly loose relation to the world of work, but with few exceptions the jobs they did hold were "low level and paid poorly": two-thirds of the jobs paid less than $125 a week, in a year when it took almost that amount just to reach the federal poverty level; just 14 percent paid more than $175.

The Vera researchers expected that the careers of these men

would exhibit fairly clear-cut and direct connections between unemployment and crime. Instead, as interviews with the men over the space of several months revealed, things were more complicated.

For some of these offenders, work and crime seemed indeed to be, as the Vera researchers put it, mutually exclusive activities; they either worked or stole. "If you're working and you see something you want," one interviewee told them, "you wonder how you're going to save enough to buy it. If you're not working and you see something you want, you wonder how you're going to take it." Some felt that losing a job had been directly responsible for their turning to crime—either because of the loss of income or indirectly, because it led to depression, idleness, and drug use. Others both worked and stole at the same time, but stole much more when they were out of work. All these patterns fit, in one way or another, the researchers' initial expectations. But other patterns also turned up. For a few of the men, working actually *encouraged* their criminality. Some used their jobs as a cover for drug sales. One worked in order to buy enough drugs to resume a career as a dealer. Another, in a truly complex pattern, worked at casual labor in order to buy enough heroin so that he would feel well enough to go out and steal at night. Others simply stole whatever they could from the places they worked. Thus, another respondent, one of the few who had found work since release , claimed he "never had a job where he did not steal."

> When he worked in a hospital, he stole baby socks, sheets, and embalming fluid (which he sold to marijuana dealers to enhance "bad reefer"). When he worked in a bank training program, he stole $50 as soon as he had the chance. His heaviest offense, for which he served four years in an upstate prison, came when he committed an armed robbery at the office building where he worked, having observed when the greatest amount of cash would be out of the safe. He claimed to have worked thirty days since his release cleaning floors at a large discount store, where he reports stealing four television sets, ten tennis outfits, and six pairs of sneakers.[16]

A more common pattern was to alternate between legitimate work and small-scale crime. Men would take jobs for as long as they could handle the boredom, harassment, and low pay that usually came with them, or as long as they felt constrained against replacing petty work with petty crime by the risks of arrest. But these jobs could not hold them for long, and they soon moved back into street crime. What comes out most clearly in Vera's interviews with these men is the relative attractiveness of crime —even the small-time property crimes most of them engaged in—when balanced against the inadequacy of the work available. "If the job pays good, I'll go to the job," one respondent acknowledged; "if the street is good, I'll go back to the street." Over and over, the interviews show how thoroughly the tenuous, unsatisfying work roles available to these men are simply outclassed by the potential rewards of the street. "That's one thing I don't like about jobs," another respondent told the interviewers. "Out on the street . . . I can make close to $300 a night if I were to stay out there 5 or 6 hours . . . whereas if I was working I would make close to $200 in two weeks."

Revealingly, the Vera respondents were "generally far more animated when discussing successful criminals and crime fantasies than they were when defining the kind of job they would 'most like to have' "; they "could more easily envision themselves in grander roles in crime than their daily lives in the legitimate world of work allowed." "Apparently," the Vera researchers conclude, "at least in imagination, there are fewer barriers to upward mobility in crime than in employment."*

It's understandable that these poor expectations for decent work might breed the patterns of alternating low-level work and petty property crime documented in the Vera study. But there is also considerable evidence that the same alienated relationship to productive work is deeply implicated in *violent* crime as well. This connection emerges starkly in interviews conducted by re-

---

* That inability even to envision clearly what kind of work they would *like* to do fits a pattern I have seen in conducting interviews with hard-core drug-addicted offenders in California. It was hard to talk with these men and women for very long without realizing that they simply did not think in positive terms, even on the level of fantasy, about what "straight" life had to offer. They could complain about the shortcomings of the jobs they sporadically held and discourse at length about both the benefits and the pains of street life, but if you asked them what they would do if they could do what they wanted—what kind of work they would like to do, what they would like to learn —they had great trouble thinking of anything and often barely understood the question.

searchers at the URSA Institute in San Francisco, who were particularly interested in any characteristics that distinguished violent delinquents from other young offenders. They interviewed sixty-three youths in juvenile prisons in four cities; each was guilty of a violent felony and had been convicted of at least one similar crime in the past. They concluded that "youth employment per se does not reduce delinquency"; but that the *quality* of work—its "status, skills, promotions, wages"—strongly affects all kinds of delinquent behavior, especially serious violence. "Where working youths perceive growth, benefits, and tangible rewards from their employment," the study concludes, "they commit fewer of each type of offense." And "work quality" was precisely what was most lacking in the communities from which these youths came; indeed, these young men "identified few lifestyle choices in their neighborhoods other than criminal activity or idleness."

One reason why this narrowing of choices so conduces to violence is that it makes *illicit* work—like selling drugs—relatively attractive, as the comments in the Vera study suggest. And since disputes over markets or "turf" in illegal occupations cannot be resolved through legal means, force and violence are typically used instead. Deadly weapons have always been a hallmark of illegal work, a fact that helps account for the appearance of peaks in American homicide rates in the twenties—during Prohibition—and from the late sixties onward, when hard drugs spread virulently in American cities. (Close to a third of the homicides in Oakland, California, in 1983 and 1984 were related to drug dealing; most of the victims were young black men—or innocent bystanders.) Reducing the central role of drug dealing in the subterranean economy of the inner cities would surely lower the violent crime rate; but it has proven hard to do (despite heavy penalties, as we saw in chapter 3) when legitimate labor markets have offered so few attractive alternatives.

The accumulating evidence, then, tells us that it is not just the fact of having or not having a job that is most important, nor is the level of crime most strongly or consistently affected by fluctuations in the national unemployment rate. The more consistent influence is the *quality* of work—its stability, its level of pay, its capacity to give the worker a sense of dignity and participation, the esteem of peers and community. In our society these fundamental needs are virtually impossible to satisfy without a job —but they are all too often difficult even *with* a job, and nearly impossible in many of the kinds of jobs available in America today, especially to the disadvantaged young. Whether work can avert crime, in short, depends on whether it is part of a larger process through which the young are gradually integrated into a productive and valued role in a larger community. Similarly, whether unemployment leads to crime depends heavily on whether it is a temporary interruption of a longer and more hopeful trajectory into that kind of role, or represents a permanent condition of economic marginality that virtually assures a sense of purposelessness, alienation, and deprivation.

Obviously, this has more than theoretical relevance. It suggests (as I will show in the last chapter) that efforts to force the young, the marginal, and the deprived into *any* kind of work, however ill rewarded and demeaning, are likely to be futile at best and destructive at worst. If we wish to build a less volatile and violent society, we will need to concentrate on improving the long-term prospects for stable and valued work for those now largely excluded from it.

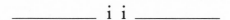

i i

Looking at the relationships between employment and crime in this broader context—to include the specific experience of marginal youths and of disadvantaged communities, as well as the significance of inadequate work—helps us to understand the apparent paradox of rising crime amidst the general economic expansion and relatively low unemployment rates of the sixties (and suggests, moreover, why a similar brand of prosperity cannot be relied on to reduce crime in the future). As some of the more prescient observers pointed out at the time, there was an ominous underside to what appeared to be an unprecedented level of prosperity. For it seemed to have an uneven, indeed contradictory, impact on different communities. Particularly disturbing was the steady and massive elimination of the livelihoods of small farmers and farmworkers, which pushed millions of displaced rural people into the cities—just when the opportunities for steady work in the cities for low-skilled newcomers were shrinking. Manufacturing jobs were leaving the central cities, lost to automation, the suburbs, or low-wage havens abroad; even many white-collar jobs were following suit. It seemed clear that this was a potentially explosive development that would surely bring rising crime, dependency, and other pathologies in its wake unless something was done to break the pattern.

Economic growth alone, while certainly necessary for reversing the increasing marginalization of the poor, was not sufficient. The Swedish economist Gunnar Myrdal went to the heart of the problem with the bluntness of a foreign observer: "As less and less work is required of the type that people in the urban and rural slums can offer," he wrote in 1963, "they will be increasingly isolated and exposed to unemployment, underemployment and plain exploitation." This prediction was strikingly confirmed when the Department of Labor surveyed the poverty areas of ten American cities in the boom year of 1966 and found rates of *subemployment*—counting the unemployed, the labor-force dropouts, and those working at poverty-level wages—that remained at Depression levels. (Thus in 1966, unemployment in the New York metropolitan area was under 5 percent, but subemployment in East Harlem was estimated at 33 percent.)

It was possible, Myrdal and other critics believed, to do something about this pattern; but the longer we waited, the harder it would be, as the new displaced of the cities became more deeply mired in a cycle of hopelessness and alienation. "There is an ugly smell," Myrdal warned, "rising from the basement of the stately American mansion."

The task of transforming masses of the rural poor, victims of decades (if not centuries) of economic exploitation and often of racial subordination, into successful participants in an urban "postindustrial" society would have been especially formidable here even given heroic public efforts. But the difficulty was greatly aggravated by the fact that such efforts were conspicuously undeveloped in this country, compared to those in most of the welfare states of Western Europe, including Myrdal's own Sweden. As Daniel Patrick Moynihan has written, among the world's industrial democracies "the United Staes alone had not instituted a postwar economic policy that gave the first priority to continued full employment." Unlike Sweden or Norway, the United States created no active labor-market policy to maintain full employment through substantial job retraining and public job creation; unlike West Germany, it developed no comprehensive apprenticeship system to guide the young from school into steady work; unlike Austria, it adopted no commitment to economic planning to anticipate the disruptive impact of technological change. Such measures were largely responsible for keeping job-less rates in many Western European countries below 3 percent throughout most of the 1970s and holding rates of *youth* unemployment at levels often lower than the American rates for adults.

In this country, on the other hand, proposals for greater public intervention in the labor market were successfully resisted, from the end of World War II onward, on the ground that both the quantity and the quality of employment should be left almost wholly to market forces. The results are apparent. The countries that developed humane and effective employment policies had both much lower unemployment and much less crime through-out the postwar period. Between 1959 and 1976 the average unemployment rate in the United States was nearly double that of its nearest European counterparts, Italy and the United Kingdom, and between three and four times the average rate in countries like West Germany, Sweden, Norway, Austria, and Japan; while its homicide rate ranged up to more than ten times that of these countries. The probability that these striking parallels are caus-ally, not randomly, connected is strengthened by the results of more complex and sophisticated research on the correlates of international differences in homicide. In a 1976 comparison of twenty-four countries, for example, Marvin Krohn of the University of Iowa found that high rates of unemployment were predictably associated with high rates of homicide.

If we want to understand the wellsprings of criminal violence in America since the sixties, we must recognize, I think, that our lack of a serious employment policy has had consequences that extend far beyond the economic realm. The failure to generate sufficient new livelihoods in the inner cities and depleted rural areas has done more than deprive a wide stratum of Americans of adequate income. Even more devastatingly, by shattering one of the principal links that bind individuals into productive and cooperative social life, it has fostered a broad culture of failure, resentment, and predation that will not be easy to eradicate. Although there is no way to quantify this effect with hard data, the corrosive social and psychological consequences of that process are surely aggravated by the fact that an increasingly acquisitive society not only excludes many people from the kind of work that could ensure them either material well-being or social esteem, but also simultaneously bombards them with the cultural message that their worth as members of society will be largely judged according to how well they meet ever-rising standards of material consumption. The results—as the Vera Institute's research illustrates—are not attractive. But no one in the 1980s should be surprised at this outcome; for twenty years we have seen it coming.

To be sure, not everyone accepts this explanation for the entwined problems of violence and inadequate employment in the United States. Traditionally, conservatives have argued that the causal process works the other way around—that it is not the state of the labor market but individual deficiencies of character (perhaps aggravated by unwise social policies) that are to blame for both unstable employment and the pathologies that often accompany it. Carroll Wright's concerns about the effects of unemployment on crime were answered by the noted Italian criminologist Cesare Lombroso, for example, shortly after the turn of the century. Lombroso didn't deny the connection between unemployment and crime, but he disputed the meaning Wright and others gave it. "One would be tempted," he wrote, "to believe that unemployment must exercise a perceptible influence upon criminality. It is, however, of little importance." The mere fact that criminals "have almost never a settled trade" did not contradict this, for criminals "never had an occupation and never wanted one"; they lacked "neither the means nor the opportunity of working, but only the willingness to work." It was not, Lombroso continued, that criminals were altogether without energy or inventiveness; but "being incapable of resisting the intermittent caprices of a character at once inert and impulsive," criminals were driven to "declare war upon a society which is not in harmony with their inclinations." "In the army of labor," Lombroso concluded, "the criminal is a guerilla."

More recent conservative arguments have usually taken one of two separate, but often related, paths. One follows Lombroso's lead with remarkable fidelity, arguing that both unstable employment and crime are reflections of an underlying personality syndrome whose origin is probably constitutional or genetic. I will come back to this argument in Chapter 6; for the moment, suffice it to say that it begs the most important question: Why should there be so many more people with these personality disorders in the United States, proportionately, than in any other advanced industrial society? And why did so many of them happen to emerge during the past two decades, concentrated in the inner cities?

To the extent that conservatives can be said to offer a response, it is contained in a second argument, which holds that public policy has demoralized the "lower classes" in the United States in ways that predictably lead to both sporadic employment and crime. In particular, conservatives have warned that purportedly beneficent measures, like the minimum wage, welfare, and unemployment insurance, cause unemployment (and crime) by inducing people to leave the labor force or (in the case of the minimum wage) making employers reluctant to hire them in the first place.

But two problems, one empirical and the other conceptual, make these arguments less than persuasive. Consider the argument that minimum wages cause unemployment by pricing the labor of low-skilled people—particularly youths—at a level higher than they are "worth" in terms of productivity, hence higher than rational employers are willing to pay. The first problem with this view is that it fits badly with the evidence. Our minimum wages tend to be considerably lower than those of most other developed countries as a percentage of average wages (and have often risen more slowly since the 1960s), yet most of those countries have had far *lower* jobless rates in the past two decades,

especially among youth. Sweden and Norway, whose labor un-
ions have successfully bargained for "solidary" wage policies—
which place the highest priority on raising the "floor" of wages
for lower-paid workers throughout the economy, thus diminishing the inequality of wages and the proportion of low-wage jobs
—have had among the most impressive employment records of
all the countries of the world since the Second World War.

Moreover, no matter how hard they have tried, econometric
studies in the United States itself have not turned up large or
consistent effects—where they show any effects at all—of the
minimum wage on employment. There is no consensus that minimum wages decrease employment at all among adults, and some
evidence that they *increase* it by shielding adult workers from
teenage competition. The results for youth are not much more
impressive. A recent review of the numerous studies of the issue
concludes that a 10 percent increase in the youth minimum wage
might reduce teenage employment by anywhere from zero to 3
percent: not an overwhelming effect, when unemployment
among urban black teenagers often reaches 50 percent.

There is a second and even more crucial reason to look
askance at the argument that minimum wages indirectly cause
crime by enforcing unemployment. Given how low minimum
wages are set in the United States—in the early 1980s, full-time,
year-round work at the minimum wage brought an income
around $2,500 below the poverty line for a family of four—it is
clear that even if they do keep some people out of low-wage jobs,
they do not keep anyone from a *good* job. And we've just seen
that it is good jobs—with reasonable pay and, perhaps even more
importantly, some chance of advancement—that provide a defense against crime. The problem is not that the young lack
"opportunities" for poorly paid, dead-end, and demeaning work;
it is that they lack opportunities for work that can lead toward
a respected future of skill and contribution.

Similar considerations apply to the argument that overgener-
ous income supports—unemployment insurance and welfare—
lure workers out of honest jobs and into lives of dependency and
crime. Once again, our levels of income support in the United
States—as I'll detail in the next chapter—are relatively lower than
in other countries whose rates of unemployment (and crime) are

far less. Since our social "safety net" is pitched so low—especially in the meaner-spirited states—even if it can be argued that welfare benefits keep some of the poor from accepting work at poverty-level wages, it cannot be convincingly demonstrated that they keep many from accepting solid jobs with adequate pay—the jobs that reliably inhibit crime. In short, as with minimum wages, the problem is less that government in the United States creates especially large *disincentives* to steady employment than that the labor market creates incentives so low and uncertain that they cannot consistently compete with the lures of street life.

The postwar experience with employment and crime suggests that the crucial point is not that we interfere too much in the private labor market, but that we intervene too little. The same point may be affirmed by looking at the opposite side of the putative paradox—the failure of crime to rise predictably during hard times. Thus conservatives have seized on the apparent failure of crime to rise during the Great Depression as evidence against any connection between economic hardship and crime—and, by extension, against the idea that crime can be significantly reduced by improving economic security. But a closer look at crime in the thirties shows that things aren't nearly so simple.

Did crime really fall during the Depression? The answer is much more difficult to establish than it might seem. The first problem is that the statistics we would need for a convincing answer don't exist; the FBI's Uniform Crime Reporting program didn't begin until the 1930s, and it was carried out haphazardly and unevenly in its early years. It did an especially poor job of covering crime in rural areas, for example, at a time when violent crime was often higher in the country than in the city. Much crime among the highly mobile and anonymous poor of that decade surely never came to official attention. Moreover, many police departments treated crime—at least property crime—more leniently under Depression conditions, a practice noted by many observers at the time. Thus crime—even serious crime—was almost certainly considerably higher than the woefully inadequate official data suggest. Even so, the numbers indicate a more complicated trend than is often assumed. If we concentrate on the most serious and best-recorded crime, homicide, the most reliable data—annual Vital Statistics collected by the U. S. Public Health Service—show homicide rates remaining remarkably high well into the mid-1930s. Indeed, the mid-thirties murder rates of 7 per 100,000 were as high as the rates during the "crime wave" of the late sixties.

Indeed, in the early years of the Depression, as the historian John A. Pandiani points out, "it was widely agreed that the economic hardship and social dislocation caused by the failure of the American economy would result in a crime wave of major proportions"—and from what we can piece together from the statistics available, those fears began to materialize, at least in some places, at the start of the Depression. Yet although the rates of many serious crimes rose in the first few years of the Depression, they unexpectedly leveled off (and in some cases dropped) thereafter. Thus, homicide rates fell after the mid-thirties. The "crime wave" most contemporaries expected never appeared. Why not?

The distinction between long-term economic marginality and other forms of unemployment discussed above offers one clue. People who are stably employed until an economic crisis throws them out of work are not the ones most likely to turn to serious criminal violence (though some do); while those who *are* likely to turn to criminal violence are most often found in the parts of the economy that are far less affected by fluctuations in the business cycle—people, in other words, who don't expect their lives to change very much, no matter what the condition of the economy.

But another strong probability is that the crime wave expected during the Depression was forestalled by the public response to economic hardship. Nowadays it's fashionable to argue that the growth of the modern welfare state has aggravated social instability and interpersonal violence. But observers during the Depression were convinced that the opposite was true—that the massive response to the plight of the unemployed by the welfare state that emerged in the Roosevelt era was at least partly responsible for keeping the crime rate from rising as the Depression deepened. More recent research suggests that they may well have been right.

It's often forgotten that the response to unemployment during the Depression—while it was never adequate to the need—took place on a scale that dwarfs anything we have had since. The explosion in public relief—welfare—for many able-bodied people (who formerly would have been denied even the most rudimentary public support) was particularly important; it couldn't fail to alter the meaning of unemployment for many of the country's poor. Robert and Helen Lynd, authors of *Middletown,* a study of Muncie, Indiana, in the twenties, pointed out in their restudy of that community during the thirties that although crime in Middletown rose in the first years of the Depression, it dipped sharply in 1932. What accounted for this unexpected pattern? "One factor in this drop in 1932," the Lynds wrote, "may be the increasing acceptance by the community as the depression wore on of the necessity for providing public relief to the able-bodied, thereby lessening somewhat their need to beg, borrow, or steal." The Lynds didn't attribute the decline entirely to the growth of relief, but they did believe that "the heavy program of public relief from 1931 on undoubtedly operated to hold down . . . crimes against property and persons."

This proposition was given more sophisticated support in a study in the early fifties by the criminologist James F. Short. Short argued that "the relation between business cycles and the cycles of various crimes" was distorted during the Depression by "the effect of the relief effort." Noting that the explosion of public relief was enormous and unprecedented, especially in the case of *general* relief—which went to the able-bodied, as opposed to special programs for traditionally served groups like the blind and the aged—Short reasoned that this massive infusion of public support mitigated the hardship suffered by many of the unemployed and would therefore have partially canceled out the increases in crime that hardship might otherwise cause. Short correlated the fluctuations in the business cycle during the thirties with the trends in crimes reported to the police and with the patterns of public relief in large American cities from 1929 to the beginning of World War II. He found that when the economy slumped, relief increased, so that public action did in fact compensate for the fluctuations of the economy. What about the crime rate? Short found that although murder and aggravated assault weren't much affected, rates of robbery and burglary were strongly influenced by the level of public aid. Both crimes peaked in 1932 and remained high until 1934, then fell to their low points for the decade in 1936, just when the amount of public relief rose to a peak.

Short's study was hampered to some extent by the limitations of the available crime statistics. But it gains credibility from more recent work that, using more sophisticated methods and better data, confirms his finding that public support for the disadvantaged reduces crime. In a study of the impact of welfare on serious crime in metropolitan areas across the country, James deFronzo of the University of Connecticut found that the level of government assistance to the poor had a strong and significant negative effect, other things being equal, on rates of homicide, rape, and burglary. Each ten-dollar-per-month increase in payments per family member under Aid to Families of Dependent Children (AFDC), deFronzo calculated, cut the urban homicide rate by about 1 per 100,000 (roughly equal to the *total* homicide rate for many industrial nations) and the rape rate by about 6 per 100,000.

The same point is affirmed in recent research on the effects of providing even modest income supports to offenders released from prison. Most former inmates reenter the community without jobs and without even sufficient funds to look for work—a condition that can't be conducive to going straight. In the seventies, the U.S. Department of Labor sponsored experimental programs in Georgia and Texas that gave ex-offenders small stipends for several weeks after their release. According to an evaluation by Richard Berk, Kenneth Lenihan, and Peter Rossi, the results were complicated by the fact that the stipends were reduced sharply if the recipients found jobs, so that they produced a *work disincentive* effect: the ex-inmates who received them were less likely to look for jobs. Because having a job *also* tended to lower arrests among these men, the overall effects of the stipends tended to cancel each other out. But the researchers argued that once the effect of the work disincentive was removed, the payments decreased crime substantially—not only property crimes but nonproperty crimes as well.

This argument has been fairly controversial, but it is strongly supported by a more recent investigation by David Rauma and

Richard Berk of a similar program in California. There, released offenders were given unemployment benefits based on the amount of time they had worked in prison; the benefits reduced recidivism over the ten months after release by about 13 percent, and in this case, work disincentives didn't cancel out the encouraging results. What is striking is that even modest amounts of income support seem to make a difference—not a spectacular difference, but given the small size of the benefits and the fact that they are granted for only a few months, we would hardly expect it to be.

What these findings tell us is that we can't understand the relations between unemployment and crime without taking into account the mediating force of public policy. Whether—and to what extent—joblessness generates crime depends on what happens to the people who lose their jobs, and that is crucially affected by the kinds of supports available to them. Another aspect of the Depression-era response to unemployment illustrates this even more powerfully. It's often forgotten in discussions of crime during the Depression that the Roosevelt administration launched, in addition to widespread public relief, the largest program of public employment in the nation's history. One of its most important components was the Civilian Conservation Corps (CCC), which between its inauguration in 1933 and the coming of World War II put over *2.5 million* poor young men to work—between a quarter and a third of the young, poor men in the entire country—mainly in national and state forests and other public-works projects. No sophisticated evaluation of the CCC's role in reducing crime was ever carried out, but contemporaries widely thought it had one; Roosevelt himself declared in 1939 that, though the program had not been explicitly designed to prevent crime, "nobody who knows how demoralizing the effects of enforced idleness may be will be inclined to doubt that crime prevention has been an important by-product of our effort to provide our needy unemployed citizens with an opportunity to earn by honest work at least the bare necessities of life." As John A. Pandiani argues in a suggestive analysis, the CCC may have controlled crime during the Depression in two ways: on the one hand, it gave young men useful, constructive work and a modest amount of money for themselves and their families; at the same time it effectively removed a substantial fraction of the highest-risk group from "the population at large," in what "might accurately be called the preventive detention of hundreds of thousands" of the country's most dangerous citizens.

That judgment of the CCC's function may be a bit harsh (though, as Pandiani points out, it was shared by the CCC's critics on the political Left), but the general point seems hard to dispute: In the face of economic collapse, the federal government put an extraordinary proportion of "high-risk" young men to work in settings that were most unconducive to serious crime and that involved them in productive enterprises that were not simply financially supportive but also meaningful and indeed enduring. For at least some of the youthful disadvantaged, the coming of the Depression, paradoxically, may have meant that they became more involved in productive work roles than they would otherwise have been.

There is also evidence that the same may have happened to other young people, more favored to begin with, who were not touched by the CCC or other public job programs. As the Cornell sociologist Glen Elder has shown in his studies of the impact of the Depression on family life, one frequent consequence of the economic losses suffered by many families was a "downward extension of adult-like experience" to the young. Adolescent boys went to work to help support the family; they became "more involved in the kind of work adult males typically do," while girls often took on a heavier load of traditionally female work, mainly in the home. For at least some young people, in other words, a major effect of the Depression was to shift them into meaningful, necessary work roles. Put slightly differently, the Depression shifted those roles, to some extent, from older adult men, who are not an especially crime-prone population, to youth, who are. Unlike the CCC, this hardly represented a conscious social policy, but its results were arguably similar. In both cases, the potential crime-producing effects of economic hardship were offset by the rise of new and valued communal roles for youth.

There is a more general point here. We know—from both studies of social life in the Depression and more recent investigations—that the impact of unemployment and economic hardship on workers and their families is mediated by a complex web of family and community supports, as well as by public policies. In the thirties, sociologists often found that the Depression's effect on families and communities was not always as disruptive as might have been expected. For one thing, the loss in real income among the jobless was reduced because rents and prices usually fell at the same time. Even more crucially, many victims of the Depression kept their families together, lived in the same houses in the same relatively stable communities, and managed to maintain much the same social life and networks of social support as they had before. Indeed, Depression-era unemployment sometimes drew families closer together, rather than splitting them apart. More recent studies of the ways in which social supports cushion the impact of job loss confirm the point. Susan Gore's research in the 1970s on the personal consequences of plant closings in two different Midwestern communities, for example, discovered that men living in a tight-knit ethnic community in one city held up much better, physically and emotionally, when they lost their jobs than workers with fewer sources of social support.

None of this, of course, is to suggest that unemployment is likely ever to be painless. But it does tell us that if we want to understand the relationships between crime and lack of work, we need to view them in a larger social context that includes the level of support—private or public, familial or governmental—available to the unemployed. That often ignored factor may help explain some part of the continuing differences in crime rates between the United States and other industrial countries that have also suffered high unemployment since the seventies. I've already argued that the more effective employment policies in most of Western Europe and Japan have helped keep their rates of criminal violence well below ours throughout the postwar era. Moreover, even though some European countries have faced sharply rising unemployment in the last few years, they have not suffered anything approaching American levels of criminal violence.

There are no hard data to tell us how much the more generous and accessible benefits for the unemployed in those countries may have suppressed crime that might otherwise have resulted from economic dislocation. But, particularly given the evidence from American investigations, the connection seems too strong to ignore. The differences in support for the unemployed between the United States and most other advanced industrial societies are striking, and they insure that losing a job in America typically entails far more hardship, deprivation, and alienation than it does elsewhere. In the late seventies, when only a little over half the unemployed in the United States collected unemployment benefits, the proportion was two-thirds in France, about three-fourths in West Germany and the United Kingdom, four-fifths in Japan, and nine-tenths in Sweden. Furthermore, the benefits granted to the fortunate half of the American unemployed who did receive them were unusually low, amounting to roughly half of the average worker's earnings—versus nearly three-fourths in Sweden.

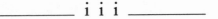

i i i

The evidence suggests, then, that it is not bare economic circumstances that most influence the crime rate, but their social context, in particular the degree of hardship and disruption of communal roles that the loss of work entails—hardships that may be cushioned and relieved by active and humane public policy and by the natural support of a stable community. This suggests in turn that the generous provision of cushions against the disruptive impact of unemployment may itself be a significant, if usually underemphasized, defense against crime. By the same token, social policies that strip away those cushions—or that disrupt the stability and effectiveness of communal networks of support and care—are likely to aggravate the impact of economic insecurity on crime. Perhaps most important, the Depression experience suggests that contrary to recent conventional wisdom, government efforts to provide meaningful training and work for the jobless can help prevent crime. That conclusion is supported, with some important qualifications, by more recent studies of the impact of job programs for offenders.

Since the late seventies, it has become fashionable to argue that publicly supported job programs have been a massive and costly failure. Conservatives have seized on the contradictory evaluations of work programs for offenders to argue that there isn't much we can realistically do to raise the benefit side of the cost-benefit ledger for those who are the most likely candidates for criminal careers. James Q. Wilson, for example, insists that job programs "can have only a marginal influence on crime"; and the supposed failure of our best efforts to improve the job situation of criminal offenders or high-risk youth becomes an argument by default for greater investment in deterrence. But is this really what the evidence tells us?

I don't think so, for two reasons. First, the evidence that some job programs can reduce crime is stronger, even on the surface, than the critics acknowledge. Second—and more important—the evidence also tells us *why* the programs developed so far have produced mixed results, and in the process tells us something about what needs to be done to make them work better.

The chief limitation is simple but fundamental, and it can be stated at the outset. With few exceptions, employment programs for offenders have been designed to improve their skills, their attitudes toward work, their ability to handle job interviews and to get to work on time, and other factors that contribute to their employability. They have only rarely sought to change the conditions of the labor market itself—by creating steady jobs or upgrading those jobs that already exist. This emphasis is partly a legacy of the sixties, when the economy seemed far more capable of providing something close to full employment for those willing to work and having basic skills and motivation. Given the expanding economy of the 1960s, the generally declining overall unemployment, and the seemingly limitless vista of continuing affluence, it isn't surprising that most of the programs that emerged from the New Frontier and the Great Society were designed primarily, in the words of the historian James T. Patterson, "to get the poverty out of the people, and afterward the people out of poverty."

The social science of the fifties and sixties offered theoretical support for this approach. In economics, the "human capital" model held that the investments that workers had made in their skills, through training and education, were the most important determinants of their success or failure in the labor market. Meanwhile, sociologists and urban anthropologists were developing the notion of a "culture of poverty" that trapped the poor in a cycle of self-defeating attitudes and values that virtually prevented their taking a place in the expanding, affluent economy. If, as economists of the time were wont to argue, a "rising tide would lift all boats," then without substantial change in their skills, education, and attitudes, a good portion of the disadvantaged would still be unable to clamber aboard at all. This meant that considerable intervention would be required to forestall some of the worst consequences expected if the poor (especially the minority poor in the inner cities) began to sink while the rest of American society rose contentedly around them.

But as critics (then and now) quickly noted, the fundamental assumptions behind this approach were shaky on closer inspection. To be sure, many of the demoralized poor *did* need help with both skills and attitudes; but that was only part of the problem. The other part was that the "rising tide" of postwar affluence was simply not providing enough jobs—of the right kinds and in the right places—to pull enough of these stragglers out of the water, even with the best training programs anyone could offer and the most radical transformations of the culture and character of the poor.

This helps us untangle the evidence from evaluations of job programs since the sixties. Some of those programs have proven more successful than others; unsurprisingly, they are those that offer more intensive training, actual jobs, or both. Programs designed to provide vocational help at the simplest levels—job counseling, tutoring in how to handle interviews, vocational education, haphazard training in tasks unrelated to the existing job market—have had the least impact on the behavior of youthful or adult offenders, measured either by their rates of rearrest or by the seriousness of their crimes. In part, this is probably because the programs have so often been poorly implemented, even on their own relatively narrow terms. Many of the earliest of these programs were established within the prisons themselves; but as the economist Robert Taggart concluded in a review of such programs in the early seventies, most of the work they offered was "degrading and irrelevant," not clearly connected to real job opportunities outside. One program (at the Riker's Island prison in New York) was more successful in placing offenders in decent jobs (in this case, jobs in data processing)—but the program was virtually unique in providing serious skill training and substantial job-development efforts for its trainees.

In the late sixties, the emphasis in job programs for offenders shifted from the prisons to the community, but the results of such community-based programs as pretrial release, work release, and others designed to get offenders out of the prisons and jails and into the labor market were not impressive. Again, part of the problem was simply that the programs provided a very limited range of services. Most offered job counseling, an attempt at placement, and perhaps some follow-up once offenders had been placed in a job. Few provided solid skills training; fewer still provided jobs, even transitional ones. But even on these levels the programs often didn't follow through; job development—finding employers willing to hire program clients—was often inadequate, follow-up was minimal, and some programs relied on overburdened probation or parole agencies to secure work for ex-offenders.

The problem of meager resources for a very large task undermined the efforts of even the best of these projects. The typical participants in the ex-offender or pretrial diversion programs of the seventies were young, inner-city, often minority, men with poor education and little work history, many with substantial criminal records and severe problems with drugs or alcohol. Yet the resources even the more serious programs could provide were usually minimal, often consisting mainly of the patience and perseverance of dedicated counselors and a Rolodex full of names of moderately sympathetic employers. And such programs were forced to try to accomplish wonders for this clientele—some of whom had been involved in crime and little else for most of their lives—within the space of a few months at most.

One of the best and most carefully evaluated of these programs was the Manhattan Court Employment Project, undertaken by the Vera Institute of Justice in the late sixties. This was a *pretrial diversion* project, in which charges against selected offenders were dismissed before trial if they participated in a three-to-four-month program of job counseling and placement.

An early evaluation had suggested that the program was successful both in improving the job situations of a relatively tough
population (though the project excluded alcoholics, addicts, and
juveniles, three of the most difficult subgroups) and in reducing
rearrests; accordingly, similar programs were widely funded by
the federal government in the seventies. But a later and more
rigorous evaluation was disappointing; the program apparently
had no effect either on job performance or on recidivism. The
reasons aren't really hard to find. Despite the seriousness and
creativity of Vera's efforts, the program was severely understaffed; moreover, it operated, necessarily, against the formidable
resistance of the unpromising job market of the mid-seventies—
and with a clientele that would have had trouble adapting even
in the best of economic circumstances. In its later years, as Vera's
own researchers point out, the Court Employment Project's services had been substantially diminished; they were "mainly
confined to limited endeavors to improve human capital"—to
improve literacy, to teach participants to read subway maps and
telephone directories, and to give job-readiness training and vocational counseling.

To say that these programs "failed," therefore, is superficially
true but not very enlightening; the "failure" of programs that had
little realistic chance for success doesn't tell us much about either
the relationships between employment and crime or the prospects for reducing crime through more substantial work-related
social programs.

More suggestive evidence comes from evaluations of more
intensive programs. The earliest confirmation that such programs
might have a significant impact on crime came from evaluations
of one of the Great Society's most rigorous social experiments,
the Job Corps. Unlike many programs for disadvantaged youth,
the Job Corps involved far more than casual summer work experience and sporadic individual counseling. It took some of the most
severely deprived youth in the country away from their own
neighborhoods and put them in residential settings, mainly rural,
where they underwent (for an average period of about six months
in the mid-seventies) a fairly tough program that mixed intensive
basic education, skills training, health care, and other supportive

services. About three-quarters of the participants in the Job Corps were minority youths, nine-tenths hadn't finished high school, and about a third had never worked as long as a month.

Yet even given this difficult population, the Job Corps apparently worked for a substantial number of its participants. Those who completed the program got better jobs, earned more, were less dependent on welfare, and cut down their use of drugs, compared to similarly deprived youth who hadn't participated. They also committed fewer crimes, measured both by their own reports and by arrests during and after the program. The biggest effect on crime came during their enrollment in the program itself —hardly surprising, since the Job Corps took them away from the inner cities and put them under close supervision—but it also continued, though at a less dramatic level, after they went back to city life.

The Job Corps experience suggested that, even short of any changes in the labor market, programs that seriously addressed the depth and complexity of the needs of these high-risk populations could make a difference. That conclusion was strongly upheld in a series of experimental *supported-work* programs beginning in the early seventies. The central premise of supported work is that people who have had great difficulty in the normal labor market need to start slowly, with a lot of help and supervision, to learn to handle the simpler tasks and personal requirements of holding a job, and then work their way up gradually to the point where they can take on more challenging tasks and greater responsibilities. Originally developed in Europe, mainly in the form of *sheltered-work* programs for the disabled, supported work was first tried in the United States in the early seventies, again through the efforts of the Vera Institute in New York. What most distinguished this program from earlier ones was that it not only offered advice, counseling, support, and training, but created an actual working environment—and real jobs—for its clientele: chronically unemployed heroin addicts and ex-offenders. Vera created a functioning corporation, the Wildcat Service Corporation, which operated several work sites (in construction and similar enterprises) across the city. The Wildcat workers were organized in small, manageable crews, given clearly defined tasks and goals, supervised closely, and given extensive feedback on their performance and rewards for doing well. They began with minimal duties and gradually worked up to larger responsibilities, with the help of counselors and a variety of support services.

Vera's careful evaluation of supported work in the late seventies seemed very promising. Compared with a control group, the addicts in the program worked more regularly, earned more, were less dependent on welfare, and had fewer arrests. All this was encouraging, despite one troubling note (which we'll observe again and again): the program's positive effects on both employment and crime were strongest up to a year after the addicts had enrolled, but steadily weakened as their time *out* of the program increased.

Nevertheless, the Wildcat results were sufficiently impressive to stimulate the creation of a much bigger experiment along the same lines. In the late seventies, the Ford Foundation, the Department of Labor, and the Department of Health, Education, and Welfare, in an unusual joint effort, established the Manpower Demonstration Research Corporation (MDRC) to develop supported-work programs in several cities across the country. The MDRC version of supported work targeted four separate categories of clients who, it was believed, should benefit from a carefully phased and intensive program of training and transitional work: ex-offenders, drug addicts, welfare mothers, and high-risk youth.

Among the four target groups, the program worked best for the addicts and the welfare mothers. The successes with addicts were particularly striking. The program didn't consistently reduce their drug use, but it did increase their rates of employment, the number of hours they worked, and their earnings—especially while they were still in the program or had recently left it, but also between thirty-one and thirty-six months afterward. Even more striking were the decreases in crime among participants as compared to a randomly selected control group with similar problems and backgrounds. Once again, the effects were strongest while the addicts were actually enrolled in the program and shortly thereafter, but they held up throughout the entire three-year follow-up period. On the average, the participants spent only half as much time in jail during those three years as the control group, and chalked up less than two-thirds as many arrests. The positive effects were particularly strong for robbery, one of the most serious of drug-related crimes. In the first nine months of the program, the control group was arrested for robberies at a rate *four times* that of the experimental group.

What, exactly, accounted for these positive effects? One interesting finding was that although the added income from employment had something to do with the drop in crimes, there was more to it than that. If simply having any job and earning a little money was what counted most, the many members of the *control* group who were employed should have done as well, in terms of reduced arrests, as the experimentals. But the experimentals did significantly better. This suggested that something about the nature of work in the program itself made a difference over and above the sheer fact of bringing home a paycheck—something one of the researchers, the economist Katherine Dickinson, describes as *work satisfaction*. To the extent that the program provided work that was genuinely useful, as well as considerable feedback and support, it offered the participant a role that was sufficiently compelling to have at least some chance of competing with the appeals of the addicts' street life.

Further evidence that the program brought satisfactions over and above the paycheck appears in a study by Sandra Danziger of the responses of welfare women to supported work. The program was clearly successful in getting many of these women off welfare and into jobs, sometimes substantial primary-sector jobs. Beyond the higher earnings, many women credited the program with stimulating a whole range of improvements in their lives. Some said their children benefited emotionally from their mothers' working. Others spoke of improvements in the quality of their social networks and relations with friends, relatives, neighbors, and coworkers. Many expressed strong feelings of pride and a newfound sense of economic independence—especially those women who had used the program to break into union jobs or traditionally male (and therefore better-paying) ones, as carpenters, for example, or fork-lift drivers. Particularly for women who moved into such good jobs, the program brought substantial gains in self-esteem, an outcome that Danziger contrasts with the tendency of the normal welfare system to reinforce a "degraded sense of self."

These results are especially important because they suggest that providing satisfying work can break the cycle of poverty and dependency all too often passed down the generations in poor families. Discussions of the relationships between unemployment and crime often adopt a cripplingly short focus on the *immediate* impact of unemployment on people who lose their jobs. But in terms of criminal violence, the longer-range impact of prolonged joblessness on the following generations are at least equally important. We know that long-term unemployment can lead to problems in prenatal and childhood health (due to impaired nutrition and drug or alcohol abuse) and to child abuse and violence within families—all of which are linked to delinquency and crime. No one doubts that it's more fruitful to prevent these problems beforehand than to try, after the fact, to alter the behavior of people who have already suffered considerable damage by the time they come before the police and courts. The success of these programs in putting *parents* to work in satisfying jobs, therefore, is one of their most encouraging results.

On the surface, the MDRC programs were less successful with youths and ex-offenders, although even here the results were not altogether discouraging. Among the youths, for instance, the evaluators found "modest" evidence that those who were more disadvantaged, younger, and more drug-abusing and criminally inclined may have benefited most from supported work; among the ex-offenders, there were strong positive effects on their employment during the early months of participation, which—again —fell off afterward. There was also what the researchers described as a "hint" of reductions in drug use and crime for ex-offenders over twenty-five.

Still, the overall results with youths and ex-offenders were unimpressive—which has sometimes been taken to mean that supported work and similar intensive employment programs won't benefit these presumably tougher and less tractable groups. But I think that this conclusion is misleading; so did MDRC's researchers. For one thing, in practice the ex-offender group was not easily distinguishable from the ex-addict group that showed substantial success; indeed, they were drawn from similar and even overlapping populations. It's surely premature, therefore, to come to hasty generalizations about the inability of these programs to work for ex-offenders, since clearly they did work for some of them. Another caveat is even more important. As MDRC's evaluators concluded dryly, "The destructiveness of poverty, poor education, discrimination, and high unemployment cannot be expected to yield entirely to an employment intervention of a year's duration." This obvious general limitation was aggravated by certain specific conditions both within the program itself and, even more importantly, outside it. The jobs provided were deliberately designed to start with pay levels well below those prevailing for the kind of work performed by the participants, ending up at or just below the prevailing rates for these usually low-skilled jobs. At these wages, the evaluators pointed out, the jobs often couldn't effectively compete against the "returns from criminal activity." More crucially, there was only a tenuous connection between employment in the program and the chances of landing an adequate job in the future—a stubborn fact of life which, the MDRC researchers felt, was especially important in explaining the program's poor results for youth. Part of the problem was that many of these extremely difficult and alienated youths had trouble with the discipline and routine of the program. But another part was "their realization that the program will at best prepare them for an uncertain opportunity for an entry-level job or a career."

So we return to the fundamental problem, which appears repeatedly in the evaluations of supported work and other partially successful programs to provide jobs and training for offenders. It shows up, too, in the finding we've seen several times already: from the Job Corps through supported work and other programs, the positive effects are strongest while the participants are enrolled in them, actually working at jobs within the program, but usually begin to peter out afterward, waning steadily with time. Even the most intensive work programs, in short, are undermined by the limits of the outside labor market, into which the participants will be thrown once the program ends. Supported work provides a special, temporary labor market in which clients are guaranteed work while in the program. But once they leave, they must compete with the rest of the low-skilled poor in a labor market that has few jobs for them in the best of times, and in hard times has virtually none. The lesson isn't that the programs don't work, much less that providing useful work cannot have much effect on crime. It is simply that the best job-training efforts we can mount for offenders are likely to be thwarted by the profound structural inadequacies of the inner-city economy.

And this reveals the deeper choices that lie beneath the current debate about unemployment and crime. Criminologists may quibble about the interpretation of particular studies of job programs or the precise impact of economic fluctuations on the national crime rate. But few could really disagree that the grim prospects for decent work that afflict the marginal poor in America produce a potent breeding-ground for crime; that as long as large numbers of people remain trapped in the dead end of the shattered labor markets of the cities, we will have great difficulty in keeping them out of crime—or at work. "If young men examining the world about them conclude that crime pays more than work," James Q. Wilson writes, "that, for instance, stealing cars is more profitable than washing them—they may then leave their jobs in favor of crime."

The real disagreement is over what can—or should—be done about this dilemma. For Wilson and other conservative critics, the answer is: not much. Employers, Wilson argued in 1975, "cannot" offer to "unskilled or semiskilled workers" either wages or nonfinancial benefits that could possibly equal the benefits they now derive from stealing; the "only alternative," therefore, is to increase the "risks" of theft so that its value is "depreciated below what society can afford to pay in legal wages." Several years later, Wilson was still insisting that "society cannot feasibly make more than modest changes in the employment prospects of young men."

This isn't true, of course. Other societies have in fact done a great deal to improve the employment prospects of young men (and others)—and so did we, for that matter, during the Depression. What *is* true is that "society" may not be able to improve those prospects very much as long as it relies almost wholly on the private labor market to do so. Hence what conservatives are really saying is not that society *cannot* make more than modest changes in the job prospects of the young, but that it *should* not, since doing so requires interfering with the ability of private employers to determine how—or whether—individuals will gain their livelihoods. The same attitude causes most conservatives to reject the provision of more generous and humane supports —unemployment insurance, income-maintenance benefits— against the *consequences* of joblessness, even though, on the evidence, doing so would also reduce crime. Both approaches require considerable public intervention in the workings of the private market in the name of larger social values. If we reject that intervention and the values that underlie it, we may indeed be forced to increase the "risks" of crime for those we have chosen to leave to the market's mercies. But we should be quite clear that this is indeed a choice, not an imperative of human nature or economic logic.

The powerful connections between crime and the absence of secure and satisfying work suggest that the issue of employment and crime is woven inextricably into the larger one of the relationships between crime and inequality. For what is crucial about not having a decent job is that it puts one squarely at the bottom of what in the United States is a particularly harsh and pervasive structure of inequality that profoundly shapes every aspect of social and emotional life. In the next chapter, I'll look more directly at the ways that structure contributes to the problem of crime in America.

5

UNDERSTANDING CRIME: INEQUALITY AND COMMUNITY

In 1983, the highest murder rate in the United States among cities with populations above 50,000 was achieved by East St. Louis, Illinois. In that year, the unfortunate citizens of East St. Louis died by violence at the hands of their fellows at the rate of about 100 per 100,000, roughly twelve times the national average. Across the state in Oak Lawn—a Chicago suburb around the same size as East St. Louis—no one was murdered. Three women were raped, giving Oak Lawn a rate of rape about one-fortieth that of East St. Louis.

Also high on the list of particularly violent American cities was Compton, California, an independent enclave of about 80,000 near central Los Angeles. Compton's homicide rate was about 50 per 100,000 in 1983; it also recorded over 1,300 robberies. Out along the freeway to the northwest is the suburb of Thousand Oaks, which, with about as many people, recorded no murders and just 55 robberies.

Or consider the still more striking case of the two Highland Parks. Highland Park, Michigan, lies within inner-city Detroit. Highland Park, Illinois, is a lakeside suburb just north of Chicago. In 1983, Highland Park, Illinois, suffered no murders, 1 rape, and 7 robberies. With a population roughly the same size (less than 30,000), Highland Park, Michigan, endured 27 murders, 55 rapes, and no less than 796 robberies.

What else distinguishes these cities? For one thing, money. Only one family in thirty in Thousand Oaks is poor; close to one in four in Compton. In besieged East St. Louis, things are even worse. There, nearly two out of five families are poor; over in Oak

Lawn, just one family in thirty-eight. The two Highland Parks, once again, offer the most extreme contrast—in Highland Park, Michigan, almost one family in three is poor; in Highland Park, Illinois, one in sixty-seven.

And there is a second striking difference. Compton's population is 75 percent black; East St. Louis's, 95 percent. In both Oak Lawn and Thousand Oaks, on the other hand, blacks are less than 1 percent of the population. In Highland Park, Michigan, blacks are 84 percent of the population; in Highland Park, Illinois, 1.5 percent.

A look at the composition of the population of the prisons and jails underscores this point. For years, every effort to determine the economic status of serious criminals who come before the courts or swell the prisons has come up with the same bleak and thoroughly predictable picture. In 1966, the President's Commission on Crime in the District of Columbia found that seven out of ten adult felony offenders in the city had incomes below $3,000. In 1979, the Bureau of Justice Statistics's periodic survey of state prison inmates found more than three-quarters with prearrest incomes below $10,000 a year. Among the inmates of local jails in 1978, the *median* prearrest income was about $3,700. In the United States as a whole, blacks are 12 percent of the population —but nearly half the population of the prisons.

The conclusion that the interwoven problems of economic and racial inequality play a potent role in breeding criminal violence seems hard to avoid. Yet surprisingly, not all criminologists would agree. "The evidence linking income (or poverty) and crime," James Q. Wilson tells us, is "inconclusive"; some criminologists go even further. "Whatever the merits of socioeconomic reform and, specifically, of greater distributive equality," writes Ernest van den Haag, "it could not replace deterrent threats and punishments as means of crime control." Few criminologists at any point on the political spectrum would venture to deny the strong associations between crime and race, but conservatives have often been remarkably reticent about the implications of that connection—and virtually silent on the obviously related question of how we might develop social policies to break it. If anything, conservative writers have been inclined to reject as unworkable, or even dangerous, most of the social programs created in the past two decades to confront racial or economic inequality head-on.

How do we square the evidence of Oak Lawn and East St. Louis, of the two Highland Parks, of Compton and Thousand Oaks, with the argument that inequality has little to do with crime and that increasing equality cannot help us reduce it? The answer is simple: we can't. The evidence for a strong association between inequality and crime is overwhelming. Denying it requires what we might politely describe as a highly selective interpretation of the facts. And we are unlikely to relinquish our status as the most violent of developed societies if we do not confront that hard and uncomfortable reality.

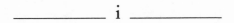

i

There is no shortage of evidence. Beyond the rough figures offered by places like Compton, East St. Louis, and Highland Park, Michigan, there is an accumulated fund of sophisticated research linking serious crime with social and economic inequality. It is a complicated linkage, because there are different ways of defining and measuring inequality; because a number of potentially confusing sources of bias lurk within both the methods of social science and the workings of criminal justice; and because, especially in the United States, it is frustratingly hard to disentangle the overlapping but partly distinct effects of income and race. Nonetheless, studies of several different kinds, both in the United States and overseas, show—strongly and recurrently —that economic and racial inequality affect not only the extent of crime but also its seriousness and violence. The relationship tends to be astonishingly linear—the worse the deprivation, the worse the crime.

These associations, which have appeared in criminological research for decades, have been powerfully confirmed in more recent research. Marvin Wolfgang's study of youth crime in Philadelphia (which we encountered in Chapter 3) found that when the city's youths were divided into two groups of higher versus lower socioeconomic status (SES)—as measured, in this case, by their parents' occupations—the "lower SES" boys committed substantially more crimes, and more *serious* ones as well. While boys from higher-status backgrounds more often went straight after one offense, the "lower SES" boys were more likely to repeat, even to become what the study called *chronic* offenders— those with at least five arrests by age eighteen.

Cutting across these substantial class differences, however, was the even more powerful factor of race. Black youths, whether of "lower" or "higher" SES, committed more recorded offenses in the first place and were far more likely to commit multiple offenses and serious offenses resulting in bodily injuries. Nonwhite youth were responsible for all the homicides, 86 percent of the rapes, and 89 percent of the robberies, though they represented just 29 percent of the entire youth cohort.

This and later research also drives home another point: the inequality associated with high rates of crime involves more than differences in income alone. The Philadelphia study found that several other characteristics of the youths' lives—school performance, IQ, and how often they had moved—were also related to delinquency. But this was true primarily because these characteristics were themselves so closely associated with racial and class position. For example, boys who were poor achievers in high school were more likely to become delinquent, but then most of the poor achievers were nonwhite. Thus, problems like school failure were best understood as aspects of a larger constellation of adverse social conditions—constituting what the researchers called a *disadvantaged* position—that were inextricable from the overriding problem of racial and class inequality. The more these conditions were combined in the youths' lives, the more they were at risk of becoming delinquent in the first place and of committing serious or repetitive crimes once delinquent. Indeed, the Philadelphia researchers noted, "the recidivists, one-time offenders, and non-offenders lie on a continuum" on all these measures of social disadvantage. Recidivists had the lowest IQ scores and levels of school achievement and the most intracity mobility, while those with no recorded offenses were at the other end of the scale, and one-time offenders fell squarely in the middle.

These general conclusions have appeared again and again in recent research on many different populations in a variety of settings in several countries. Wolfgang's own later study of Philadelphia youths born in 1958 found, for example, that although the second cohort was significantly more violent than the first, racial imbalance remained pervasive and startling. The nearly 6,600 white boys committed 4 homicides, 9 rapes, and 103 robberies; the 7,200 nonwhite boys accumulated 52 homicides, 96 rapes, and over 1,200 robberies. More than a quarter of the nonwhite boys were recidivist delinquents, with one in every nine a "chronic"; among the white boys, only one in nine was a recidivist and one in twenty-eight a "chronic." Similarly, in a 1978 study of violent juvenile delinquents for the Vera Foundation, Paul Strasburg found that black youths accounted for 62 percent of all violent offenses, though they were 49 percent of the study's sample of arrested delinquents. Just over half of the black delinquents in the sample had been charged with a violent crime at least once, compared to just under half of Spanish-speaking delinquents and only 29 percent of whites. More than twice as many blacks as whites—and nearly twice as many blacks as Spanish-speaking youths—had committed three or more violent offenses (though the Spanish-speaking delinquents were slightly more likely than the whites to have committed at least one violent crime). Arrest data from a Rand Corporation study of youth crime and juvenile justice in California uncovered an even more striking racial and ethnic imbalance. In 1980, white youths in Los Angeles were arrested for homicide at a rate of about 15 per 100,000. Among Hispanics, the rate was 103 per 100,000; among blacks, 292. For robbery, the rate for white youths was a shade under 250 per 100,000; for Hispanics, 918—and for black youths, more than 5,500 per 100,000.

The picture is the same if we look at the racial and economic characteristics of youths who are not just arrested but behind bars. As the California Youth Authority's researchers dryly note, their analysis of the factors distinguishing "chronic" and violent youthful criminals from other delinquents contains "few surprises." Like Wolfgang's research, the CYA study found that the relationship between crime and socioeconomic disadvantage was depressingly linear. The most troubling and dangerous youths—

the *chronic violent-aggressive* delinquents who had committed multiple crimes, at least one of which was a murder, manslaughter, rape, or serious assault—were at one end of a spectrum of social deprivation. The nonchronic, less violent delinquents were at the other, while chronic but less violent property offenders were in the middle. "Degree of chronicity and violence-proneness," the Youth Authority researchers concluded, "appears closely paralleled by degree of social deprivation and psychological deviance."

The finding was all the more striking because this was such a tough population to begin with: most of these youths were chronic offenders. But even among them, the less chronic and less violent had several things in common. They were more often white, their parents were much less often of "below-average" socioeconomic level and less likely to have been on welfare, and the boys themselves were likely to have been rated higher on mental ability and to have gone farther in school. Among a sample drawn from one of the institutions in the study, the Preston School for youth, the largest single group was the chronic violent-aggressive offenders. Who were they? Only a fourth had parents who had graduated from high school, versus nearly two-fifths of less chronic or less violent delinquents. Two-thirds of the chronic violent-aggressives came from families of below-average socioeconomic level, versus just two-fifths of the nonchronics. Twice as many chronic violent-aggressives came from families receiving public assistance. Less than half as many had gone past the junior year of high school.

Given America's racial history, it is difficult to sort out exactly how much of the variations in rates of serious crime reflect inequalities of class versus those of race. Where both historical and current forces have kept some minorities disproportionately trapped in the lowest reaches of the economy, the distinction between economic and racial inequality itself is in danger of being uselessly abstract. On balance, however, the evidence suggests that in the United States the effects of class and race on criminal violence in the United States are inextricably intertwined—but that race probably does have an independent effect. In a recent study of the 125 largest American metropolitan areas, for example, Judith and Peter Blau found that greater inequality of family incomes in an urban area "substantially raises its rate of criminal violence"—as does the proportion of blacks in the population. When the Blaus tried to tease out the relative importance of racial versus economic inequalities, they found that most of the influence of race on the crime rate could be accounted for by the fact that blacks were so predictably at the bottom of the socioeconomic ladder—but even when that association was statistically controlled, a significant racial effect remained.

The repeated connection between inequality and crime holds for other industrial societies as well. Though serious street crime is less widespread in Britain than here, its distribution within the social structure is broadly similar. Donald West's Cambridge Study of Delinquent Development found that being from a low-income family "effectively doubled" the chances of delinquency among London working-class boys. Like their American counterparts, the London delinquents were also more likely to become repeat offenders (and to persist in crime longer) if they came from poor families. And here too, low income was an indicator of a larger set of "interlinked circumstances." The delinquents came disproportionately from families that moved often and were more often on welfare.

In another long-term study of British children born in the 1950s, Michael Wadsworth came to strikingly similar conclusions. Unlike West, Wadsworth measured socioeconomic inequality by occupation and education, not income; but the results were essentially the same. Sons of unskilled manual workers had a rate of delinquency more than three times higher than sons of professional workers. The likelihood of serious delinquency increased, again in predictable linear fashion, as the level of parents' occupation and schooling fell. Among the more than four thousand children in Wadsworth's sample, only a small percentage ever committed a serious crime resulting in physical injury (this was, after all, England, not the United States). But the rate of such crimes among youths from what Wadsworth called the *upper-middle* group was so small it was not even recorded, while it was 1.2 percent in the *lower-middle* group, 2.0 percent in the *upper-manual*, and 2.7 percent in the *lower-manual*.

Similar results come from a recent long-term study in Denmark. The Danes have one of the industrial world's lowest rates of criminal violence, as well as one of the world's most advanced welfare states (two facts that, as I'll argue below, can hardly be coincidental). Denmark boasts a relatively narrow spread of income inequality, but has by no means eliminated disparities in income and living conditions. And, as Tavs Folmer Andersen discovered, it is from the most deprived sectors of the Danish welfare state that most of Denmark's relatively few serious delinquents and adult criminals have come. Andersen compared children born between 1941 and 1952 who had suffered what he called "rough conditions during childhood"—working-class children who had grown up in poor, overcrowded housing in slum-clearance sections of Copenhagen—with a random sample of all children born in the city during those years. By 1979, the slum children had racked up a rate of imprisonment between four and five times higher than the others and a rate of early delinquency (measured by youth imprisonment or being sentenced to the custody of child-welfare authorities) eight times greater.

i i

These findings are both remarkably sturdy and remarkably consistent over time and in different countries; their implications for social policy seem transparently obvious. "The high concentration of serious delinquents of the future among children exposed to a characteristic constellation of social deprivation," writes Donald West, "points inexorably to the need to include anti-poverty measures in any coherent policy of delinquency prevention." Yet that seemingly unavoidable conclusion is far from universally accepted. Despite compelling evidence, conservatives have still maintained that the influence of inequality on crime is minimal and that we will prevent little crime by trying to reduce it.

Those who insist that the links between inequality and criminal violence are overstated have offered several different arguments. One is that the commonly observed association is largely spurious, an artifact of the biases of social scientists and of the criminal-justice system itself. A second is that the observed associations are real enough, but they are the result of cultural proclivities or personality deficiencies of some groups, which are regarded as causes rather than consequences of their disadvantaged position in society. In other words, it is not inequality or deprivation that leads to crime, but something about the culture, temperament, or upbringing of a small fraction of the population that leads to both crime and economic disadvantage. This is the most recent variant of the traditional conservative argument that the poor deserve what they get, and that delinquency and violence are merely dramatic expressions of the generally flawed character of those who wind up at the bottom of the social order. A third argument, favored by some of the more extreme proponents of dismantling the welfare states of the Western democracies, goes still further: it is not inequality that generates crime, but our misguided efforts to *reduce* inequality—efforts rooted in a naïve egalitarianism and enforced by the political mechanism of the welfare state.

The first argument—that the link between inequality and crime is largely if not entirely spurious—is based on a genuinely important perception: that the statistical evidence on which it rests is subject to powerful biases. For in a society run by the white and the well-to-do, it's argued, the decisions that determine whether individuals who break the law will be channeled through the stages of arrest, conviction, and imprisonment—and thus appear in the official crime statistics—cannot fail to be profoundly affected by racial and class prejudices. Police, in this view, are more likely to stop and arrest minorities and the poor in the first place; judges and juries more likely to convict them and to give them harsher sentences once convicted. Therefore, any apparent relationships between inequality and crime that are derived from official data on arrests, conviction, or the composition of the prison population are at least as much a measure of the behavior of the criminal-justice system as they are an accurate description of variations in the actual behavior of people at different points on the social spectrum.

This case cannot be easily dismissed. No one seriously argues

that criminal justice in America has been either color-blind or free
of class prejudice. In its more restrained versions, this argument
sensitizes us to important pitfalls awaiting researchers who use
official criminal statistics. But in its extreme form, the argument
requires us to believe not only that the criminal-justice system
discriminates against poor and minority offenders, but that it
discriminates enough to explain the enormous class and racial
variations that appear in the official data on arrest, conviction, and
imprisonment. The first belief is doubtless true, at least in some
jurisdictions—true enough, at any rate, to warrant serious concern. The second is false.

This is most obvious in the case of racial differences in crime.
To take the clearest case, there is no serious argument that the
racial disparities in homicide can be credibly attributed to criminal justice biases. And those disparities are stunning indeed.
Other things being equal, people in their late adolescence and
early adulthood are far more likely to die by violence than infants
and young children. But a black infant is more likely to be murdered in the United States than a white person of any age. Similarly, it's a truism that men—other things being equal—are more
likely to meet death by violence than women. But other things
are *not* equal. At every age until the late forties, a nonwhite
woman faces a higher risk of death by homicide than a white man.
All this, to be sure, would tell us little about the race of the
perpetrators, were it not for the fact that we know the great
majority of homicides are intraracial, not interracial.

Public Health Service data on racial differences in death rates
tell us the same thing. These figures are subject to uncertainties
of their own, but they are not affected by the prejudices of police,
prosecutors, or judges. And they too show that, apart from the
relatively constant factors of age and gender, race is the most
important determinant of the risks of death by violence. Homicide is the leading cause of death for blacks of both sexes between
the ages of fifteen and twenty-four: 39 percent of black men and
25 percent of black women who die at these early ages are murdered. At this age, homicide death rates are five times higher for
blacks than whites among men and four times higher for women.
For men only, homicide is the leading cause of death for blacks

153

aged twenty-five to forty-four as well; black men in this age range are roughly eight times as likely to meet death by violence as their white counterparts.

These great disparities are also confirmed in *victimization* studies, in which victims are asked to report some characteristics of their attackers, including sex, age, and race. These studies, too, can be biased by victims' misperceptions or even deliberate falsification, but investigations of this problem suggest that victims are in fact reasonably accurate in identifying their attackers. As the criminologist Michael Hindelang has demonstrated, these studies show a remarkable concentration of crimes against the person committed by young black men, a pattern little different from that shown by official police data. Thus, black men aged eighteen to twenty commit personal crimes (rape, robbery, assault, and larceny from the person) at a rate more than five times higher than white men the same age. Indeed, the factor of race is sometimes strong enough to cut across the otherwise definitive effects of age and gender. For example, although violent crime is generally highest for men aged eighteen to twenty, black men over twenty-one have much higher rates of robbery and rape than white men of any age. Among youths under eighteen, black women have slightly higher rates of robbery and assault than white men.

These findings all suggest that, at least for serious crimes of violence, the official criminal-justice statistics are not as far off the mark as critics have sometimes thought. And they are supported by studies that have sought to uncover the extent of racial discrimination in the criminal-justice system. Certainly no one can boast that discrimination has been eliminated. In a recent study of felony offenders in California, Texas, and Michigan, for example, Joan Petersilia of the Rand Corporation found little or no evidence of discrimination by race in arrests, prosecution, or conviction, but did uncover significant and otherwise inexplicable differences at the stage of sentencing in several jurisdictions: both blacks and Hispanics got longer sentences to begin with and served longer stretches in prison.

But the level of discrimination in sentencing found in this and other studies is not nearly great enough to account for the overrepresentation of blacks in prisons (especially since the evidence shows that, if anything, there is still an equally discriminatory countertendency, making for greater leniency in the courts toward blacks who commit crimes against other blacks). The overall incarceration rate for blacks in the state prisons exceeds the white rate by almost seven to one; on an average day, about three out of every hundred black men are behind the walls of a state prison and half that many more in a federal prison or a local jail. Almost one in five black men, versus one in thirty-seven white men, can expect to do time in his lifetime. As Alfred Blumstein has calculated, most of this disparity—about 80 percent—can be accounted for by the much higher crime rate among blacks in the first place. That leaves 20 percent unaccounted for, some of which doubtless reflects racial bias.

Unequal treatment in the courts is more likely with somewhat less serious crimes, where there is more room for discretion in sentencing. Thus, Blumstein calculates that the proportion of the racial gap in imprisonment that does not simply reflect higher crime rates may be as high as 33 percent for burglary, but just 5 percent for aggravated assault and less than 3 percent for homicide. This isn't to deny that racial bias may be more severe in some places than others, nor, certainly, to deny the importance of vigorous efforts to eliminate bias from the system wherever it's found. But it does confirm that only a part of the racial differences in incarceration rates can be explained by official bias. And it reminds us that, as Blumstein puts it, "any significant impact on the racial mix in our prisons will have to come from addressing the factors in our society that generate the life conditions that contribute" to the disparity.

Most criminologists would now agree with that judgment, though it would be hard to find a consensus on the specific "life conditions" that need changing in the black community—or on who should change them. But there is far less agreement on the role of bias in accounting for the relationship between economic inequality and crime. Indeed, this has long been one of the most vexed issues in American criminology, not least because it is bound up, in complex ways, with much deeper ideological concerns. Curiously, the argument that conventional statistics exaggerate the links between economic inequality and crime has been promoted both by criminologists of liberal sympathies and (though less frequently) by conservatives.

The idea that the poor are given a raw deal by the criminal-justice system has been with us since time immemorial, but the modern debate over the uses of statistics on class and crime is based on studies from the forties and fifties. They seemed to show that, contrary to what official data indicated, delinquency (this early research was largely concerned with youth crime) was widespread throughout the American class structure. Instead of comparing arrest, conviction, or imprisonment rates among different strata, or comparing poorer cities or communities with richer ones, these studies asked people to report in confidence what kinds of crimes they had committed and how often. In these *self-report* studies, middle-class youths readily admitted having done a variety of things that could have gotten them in trouble with the law—and to have done them as often, or nearly as often, as lower-class or working-class youths.

The implication was that only the biases in a criminal-justice system deeply imbued with middle-class prejudices accounted for the overrepresentation of poorer kids in the official figures. This conclusion was warmly received by both liberals and conservatives. To liberals it offered useful ammunition for attacking the (often real) class biases of the criminal-justice system and the hypocrisy of a society that came down hard on the crimes of the poor while ignoring the crimes of the affluent. To conservatives, it seemed to lend some support to the idea that crime was less influenced by the stock villains of traditional liberalism, like inequality and poverty, than by their own social pathologies of choice—like defective character and faulty upbringing.

Thus, in a controversial review of the evidence published in 1978, Charles Tittle, Wayne Villemez, and Douglas Smith argued that criminologists should abandon once and for all what they called the "myth of social class and criminality," a myth they attributed to "the tendency of sociologists, criminologists, and laymen to begin with the preconceived notion—the prejudice— that lower-class people are characterized by pejorative traits such as immorality, inferiority, and criminality." Farther to the Right, Travis Hirschi and his colleagues similarly announced in 1982 that "the class issue is a diversion the field can no longer afford."

But as many critics have pointed out, this peculiar consensus rested on remarkably fragile evidence, highly suspect on grounds of method as well as those of common sense. In particular, in their haste to adopt what seemed to be the egalitarian implications of the self-report studies, liberal criminologists (and the conservatives who also saw these studies as ideological fodder) ignored the studies' fairly obvious limitations. For one thing, the self-report researchers had to make do with whatever research subjects were available. In practice they usually studied high-school or college students, mostly in semirural areas or small towns, and thus systematically under-studied the kinds of young people most likely to be involved in serious crimes, notably ghetto dropouts and the "underclass" in general, whether urban or rural. At the same time, these studies curiously lumped together a few serious offenses with an enormous number of trivial ones. The bulk of the questions had to do with what might best be called youthful hijinks—many, in fact, weren't even violations of the law, much less serious ones. In many of these studies, it was thus quite possible for relatively insignificant acts to be counted as "serious" delinquency, thus ensuring that nearly every youth from whatever background *could* have been considered a serious "unofficial" delinquent—and therefore stacking the deck from the outset. For example, as John Braithwaite has noted in an incisive critique, one self-report questionnaire used by Travis Hirschi in a study published in the late sixties asked youths if they had ever "taken little things worth less than $2 that did not belong to you" or "banged up something that did not belong to you on purpose." Braithwaite points out that a child who takes a schoolmate's pencil and breaks it in a moment of anger is guilty of both "offenses" and, in this study, would have been placed in the *most* delinquent category. Most of these studies were overloaded with questions asking young people to report whether they had ever disobeyed their parents or told lies or gotten into fistfights—all activities that nearly any moderately honest youth would have had to acknowledge.

Hence, at best, the self-report studies were more or less accurately recording the fact that American youths of all backgrounds sometimes acted up and got out of hand—a conclusion that was surely true, though hardly surprising enough to any parent or teacher to warrant the commotion it caused. The studies simply were *not* about serious crime, for the most part, and the attempt to stretch their unremarkable findings about the prevalence of youthful misbehavior to encompass the much more disturbing issue of criminal violence was bound both to fail and to discredit the larger social and theoretical vision that lay behind it.

More recent and sophisticated self-report studies that have tried to overcome these methodological problems show, in fact, that the "myth" of the connection between class and serious crime is no myth at all. Some of the most compelling evidence comes from a study by Delbert Elliott and David Huizinga at the Behavioral Research Institute in Colorado, based on a national sample large enough to represent youth from the bottom of the social ladder adequately (and minorities as well). Elliott and Huizinga also used measures of delinquency that enabled them not only to distinguish serious offenses from the vast bulk of less serious ones, but in addition to distinguish between the *prevalence* and *incidence* of offenses—that is, between the number of people who have committed a given offense at *some* point versus the frequency with which they do so—an issue often ignored in earlier self-report research.

The respondents were divided into three groups according to their parents' occupations and education. *Middle-class* youths came from professional or managerial families with college educations, *working-class* youths from clerical, sales, or skilled blue-collar families with high school or some college, and *lower-class* youths from families of unskilled or semiskilled manual workers with high school educations or less. As in many earlier studies, Elliott and Huizinga found few class differences in the prevalence of delinquency *in general,* but this was because the vast majority of offenses were trivial ones that nearly everybody committed at one point or another. When it came to serious crime, however, and particularly its *incidence,* there was a sharp split between the lower-class and the middle-class youths; indeed, the familiar linear association between class level and delinquency surfaced once again. Middle-class youths were less seriously delinquent than working-class youths—who, in turn, were usually less delinquent than lower-class youths.

A similar relationship between lower status and the frequency and seriousness of crime appears in several other recent, more sophisticated studies using self-report data. (The findings linking class and delinquency in the Cambridge study of London adolescents, for instance, are based on self-reports as well as official data.) And, as in the case of racial differences, studies of victimization strongly suggest that the official statistics are less wide of the mark than their critics have often assumed. Using victim surveys, for example, Robert Sampson and Thomas Castellano found that offense rates for both juveniles and adults were at least twice as high in low-income as in high-income neighborhoods.

The rush to interpret the self-report studies as definitive proof that lower-class people were not more likely to be involved in serious street crime than middle-class people was one of the most egregious failings of liberal criminology, one of the most vulnerable links in its understanding of crime. In its milder versions, to be sure, this perspective told us important things about the way the police, courts, and parole boards worked in practice as opposed to theory, and it did show that on balance the system tended to go easy on those who—by reason of class and family background, personal style, or demeanor—happened to be rather like the people who ran the system. There was, in other words, genuine, sometimes pervasive bias in the system, and it is very likely that this bias had (and has) something to do with the overrepresentation of poor and, to a lesser extent, working-class people in the statistics of arrest, conviction, and incarceration. (It is also true, of course, that the more lenient treatment of white-collar or corporate crimes adds another kind of bias all its own.) But it is a very long leap indeed from this useful perception to the more extreme argument that interpreted these biases as providing evidence against *any* class differences in street crime. For after all, this extreme position simply violated common sense. In their personal lives, it was unlikely that many liberal criminologists were ignorant of the different risks of being robbed or raped in different parts of their own cities, or that they really lacked sufficient savvy to know the difference between "bad neighborhoods" and good ones.

But the fact that economic inequality and criminal violence are closely and predictably linked raises a far deeper and, I think, more compelling point than that the courts and the police may treat poor people differently from others. It reminds us that harsh inequality is not only morally unjust but also enormously destructive of human personality and of social order. Brutal conditions breed brutal behavior. To believe otherwise requires us to argue that the experience of being confined to the mean and precarious depths of the American economy has *no* serious consequences for personal character or social behavior. But this not only misreads the evidence; it also trivializes the genuine social disaster wrought by the extremes of economic inequality we have tolerated in the United States.

i i i

This insight also helps us evaluate another argument raised by those who reject the importance of inequality as a source of crime: that it is the culture or character of the disadvantaged, rather than inequality, poverty, or current discrimination, that accounts for their high levels of criminal violence. I will save the question of individual personality problems versus race or class as explanations of crime for the following chapter, which examines the role of the family and early childhood experience in crime and delinquency. Here let me consider, briefly, the related argument about "culture."

The debate over the relative importance of *cultural* versus material or *structural* factors in crime is a long one in American social science, but one that has shed more heat than light, in good part because the meager and inconclusive evidence it has generated has been overwhelmed by the ideological purposes to which it has been put. In order to make sense of that frustrating debate, it helps to distinguish between two different versions of the argument that criminal violence is the reflection of cultural attitudes or values—the *soft* version and the *hard*.

The *soft* version rests on the commonsense argument that there is inevitably an *interaction* between the structural and the cultural: the external conditions surrounding a group will have an effect, especially in the long run, on the attitudes and values they hold about themselves, about society as a whole, and about the moral weight of illegal activities and the use of violence. These attitudes, over time, may crystallize into more or less coherent value systems that may persist to some extent even if the original conditions change. Nevertheless, the values cannot be usefully *detached* from the structural conditions that gave rise to them. It is therefore highly probable that significant changes in those conditions will be followed by shifts in the values as well.

Some variant of this soft cultural argument underlay much of the most influential criminological theory of the 1950s and 1960s. The chief problem that the theory sought to explain was the emergence of delinquent youth gangs in the cities of the "affluent" society. Beneath the specific concern over the troublesome behavior of the gangs was the deeper question of the reasons for the paradox noted in the previous chapter: the persistence—or indeed growth—of alienation and violence in the midst of abundance. Students of delinquency began to argue that the rise of the gangs reflected the growth of "subcultural" values stressing "toughness" and predatory behavior in place of legitimate achievement. These subcultural values in turn arose out of a crucial contradiction of postwar affluence: the fact that some groups were systematically blocked by race and economic disadvantage from achieving the goals of status and material well-being encouraged by the larger culture.

This argument drew to a great extent on the theoretical work of the Columbia sociologist Robert K. Merton and was most forcefully expressed in the classic 1950s study *Delinquency and Opportunity,* by Richard Cloward and Lloyd Ohlin. In addition to offering an explanation of why delinquent gangs behaved as they did, the contention that blocked opportunities generated delinquent subcultures offered one answer to the question of how such widespread and virulent delinquency could appear in such a rich country. It suggested that more important than the sheer material impact of *absolute* deprivation was the social-psychological wound of *relative* deprivation—of being hindered from attaining what others were able to attain. The implications for social action seemed clear. Urban delinquency would continue and perhaps increase even in the face of economic growth and abundance unless the barriers to opportunity were removed. This theme was an important intellectual influence on the War on Poverty in the sixties, particularly its efforts at education, job training, and community organization.

A similar approach appears in Judith and Peter Blau's more recent study. As we've seen, the Blaus found strong associations between homicide rates and economic inequality, and even stronger ones for racial inequality. They also found that sheer poverty was a less powerful explanation for variations in homicide than inequality. Hence they, too, concluded that what most predictably generates violent crime is not the simple absence of material goods, but rather the deeper attitudes of hopelessness and alienation produced by inequalities that are perceived as unjust. Great inequalities of any kind, they argue, cause corresponding alienation in those at the bottom; but in professedly democratic societies, the experience of *ascribed* inequalities—justified by group membership rather than performance—are especially alienating. "Pronounced ethnic inequality in resources implies that there are great riches within view but not within reach of many people destined to live in poverty." The result is "resentment, frustration, hopelessness, and alienation." Once again, it is *relative* deprivation that is most salient—the sense of being unjustly deprived of what others have. Violence results "not so much from lack of advantages as from being taken advantage of." Those attitudes, moreover, often wreak havoc on close personal relations (especially in the family), thus compounding the problem by weakening some of the most important "informal" bulwarks against crime.

This sort of argument does not deny the importance of attitudes and values in understanding crime; far from it. To do so would amount to suggesting that human beings are simply automatons who respond in some visceral fashion to the bare fact of material conditions. But the soft cultural argument regards those values as the reflection of circumstances—in particular, the systematic exclusion of the poor and especially the minority poor from realistic chances of success and well-being in the terms prescribed by the larger culture.

. . .

The *hard* version of this argument, on the other hand, makes culture into something close to an independent force that shapes the fates of the minority poor. In the sixties this was often phrased in terms of a "subculture of violence" afflicting certain groups, most notably American blacks. The "subculture of violence" turned the norms of the larger culture upside down by placing a positive value on the use of violence to resolve personal problems. Sometimes this was just another expression of the soft argument that persistent discrimination often created tragically self-defeating attitudes among its victims, a line of reasoning that led logically to a sense of urgency about ending discrimination. But the harder version saw discrimination as mainly if not entirely in the past (indeed, the subculture was seen as primarily a legacy of slavery); by now it was the subculture itself, not current discrimination or the systematic blockage of opportunities through economic and technological change, that kept many blacks from achieving a successful and orderly life in the more open society of the sixties. A more recent variant of the argument has often been deployed by conservatives to explain the apparently paradoxical divergence in social conditions among American blacks since the 1960s—the glaring contrast between an increasingly successful majority and an an increasingly impoverished, demoralized, and violent minority within a minority. That growing numbers of blacks have succeeded in the American economy in recent years is taken as evidence that there are no longer substantial racial barriers to success, and that what must therefore explain the demoralization and violence of the black poor is mainly their culture—what one observer calls the "burden of background."

If all that was being said here was that a history of brutal discrimination and exclusion has often left its mark, fostering attitudes and behavior that can be brutal, self-defeating, and difficult to change, not many would now disagree. But the hard subculture argument says more; it says that these attitudes are no longer significantly generated by the current conditions of minority life in America, and thus that they are therefore unlikely to be much affected by improvements in those conditions.

The argument raises a host of complex historical questions, most beyond the boundaries of this book. But several crucial limitations of the hard view of crime and culture may be quickly stated. To begin with, it fits poorly with the historical trend in violent crime in recent decades—a fact noted by some critics as early as the sixties. It isn't unreasonable to argue that the inheritors of a legacy of slavery and harsh discrimination might carry a repertoire of violent responses with them as they moved away from their rural roots and into the cities. But the cultural argument is far less persuasive as an explanation of why criminal violence *worsened* as the descendants of slaves moved farther and farther from that experience, chronologically and geographically. (Studies of the careers of recent migrants to the cities drove home this objection; it was repeatedly shown that new entrants to the cities exhibited less social pathology than those who had been there longer and had thus been more heavily exposed to the demoralizing forces of urban conditions.) Moreover, the fact that some blacks have moved rapidly into the ranks of the stable and steady middle class while others remained trapped in instability and poverty would seem logically to contradict rather than support the hard cultural argument. After all, the culture at issue is presumably common to American blacks in general, most of whom are descended from slaves. Since the culture is common to the black community while the demoralization is not, it remains for us to explain—in terms *other* than the common culture—why some have managed to escape it and some not.

At the same time, there is an even more stubborn difficulty with the hard cultural argument: no one has yet been able to *find* the subculture of violence—and not for lack of trying. Many sophisticated quantitative studies have sought to determine just how much of the variation in criminal violence between different states or cities can be attributed to such cultural values versus the more *structural* forces of low income, poor education, and so on. Obviously, separating these things is harder in practice than in theory, and it is not surprising that the results have been inconclusive. Usually the research strategy is to use race itself (or sometimes Southern origin) as *indirect* indications of the subculture of violence—a dubious practice made necessary by the fact that the subculture itself has proven impossible to measure more directly. Several studies have concluded that once the structural factors have been accounted for, there is no remaining effect of race or region on the rate of violent crime; others find that some—usually small—effect remains. Yet it is difficult to attribute that differential—where it appears—reliably to culture without becoming circular, since we're never sure whether the research has managed to isolate and control for every structural feature of black life in America that might just as effectively explain it.

Again, however, the point is not to reject the influence of cultural forces on crime altogether, but to steer a middle course between the extremes of this increasingly fruitless debate between structure and culture. To say that there is little evidence for a distinctive subculture of violence is not to claim that violent attitudes and responses are not evident among the minority poor; that would be to fall once again—as liberals often have—into the trap of the denial of pathology. It *is*, however, to argue against the implications of intractability and permanence that pervade the hard version of the argument and the smug defeatism about the possibilities of social action that often accompanies it. The hard cultural argument exculpates contemporary institutions and policies far too blithely. It implicitly denies that society bears any responsibility to address these problems or has any realistic hope of doing so in ways that will prevent violence. The soft version is not only compatible with a more generous and active approach to the problems of the disadvantaged, but lends itself to it, as we've seen in the case of "opportunity" theory. The existence of self-defeating values and attitudes among some of the poor thus becomes a signal for redoubled efforts to confront the mutable conditions that nourish them. The exact form those efforts should take is a complicated question; I do not think that the answers of the liberals of the 1960s were entirely adequate, but I will leave that issue for the final chapter. Suffice it to say here that the question of how stubborn the culture of the deprived may be is an empirical one. The answer is not dictated by fate or even by our tragic racial history; we will know it only when we begin to move decisively against the continuing inequalities of American life.

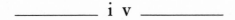

i v

The understanding that harsh inequalities might damage those who experience them would seem to lend particular urgency to efforts to redeem the lost promises of the War on Poverty and mitigate the extremes of inequality in America. Those opposed to this course of action, however, have countered with still another line of argument. Conservatives have not only denied that reducing inequality will reduce crime, but have recently managed to argue that it *causes* crime. Writing in the journal of the arch-conservative Heritage Foundation, for example, one Christie Davies, a British author, blames the rising crime rate in modern industrial societies on the "corrosive ethic of socialist egalitarianism." "Since inequality is not a cause of crime," Davies tells us, "crime rates cannot be reduced by the political pursuit of social equality." In fact, "policies that have aimed at producing equality through political and bureaucratic intervention have been the underlying cause" of rising crime rates in recent years.

Davies's attack focused mainly on Britain and Sweden, but the larger target is the creeping egalitarianism of all the Western democracies. This is an extreme version of a more familiar conservative theme: not only crime but many other contemporary symptoms of social disintegration can be linked to the insidious effects of equality in general and of the welfare state in particular. Sometimes the villain of the piece is the rise of "egalitarian" sentiment itself, which has come to replace (as Davies puts it) the "sense of personal moral responsibility." Or the growth of public welfare has boosted the crime rate by eroding family stability and the work ethic. Whatever specific mechanisms are held responsible for the welfare state's pernicious impact, the general attitude is one of nostalgia for the days when the forces of the unfettered "market" held the baser impulses in check (along with the ancillary institutions that enforced its discipline, including the penitentiary and the workhouse). This argument faithfully expresses the conservative vision of the ideal social order governed by the stern but ultimately benign dictates of the private market, and reflects the visceral distaste for measures that might cushion the market's impact on personal and communal life. But it is also one of the most egregious examples of the triumph of ideology over evidence in the short history of neoconservative thought.

It's true that crime has recently increased in most of the welfare states of Europe, though in many of them the increases in serious criminal violence have been small, and all pale in comparison to the levels of violence Americans routinely expect. And since—at least until recently—many of the provisions of the welfare state have also expanded in most of those countries, it is possible to argue that the two trends are causally related. But many other things have also increased at the same time, any or all of which might, by the same logic, be related to crime: the migration from countryside to city, the international drug traffic, the intensity of consumer advertising, the level of youth unemployment, or the number of conservative think tanks, to pick only a handful of possible candidates. To convince us that "egalitarian" welfare measures cause crime, conservatives should be able to show that those industrial societies with greater commitment to the welfare state suffer more crime. Here, however, the argument disintegrates, for all the evidence points in the opposite direction. The industrial societies that have done the most to blunt the inequalities produced by the market system have low rates of crime—particularly when compared to the one major industrial society that has done the least: the United States.

Consider first some simple comparisons. According to figures from the Organization for Economic Cooperation and Development (OECD), we had the widest spread of income inequality in the late sixties and early seventies of any comparable developed country. The narrowest spread was in Holland, where the share of total personal income going to the poorest fifth of the population was more than double that in the United States. During the same period, according to Dane Archer and his associates, the homicide rate in America averaged more than thirteen times the Dutch rate, and the murder rate in New York City about ten times that in Amsterdam. In Denmark, where public expenditures amount to about half of the gross national product, versus a third in the United States (a comparison that greatly understates the real difference in social priorities, because so much of America's public spending—and so little of Denmark's—goes for defense), the homicide rate in the late seventies ranged between about one-tenth and one-nineteenth of the American rate.

Some conservative writers have argued that the relatively low Japanese crime rate is evidence that more market-based societies are relatively free of crime because they have eschewed the destructive lures of egalitarianism and public responsibility for the collective welfare. But this betrays a fundamental misconception about Japanese society. Among OECD countries, the Japanese are exceeded only by Holland, Sweden, and Norway in the extent to which they have narrowed the range of income inequality between rich and poor, and by Holland and Sweden alone in the proportion of personal income that goes to the bottom fifth of the population. Moreover, the elaborate provisions for job security and other private cushions against the impact of the market in Japan have been held up for years as models that the United States might wish to follow. In this respect, Japan is far closer to the welfare states of Western Europe than to the United States, which is uniquely lacking in the mechanisms of reciprocity and mutual obligation that have been developed in other industrial societies.

There are many ways to describe this difference in numbers; let me borrow a few from Robert B. Reich's powerful discussion of America's relative failure, among industrial societies, to develop effective social-service programs to ensure the well-being of its work force—worker's compensation and benefits for the unemployed, children, the aged, the handicapped, and the disabled. The United States spends just 14 percent of its GNP on these programs; Sweden spends 33.8 percent, West Germany 30.6 percent, the Netherlands 27.7 percent, France, 22 percent. The Japanese government spends 17 percent of its GNP on such services, but this figure is misleadingly low because it does not reflect the substantial contributions made by Japanese employers, in contrast to their American counterparts.

This isn't just a matter of levels of spending. What these figures represent is a historical commitment—often achieved through long and painful political struggle—to shift the moral balance of these societies toward greater concern for social solidarity and mutual support. The United States is the industrial country whose cultural and political traditions have been least favorable to that kind of commitment, the country in which the "forces of the market" have been least cushioned and regulated in the name of the wellbeing of its people. Can it be merely coincidental that it is also the country most torn by interpersonal violence?

These relatively crude comparisons, moreover, are supported by every sophisticated study we have of the cross-national relationships between inequality and violent crime. The problems in comparing different countries' crime rates are formidable, but—used carefully—international statistics on homicide are reliable enough to permit useful comparisons. The results have been consistent and revealing. Around the world, at every level of economic development, increasing equality goes hand in hand with lower risks of homicide.

Thus, in a careful analysis of murder rates in thirty-one countries, from poor ones in the Third World to advanced industrial societies, John and Valerie Braithwaite concluded that higher homicide rates were linked with several measures of economic inequality—a broad gap between the rich and the average wage earner, large disparities in income between workers in different sectors of industry, and a low per capita consumption of protein —usually indicating a "wide gulf between the poor and the remainder of the population." Using only slightly different measures, Stephen Messner of Columbia University arrived at similar conclusions in a study of thirty-nine countries, again spanning the range of economic development. Income inequality explained a very substantial 35 percent of the differences in homicide among these countries, even when several other factors—including population density, degree of urbanization, and level of economic development—were taken into account. (The findings are all the more compelling because—in both studies—methodological problems prevented the researchers from including socialist countries. Thus all variation in income inequality found is variation within the range of capitalist societies.)

Not surprisingly, the same patterns appear if we focus on the uneven growth of "egalitarian" welfare measures within the United States. Conservatives like to argue that the "demoralizing blandishments" of the welfare system (in George Gilder's phrase) caused the rise in crime (and a host of other social pathologies) during the sixties. And it's true that some of the most rapid increases in crime in America occurred then, roughly parallel with the rapid growth of public assistance programs, especially Aid to Families with Dependent Children (AFDC).

No one denies the existence of this association; the question is what it means. Historians and social scientists have often argued that growing welfare and growing crime in the sixties were both *responses* to the same set of underlying conditions—especially migration to the cities prompted by mechanization of agriculture (particularly in the South) and the resulting breakdown of traditional livelihoods and of patterns of informal social support and control. If welfare was a *cause* of crime, we'd expect crime to be worse where the welfare system was more generous and less so where it was more sparing (just as we'd have expected crime to rise in response to the public assistance programs of the thirties). But stubborn reality once again asserts itself. Not only is the American welfare state the least generous among modern industrial societies, but within the United States welfare is most meager in many of the states with the worst levels of criminal violence, and relatively generous in some of the most tranquil.

Consider two states whose approaches to social welfare have traditionally been at opposite extremes of generosity. In Texas, the average welfare payment for an AFDC family in 1980, one of the lowest in the country, amounted to all of $109 a month (and had dropped from its level of ten years before, even in constant dollars). In Wisconsin, the average AFDC payment was $366 a month, one of the country's highest—up by more than two-thirds since 1970. With three times the population and more than five times the number of poor people, Texas actually had only slightly more total AFDC families than Wisconsin. Few states left their citizens more at the beneficent mercy of the market system than Texas; few so cushioned them from its vicissitudes as Wisconsin —thus few presumably so wantonly exposed them to the risks of demoralization, depravity, and violence. And the effect on crime? In 1980, the homicide rate in Texas was about six times that in Wisconsin; Houston's murder rate was five times higher than Milwaukee's.

What little specific research we have on how economic assistance to the poor affects crime supports these observations. James deFronzo's analysis of AFDC levels and crime rates (see Chapter 4) found that higher AFDC payments had a clear and consistent negative effect on rates of homicide, burglary, and rape. De-Fronzo calculated that increasing the AFDC payment by just $10 a month for each member of a welfare family would reduce the murder rate by about one per one hundred thousand.

Those who argue that public assistance causes crime must also be prepared to explain why criminal violence rose in the late seventies and early eighties, when income supports were dropping significantly. It's more plausible to argue the other way around—that declining support may have been a factor in the surge of criminal violence in those years despite enormous increases in imprisonment. Precisely to what extent the shrinking of the American welfare state may help explain that phenomenon, we do not know. But it is difficult to maintain that our excessive generosity, fueled by misguided egalitarian zeal, was to blame.

I don't mean to exaggerate the achievements of the welfare state. Welfare in the United States remains a demeaning and alienating system that all too often is a mean-spirited and inadequate substitute for the provision of sustaining employment. Even in more generous countries, the welfare state has often represented a series of ad hoc, sometimes reluctant, attempts to moderate but not to correct the stresses and dislocations of a still largely unregulated market system—what the British social theorist Richard Titmuss called the "diswelfare state." But in our time the more common and more destructive error is in the opposite direction—to deny or to minimize the important victories of the welfare state in humanizing life under modern industrial capitalism. Lowering the level of interpersonal violence is only one of those victories; but it is not a minor one.

———————— V ————————

It isn't accidental, then, that among developed countries, the United States is afflicted simultaneously with the worst rates of violent crime, the widest spread of income inequality, and the most severe public policies toward the disadvantaged. The industrial societies that have escaped our extremes of criminal violence tend either to have highly developed public sectors with fairly generous systems of income support, relatively well-developed employment policies, and other cushions against the "forces of the market," or (like Japan) to accomplish much the same ends through private institutions backed by an ethos of social obligation and mutual responsibility. By any measure we can construct, these countries have been less plagued by the extremes of inequality and economic insecurity. Our pattern of development into an advanced industrial society, on the other hand, has been unusually harsh and disruptive of the conditions that inhibit interpersonal violence.

This distinctly American pattern helps us to put in perspective another common argument—that prosperity causes crime. We've already examined the "paradox" of rising crime amid rising affluence. But some argue further that improvement in the material conditions of life, by itself, increases crime. Proponents of this view cite the rising crime rates in some affluent societies after the Second World War, especially the United States during the economic expansion of the sixties. Like the related argument that equality generates crime, this one implies that the crime problem cannot be made better by efforts to improve social conditions, particularly for the disadvantaged, and may be made worse. Sometimes this leads to a passive and fatalistic insistence that crime will always be with us, since it is caused by trends we wouldn't want to interfere with, even if we could; sometimes, to regressive yearning for a past when there was more poverty but also less crime—a form of nostalgia that lends itself nicely to demands for the restoration of authoritarian controls in the family, the classroom, and the justice system.

In this simplistic form, the argument is quite wrong. It is not true that material prosperity, in itself, causes criminal violence or that violence is fostered by "improving social conditions." But there are different *varieties* of prosperity—and the variety we have encouraged in America powerfully intensifies the social conditions that do generate violent crime. Recognizing this will help us comprehend why the American experience with criminal violence has been so crucially different from that of other developed societies. It also has vital implications for social policy in the future.

The issue is complicated by the fact that prosperity may affect violent crime differently than it does property crime. Most evidence suggests that property crimes may increase with affluence (though those crimes have been reported so unreliably that conclusions must remain tentative). When there is more to steal, more will be stolen, other things being equal; the declining need for theft may be outstripped by increasing opportunity. But serious criminal violence is another story. It is hardly the prosperous, after all, who now fill the prisons—with a few spectacular exceptions. Nor is it among the prosperous countries—except for the United States—that we find those most afflicted with criminal violence. The worst violent crime is found in some Third World countries wracked by desperate poverty, especially parts of the Caribbean, Latin America, and Africa. In the late sixties, when some pundits were shaking their heads over the tendency of "affluence" to produce crime, Mexico's homicide rate was twenty-six times Holland's, Trinidad and Tobago's about eighty-eight times New Zealand's, and Manila's about twenty-seven times Vienna's.

The evidence is strong that violence ordinarily *declines* as societies become more prosperous. A familiar sociological argument holds that the transition from the presumably more cohesive communities of the preindustrial era to the more fragmented ones of modern industrial societies *necessarily* involves a decline in social integration and a corresponding rise in crime and other social pathologies. But the record has actually been more complicated—and more encouraging. The best historical evidence shows that interpersonal violence was generally high in preindustrial Europe. It probably increased temporarily—at least in some places—with the first drastic disruptions wrought by early and harsh industrialization, which threw millions—especially the young—off the land and into the cities, without livelihoods, income, or the traditional supports of family and local community. But then, in most cases, things got better. In much of Europe and, with reservations, the United States, criminal violence seems to have declined in the late nineteenth century as the displaced were gradually, if imperfectly, integrated into stable occupational and communal roles in the industrial order and granted broader access to education and political participation. (One important reservation is that criminal violence remained high in urban black communities in America—another indication that blacks in the United States underwent what the historian Roger Lane describes as a "separate path of development.")

What the historian Ted Robert Gurr calls the "humanizing" effect of industrialization and democratization can also be observed in cross-national studies. As Steven Messner has recently shown in a study of fifty countries, economic development—as measured by the growth of Gross National Product per capita—is associated, on balance, with declining rates of homicide. Why? Economic development ordinarily reduces the level of violence because, over the long run, it reduces economic inequality. As Messner puts it, "The more developed societies do not exhibit especially high levels of homicide, in part because the greater equality in the distribution of income accompanying development serves to deflate the homicide rate."

But it is true that economic growth in some countries *has* been accompanied by increasing criminal violence, even while the general level of affluence has been rising. What this tells us, though, is not that increasing affluence necessarily causes crime, but that something has gone badly awry in the process of growth itself.

To understand what has gone wrong, it is helpful to look at the social forces that keep crime relatively low in certain communities that are poor in material terms. Though the case is often overstated, it is true that some (though not all) poor countries have fairly low crime rates. This is not, however, a mysteriously benign effect of poverty; rather, as students of crime in the Third World have often pointed out, it is usually attributable to a strong and encompassing community life that offers meaningful work and family roles in the midst of material deprivation. In such a context, even the very poor may have socially valued occupations, as well as close, supportive relations with their families, religious associations, and other local institutions. These relationships provide not only material assistance, but also a less tangible but no less important sense of social purpose, cooperation, and mutual responsibility. (At the same time, in communities where *most* people are poor, inequalities of material well-being are likely to be less glaringly evident, and their implications for self-esteem and social status less encompassing.)

How these circumstances may influence crime is illustrated in a recent study of delinquency in rural India by the sociologist Clayton Hartjen, who found a surprisingly low level of juvenile crime, despite widespread poverty. Why? According to Hartjen, part of the answer is that "Indians are immersed in a network of role relationships that involve a variety of obligations toward kin, *jati* [subcaste], and community." Children and youths are "included in almost all forms of social activity," notably meaningful work; this is especially true in agriculture, but "even in nonagricultural commercial enterprises, children are working: filling tires with air, packing groceries in the tiny shops along the streets, or working with their parents on construction and highway crews." Above all, the place of Indian citizens in the larger community is not so thoroughly dependent as in many wealthier societies on their economic performance. "Regardless of one's position in the economic structure," Hartjen writes, "one still belongs to the larger social system in terms of family, *jati*, and community membership. An Indian may be low on the membership hierarchy, but he or she is still a member."

Such relationships are important bulwarks against interpersonal violence both because they provide a fundamental sense of belonging to a larger supportive community and because they provide the setting in which informal social sanctions against aggression and crime can operate effectively. And this helps explain what has gone wrong in those countries where growth has, if anything, brought intensified violence. Economic development within the market system tends to undermine traditional institutions of support and mutual obligation; what is most crucial in influencing the pattern of violence and crime is the extent to which these traditional supports manage to survive in the face of that disruption (recall Japan's private mechanisms of social obligation) or are supplanted by new ones (Western Europe's welfare states). Where this happens, the overall effect is to decrease interpersonal violence over time. Where it fails to happen, economic growth may weaken or destroy the supportive relations that existed in more traditional communities without putting anything of substance in their place. The result is an impoverished rural and urban underclass deprived of respectable livelihoods, torn away from personal attachments and informal controls, and dependent on an often inadequate labor market as the exclusive provider of social integration, material welfare, and self-esteem.

This is precisely what has happened in many Third World countries that have experienced the wrenching transformations of unregulated economic development. Rural livelihoods and ways of life have been eroded, often shattered, but there is no strong, labor-intensive industrial economy to absorb the displaced and to provide new occupations and new resources for stable community life. That condition—bad enough in itself—is typically exacerbated by the simultaneous growth of a small but glittering sector of extravagant affluence with which the displaced poor must necessarily compare themselves. The same profit-driven growth also tends to replace older values of mutuality and cooperation with a culture that encourages competitive, individual striving for a level of material consumption that only a fraction of the population can conceivably afford. The combination is volatile, and it goes a long way toward explaining why some cities of the developing countries are the most dangerous places in the world.

This process of disruptive development—in which a selective prosperity is accompanied by the persistence or even increase of inequality, the breakdown of communal bonds, and the destruction of stable work roles—not only helps account for the dreadful rates of criminal violence in places like Brazil, the Philippines, parts of the Caribbean, and Africa, but it also illuminates the seeming paradox of violence amidst prosperity in the postwar United States, where these disruptions took place within a society and culture already deeply distorted by racial inequality.

I've argued already, in Chapter 4, that the growth of the postwar American economy was unusual among advanced industrial societies in the extent to which it eliminated traditional livelihoods, yet failed to replace them with new opportunities. This helped ensure that the American distribution of income remained highly unequal in spite of the overall rise in the standard of living. To this aspect of economic deprivation must be added the fragmenting impact of a largely unbuffered market economy on less quantifiable but critical dimensions of communal life— local networks of support, traditions of mutual help, values of cooperation, and common provision of basic needs. In particular, the loss of agricultural employment and the large-scale movement from country to city broke older communities apart, while the relative absence of mechanisms to integrate the displaced into new jobs inhibited the development of a stable and supportive urban community life. In a familiar pattern, these transformations brought the unskilled of the rural South, Appalachia, and even the Caribbean and Latin America into American cities just as the capacity of the urban-industrial economy to absorb them was declining, trapping the newcomers in neighborhoods too rapidly changing to sustain strong networks of social support, and placing the marginal and uprooted poor in demoralizing proximity to the prosperous, while saturating them with the lures of an increasingly frenetic consumer culture.

As in the Third World, the combination was (and is) an explosive one—and one that sharply distinguishes the American pattern of economic development. Many other industrial societies suffered similar strains; none suffered them in such extreme form. It is precisely the minimization of inequality and unemployment and the preservation of strong communal institutions that, for example, help account for the experience of two modern industrialized countries noted for their low rates of serious crime—Switzerland and Japan. As the criminologist Marshall Clinard has argued, Swiss economic development was far more decentralized than that in most other countries and took place in the context of a political system strongly based on local self-government and broad community participation. As a result, Switzerland's rise to affluence entailed considerably less disruption of local communal life than occurred in most industrial societies. Similarly, scholars have often pointed to the persistence of strong ties of community and kinship in the face of rapid industrialization in postwar Japan. In both cases,too, economic development was accompanied by a relatively narrow spread of income inequality and very low rates of unemployment, assuring a more egalitarian distribution of the fruits of growth.

It is important to be clear about what this evidence means and doesn't mean. That some forms of economic growth can generate crime doesn't mean that we should romanticize the supposedly harmonious life of poor countries—countries that are often both wretchedly deprived in material terms and ridden with their own forms of institutionalized violence and traditionally accepted brutality. Nor does it suggest that poverty and material deprivation have nothing to do with crime (as comfortable observers in affluent nations sometimes prefer to believe) or justify a less-than-benign neglect of the material needs of the poor at home or overseas. It *does* tell us that if we want to understand the relationships between crime, inequality, and prosperity, we will need a broader conception of what we mean by impoverishment—and prosperity. It tells us that statistics on the growth of Gross National Product or personal income alone are not very precise guides to the extent of social deprivation; that the supports of community and kinship can inhibit violence even where there is little money and few material goods; and that the enforced separation of people from these communal supports in the name of economic growth can be among the worst forms of impoverishment of all. By the same token, it follows that if we wish to mount an effective attack on criminal violence, we cannot be satisfied with simply doling out funds, grudgingly and after the fact, to people who have been stripped of livelihoods and social networks by the dynamics of the private labor market.

This conclusion, most emphatically, does not mean that we should dismantle the welfare state and replace it with nostalgic calls for a revival of volunteerism and a vaguely defined community spirit; nor that we should diminish the role of government in the futile pursuit of an imagined vision of the industrial discipline of the nineteenth century or the traditional cohesiveness of the preindustrial village. Conservatives often forget that the unity and tranquillity of these traditional communities—where they existed—depended on the stability of institutions that have increasingly been undermined by the market economy itself. In the face of that development, there are two logical responses. One is to try, through force and fear, to impose new forms of discipline and control on the uprooted and marginal poor of the cities, while allowing the disintegrative effects of a chaotic and disruptive economy to take their natural course. The other is to develop social and economic policies to forestall this volatile and tragic pattern in the first place, or to reverse it.

But this gets a bit ahead of the story. Before coming back to these issues, we need to look at a further objection to the argument I've been making about the intimate connection between harsh social inequalities and violent crime—that this relationship has more to do with individual differences in character or upbringing than with the more "external" circumstances of social and economic deprivation. As I'll demonstrate in the following chapter, the value of this objection is that it directs attention to important questions that liberal criminology has traditionally neglected—particularly the role of patterns of child-rearing in crime and delinquency. Taken to the extreme, however, as it frequently is, this point of view serves to obscure many of the things we might do to reduce crime, while pointing us toward responses that cannot do much good, and might do considerable harm.

6

UNDERSTANDING CRIME: FAMILIES AND CHILDREN

As far back as 1816, one of the earliest forerunners of the modern blue-ribbon commission—the Committee for Investigating the Causes of the Alarming Increase of Juvenile Delinquency in the Metropolis—placed faulty upbringing at the head of the list. The metropolis in this case was London, and the committee included such eminent students of social and economic questions as James Mill and David Ricardo. In order to "obtain every possible information respecting the nature and causes of the evil in question," as well as the "most efficient means of removing or diminishing it," the committee undertook the arduous task of visiting the youths confined in the city's prisons, where they were to be "separately examined and privately admonished, the evil consequences of their conduct represented to them, and every persuasive used for their recovery which kindness could suggest." The investigators then went on, with admirable perseverance, to interview and "admonish" the friends and associates of the imprisoned youths as well. On the basis of these investigations, the committee concluded that the primary causes of the alarming rise in delinquency were the following:

The improper conduct of parents. The want of education. The want of suitable employment. The violation of the Sabbath and habits of gambling in the public streets.

The committee also listed as contributory causes the severity of the criminal code, the "defective state" of the police, and "the existing system of the prison discipline." Nonetheless, they clearly regarded parental misconduct as, if not the sole cause of the alarming increase of delinquency, at least the first among equals.

Since the committee's report, concern over the relationship between family life and crime has waxed and waned, more as a function of broader social and ideological trends than of the accumulation of new evidence one way or the other. With some important exceptions, conservative writers have focused on the familial determinants of delinquency to the exclusion of larger social forces, while liberal criminologists have tended to denigrate family influences in favor of broader environmental forces. In England, the emphasis on family factors was for years most closely associated with the psychologist Cyril Burt (later best known for having falsified data in order to demonstrate the overriding role of genetic factors in intelligence). "Of environmental conditions," Burt wrote in the twenties, reasoning along lines that have changed remarkably little among conservative scholars since, "those obtaining outside the home are far less important than those obtaining within it; and within it, material conditions such as poverty are far less important than moral conditions such as ill discipline and vice." In the United States, the same stance was adopted most forcefully by the Harvard criminologists Sheldon and Eleanor Glueck, in a series of studies of young delinquents beginning in the 1930s. The Gluecks argued that what they called "under-the-roof culture"—the moral climate of the youth's home—was far more influential in shaping behavior than the often-cited effects of material deprivation.

The frequently strident and one-sided character of these claims—the fact that scholars like Burt and the Gluecks found it necessary to view material disadvantage and the quality of family life as somehow mutually *exclusive* explanations of delinquency—coupled with some egregious methodological flaws helped discredit this line of thinking during the heyday of liberal criminology in the sixties. Research of the Burt or Glueck variety seemed all too transparently to provide the comfortable with a way of explaining crime and delinquency that blamed individual parents —especially poor, immigrant, or minority parents—for problems whose ultimate origins lay far beyond their control. In response, many, though by no means all, liberal criminologists took the position that there was something suspect about the very idea of investigating the role of the family in crime. With some exceptions, the study of these relationships languished during the sixties.

Since the seventies, however, there has been a resurgence of interest in the influence of family and child-rearing patterns on crime and delinquency. On the whole, this has been a healthy development, for these issues *are* important and their neglect by liberal criminologists is difficult to justify. Yet much of the recent writing on crime and the family has progressed little from the days of Cyril Burt and the Gluecks, as James Q. Wilson's summary statement makes clear:

> When I published the first edition of *Thinking About Crime* in 1975, I argued that a free society lacked the capacity to alter the root causes of crime, since they were almost surely to be found in the character-forming processes that go on in the family. The principal rejoinder to that argument was that these root causes could be found instead in the objective economic conditions confronting the offender. Labor-market or community conditions may indeed have some effect on the crime rate, but since I first wrote, the evidence has mounted that this effect is modest and hard to measure and that devising programs—even such extraordinary programs as supported work—that will have much impact on repeat offenders or school dropouts is exceptionally difficult.
>
> By contrast, a steadily growing body of evidence suggests that the family affects criminality and that its effect, at least for serious offenders, is lasting. Beginning with the research of Sheldon and Eleanor Glueck . . . we now have available an impressive number of studies that, taken together, support the following view: Some combination of constitutional traits and early family experiences accounts for more of the variation among young persons in their serious criminality than any other factors, and serious misconduct that appears early in life tends to persist into adulthood. What happens on the street corner, in the school, or in the job market can still make a difference, but it will not be as influential as what has gone before.

These themes represent an increasingly popular view among conservative writers. But is this really what the "steadily growing body of evidence" suggests? I think not. Indeed, the first part of Wilson's passage contains a clue that the argument stretches the available evidence considerably, for we've already seen in earlier chapters that the effects of "labor-market or community conditions" are far stronger than Wilson acknowledges, and the results of social programs to confront them far more encouraging.

Beyond this, Wilson's argument illustrates two fallacies that pervade the new writing with stunning regularity. The first is what we might call the *fallacy of autonomy*—the belief that what goes on inside the family can usefully be separated from the forces that affect it from the outside: the larger social context in which families are embedded for better or for worse. Consequently, factors like "early family experiences" on the one hand and "labor-market or community conditions" on the other are seen, curiously, as competing explanations for the course of human development, rather than closely related parts of a larger set of interlocking circumstances. The second might be called the *fallacy of intractability*—the belief that because childhood problems often appear early in life they are therefore fundamentally irreversible, portents of criminality worsening into adulthood. Both fallacies lead to the argument that the family problems implicated in crime are beyond the reach of conscious social action. Armed with these fashionably pessimistic themes, the new writing on crime and the family often becomes little more than further ammunition in support of a less-than-benign neglect of the social hardships endured by many American families, or—at its worst and most troubling—an argument for the early screening of children in order to isolate and incapacitate those who presumably won't change and can't be helped.

The revived concern with family problems and early childhood development has taken this unfortunate form partly because of the limited results of our decade-long reliance on massive imprisonment. As it has become less plausible to defend the idea that simply raising the "costs" of crime will reliably or enduringly bring down the crime rate, there has been a movement toward explanations of crime that can account for the limitations of the prison while maintaining the deeper argument that crime is caused by insufficient controls imposed upon a fundamentally destructive "human nature." The argument, in essence, is that the prison comes too late to be of much use in managing people who have already been ruined, either by faulty upbringing or by constitutional or genetic inadequacy.

To be sure, it is painfully true that by the time some young offenders have arrived at the juvenile or adult justice system, they have suffered an enormous amount of damage that cannot easily be undone; to that extent, the renewed emphasis on the importance of early childhood experience is salutary. Clearly, we are better off if we can prevent that damage than if we wait for someone to get hurt before we intervene. The issues are two: what it is about family life and its social setting that causes the damage, and whether (and how) those conditions can be improved through public action. On both counts, a hard look at the evidence suggests that the conservative analysis of these issues is misleading. At every turn, the family problems most clearly connected with delinquency and crime are closely related to larger social conditions over which we can have some control—if we will. And the evidence that destructive family patterns can be changed, and that the damage they create can be reversed, is much stronger than these arguments assume.

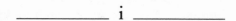

i

One strand of conservative thought blames rising crime —along with much else that is wrong with contemporary society—on the "decline of the family." The erosion of the "strength" of the family, Senator Jeremiah Denton declared at a congressional hearing in 1982, is responsible for "not only the juvenile crime rate, but the adult crime rate," as well as the spread of drug addiction and, for that matter, "the fact that we have so much loss of drive in terms of the work ethic" and that "only one-eighth of our youth have got enough sense of responsibility to register for the draft." Something resembling the senator's view has become close to an article of faith among conservatives, who have linked the growth of crime and delinquency to a series of unfortunate departures from what are believed to be "traditional" family structures and values—especially the growth of single-parent families, the rising participation of women in the labor force, and above all, the spread of "permissive" techniques of child-rearing.

These themes are concisely expressed in a recent article by the criminologist Travis Hirschi. To Hirschi, the central problem is that "modern" trends in family life have undermined the capacity of parents to "monitor, recognize, and punish the misbehavior of their children." The extended family, once so successful in "controlling everybody's behavior," has declined in importance, while the modern nuclear family is increasingly besieged by attitudes of "tolerance" for a diversity of lifestyles and values. Criminologists, Hirschi believes, have failed to give sufficient attention to these developments because they share with "modern" social thought generally a fundamental misconception about human nature—the assumption that "the individual would be noncriminal were it not for the operation of unjust and misguided institutions." But in Hirschi's darker view, criminal behavior is "not something the parents have to work to produce; it is something they have to work to avoid"; it is "part of the child's native equipment, and will remain unless something is done about it."

The main difficulty with this view of "human nature" is not that it is necessarily wrong—for on this rarefied level it's impossible to know how to judge it—but that it is simply far too abstract to be of any help in explaining criminal behavior in the real world. Whatever one may think, on a purely philosophical level, about Hirschi's attitude toward human nature, it cannot tell us why some times, some places, and some groups are more criminal than others. In order to accomplish this, Hirschi must go on to blame a variety of changes in contemporary values and attitudes for weakening parents' capacity to quash their children's unruly impulses. Some of the villains in the ensuing drama are quite predictable—working mothers, single-parent families, schools that "preach toleration for natural tendencies"—but others are rather unexpected; in Hirschi's curious demonology, for example, youth *employment* becomes an important, if heretofore unappreciated, cause of crime.

Why this should be so in Hirschi's scheme is instructive. It is not, Hirschi acknowledges, that getting a job necessarily diminishes the quality of supervision a youth receives (since an employer can monitor his behavior as well as parents can) or decreases his parents' affection for him—both of which might be expected to increase his risks of delinquency. The problem is rather that employment gives a youth enough resources to enable him to be less dependent on his parents; as a result, "his parents no longer have the material means to punish him, and the entire system of family control is vulnerable to collapse." What this says about Hirschi's conception of normal family life is revealing; it is a vision in which children respect and obey their parents only because the parents control the purse strings, and it's probably true that the quality of life in such families is fairly grim. But more importantly, the argument as it stands doesn't bear much reflection: it isn't easy to take seriously an argument that predicts worse crime rates among solidly employed blue-collar youths, say, than among unemployed or subemployed ghetto dropouts.

The emphasis on control to the exclusion of other factors clouds the conservatives' understanding of other aspects of family structure that are more plausibly linked to delinquency. Consider Hirschi's treatment of the relationship between the experience of being raised in a very large family and the likelihood of becoming delinquent. The association has turned up repeatedly in criminological research for decades, but its interpretation has varied depending on the ideological preoccupations of the observer. For Hirschi, large families are predictable breeding grounds for delinquency because parents in large families are likely to be less able to *punish* their children's misbehavior, since their authority is overextended. But more serious research suggests another line of explanation: large families often mean low incomes, overcrowded living conditions, and other deprivations; and when these are taken into account, not much, if anything, remains of the association between family size and delinquency. Michael Wadsworth's long-term study of British children found that coming from a large family significantly increased the likelihood of delinquency —but *only* for boys whose fathers were manual workers. In their London study, Donald West and his coworkers also found a sizable relationship between delinquency and large families, but if the family had "adequate living accommodation," the relationship disappeared. The connection between families that are too large, *relative to their resources*, and the risks of delinquency is a real one—and one that has important implications for social policy, for it suggests that we may achieve some gains against crime and delinquency through policies that encourage either smaller families or more resources for low-income families, or both. Neither approach, however, has drawn a great deal of enthusiasm from conservatives.

The same neglect of broader social factors in favor of an almost obsessive concern with control is evident in the conservatives' treatment of two modern changes in family life that, they believe, are partly to blame for rising crime: the growing proportion of women in the labor force and the increase in single-parent families. In each case, the thrust of the conservative argument is that these changes lead to increased crime because they erode the family's traditional capacity to discipline and punish children. Another possibility—that something about the larger conditions surrounding the families of some single mothers or of some working women may negatively affect family life and thus lead to delinquency—receives little attention.

Take Hirschi's argument about working mothers: "The tremendous increase in the number of women in the labor force," he insists, has "several implications for the crime rate." One of them is that women's working contributes to the instability of marriage—which, in turn, leads to the proliferation of female-headed families in which mothers cannot devote enough time to "monitoring and punishment." But Hirschi also argues that women's work, whether it leads to a broken home or not, has a "direct effect" on child-rearing, and thus on delinquency. What that effect may be, however, he seems at a loss to explain. Citing an early finding by the Gluecks that working women were more apt to have delinquent children, Hirschi acknowledges that the Gluecks also found that *all* of this effect was accounted for by differences in the level of supervision the mother was able to provide or to arrange. That finding might well be taken (and has been) to mean that such amenities as accessible child care and flexible working arrangements should cushion any adverse effects of women's employment on patterns of child-rearing and hence on the risks of delinquency.

But Hirschi is not so easily deflected. Citing as his most recent evidence some work of his own published in 1969, Hirschi insists that "more recent research" finds a "small effect" of mothers' employment on children's delinquency even when supervision and other characteristics of the mother and the family are taken into account—an effect that, however, the research is curiously "unable to explain." The effects of mothers' employment, Hirschi finally suggests, "influence children in ways not measurable except through their delinquency." This is sheer circular reasoning, of course; equally importantly, it is quite misleading, for genuinely recent research fails to support the belief that mothers' employment in itself has a pernicious impact on their children's behavior—and reaffirms that the relationship between women's work and delinquency is mediated by such larger social and economic factors as the family's income (and hence the quality of work) and the supports available to working mothers.

West and his coworkers, for example, in their study of London delinquents, found that delinquency was in fact significantly *less* common among boys whose mothers held full-time jobs. They attributed this result to the higher family income that working mothers generated and to the fact that mothers who worked full time tended to have fewer children, which similarly improved their families' effective standard of living. Taking due account of the families' social condition usually explains any relationship between women's employment and delinquency that careful investigations turn up; the failure to do so likewise explains why some *less* careful studies have emphasized the deleterious impact of women's work on children's behavior. The Gluecks' early finding in support of that assertion—47 percent of the mothers of delinquents in one of their studies worked outside the home, versus 33 percent of the mothers of nondelinquents—remarkably failed to control for the different social class of working versus nonworking mothers, as the British criminologist Michael Wadsworth notes. Wadsworth's own long-term study of British children initially found a slight association between mothers' working full time (when their sons were under six) and higher rates of delinquency in the boys later on. But when he included in the analysis such "income sensitive" characteristics of the families as social class and overcrowded housing, the relationship vanished.

Similar points emerge from more general studies of the relationship between maternal employment and child development. Some studies have found evidence that mothers' working can be associated with developmental problems in children; others—including a recent UCLA study of the developmental impact of various "alternative" family patterns—conclude that, if anything, the opposite is true: the children of working mothers turn out *better* on standard measures of cognitive development, for example, than others. What seems to make most sense of these conflicting findings is the *quality* of the work involved. Not surprisingly, child-development research turns up greater developmental problems in children of mothers who are highly stressed at work or dissatisfied with their jobs; no such problems appear among children of mothers who are satisfied with their work. The same theme appears in research on the developmental effects of child care outside the home; it is the quality of care, not the mere presence or absence of the child's mother, that seems to matter most. Overall, as a recent exhaustive review by the National Academy of Sciences puts it, the experiences of children with working mothers are "not significantly different from those of children whose mothers are not in the labor force. Moreover, even when the experiences are different, their development and educational outcome do not seem to be."

Once we abandon the ideological commitment to women's traditional family role, these findings seem hardly surprising. As usual, the experience of other countries is instructive. There are nations—West Germany is one—where women's labor-force participation is lower than ours and violent crime rates are, too; there are others, like Sweden, where women's labor-force participation is much higher than in the United States and where rates of serious criminal violence are *also* lower. On the other hand, there are striking differences between the United States and otherwise comparable industrial societies when we compare their provisions for child care, flexible work schedules, and other tangible supports to ease the stresses facing working parents. Where the Swedes, the French, and many other Europeans have at least begun to move toward making day care accessible for even very young children as a matter of right, in the United States day care remains harshly stratified by income and is especially inaccessible for infants and very young children. At the same time, as Edward Zigler and Susan Muenchow observe, the United States "does little to make the use of out-of-home care for infants less necessary." For example, it "stands alone among advanced industrialized nations in having no statutory maternity leave policy." In this regard, as Sheila Kamerman puts it, the United States is a uniquely "unresponsive society" when it comes to the needs of families with working parents. It is in *this* difference, rather than in the increasing role of women as breadwinners, that we may begin to understand some of the connections between delinquency and the conditions of family life in the United States.

Awareness of the crucial role of the social context also helps us evaluate the much-debated question of the relationship between "broken" families—especially those headed by women —and crime. In the past several years, the visceral belief that female-headed families breed crime has been a recurrent theme in discussions of the urban "underclass," where it serves as part of a larger attack on the supposedly demoralizing effects of the welfare system and of "excessive government" generally. The acme of this line of argument may be found in the conservative critic George Gilder, who managed to argue in his *Wealth and Poverty* not only that female-headed families demoralized by welfare benefits were responsible for most of the problems of the contemporary urban ghetto (including crime and disorder), but also that a similar disruption of the family (caused—though Gilder never makes clear how—by too many government jobs) created the high levels of crime and rioting among the nineteenth-century Irish in American cities. In less bizarre forms, the contention that the increase in families maintained by women is responsible for the crime rate has become common among pundits of the Right. But the connection between crime and the broken family is actually quite tenuous—a fact acknowledged even by some conservative criminologists (Hirschi, who believes that the spread of single-parent families is yet another reason for the contemporary family's weakened ability to "monitor and punish," is not one of them).

Concern over the role of family structure in crime and delinquency is not new. Early students of delinquency in America emphasized the importance of the broken home as a cause of crime among new immigrants in the cities and, more generally, of the delinquency of working-class youths. A number of not very careful studies early in this century presented alarming figures on the proportion of delinquents' homes broken by separation, divorce, or death of a parent. Characteristically, though, few of those studies bothered to count the proportion of broken homes among the families of *nondelinquents*, an omission that helped confirm the suspicion among some sociological critics that the focus on broken homes as a cause of delinquency reflected an ideological commitment to the conventional family structure thought to have been typical of a less urban, less heterogeneous America, rather than any serious concern for uncovering the causes of crime. The noted American criminologists Clifford Shaw and Henry McKay unleashed a withering attack on the methodological inadequacies of the literature on broken homes and delinquency in 1932, demonstrating that in several ethnic groups broken homes were common among both delinquents and nondelinquents, and that the incidence of broken homes within a group did not correlate with its rate of delinquency. Moreover, in at least one of the Chicago neighborhoods that Shaw and McKay studied, the proportion of broken homes turned out to be higher among *nondelinquent* boys than among the delinquents. For Shaw and McKay, this didn't necessarily mean that the "more subtle" aspects of family relationships might not play a role in generating delinquency. It did mean that the "broken home" itself was relatively unimportant in explaining delinquency. More recent studies confirm that this distinction remains useful.

On the surface, the connection between the "broken" home and serious crime still looks impressive. In a sample of state prisoners interviewed by researchers at the Rand Corporation, 56 percent came from broken homes and lived with a single parent during adolescence. Only 29 percent of male and 19 percent of female wards of the California Youth Authority in 1980 came from "unbroken" homes. In the sample of institutionalized juvenile serious offenders assembled by Charles A. Murray and Louis Cox in their study of the UDIS program in Chicago, less than a quarter had been living with both natural parents. But the superficially compelling link between disrupted family structure and delinquency is much less sturdy than it looks at first glance.

The first complication involves the perennial issue of whether the population of "official" criminals or delinquents is characteristic of the delinquent population as a whole. This is especially troublesome in studies that use samples of incarcerated offenders to assess the influence of family structure on crime. As far back as 1931, Shaw and McKay, in their wide-ranging attack on the belief that broken homes were an important precursor of delinquency, argued that coming from a broken home meant "a greater likelihood" that a boy would be brought to court in the first place for any given offense, rather than let off with a warning. Much research since then, both in the United States and elsewhere, confirms their point: police, probation workers, and others along the way tend to channel youths whose families are thought to be less wholesome or less capable of controlling them into formal processing by the courts. The American criminologist Kenneth Polk found that although youths from broken families were somewhat overrepresented at every stage of the juvenile-justice process, they became more and more so as they moved along the path toward imprisonment. The sociologist F. Ivan Nye, whose *Family Relationships and Delinquent Behavior* was the most comprehensive analysis of its sort in the 1950s, came to a similar conclusion by using self-reports of delinquency gathered from interviews with high-school youths and comparing them with official delinquents. About a quarter of the high-school youths who reported the most delinquency came from broken homes, versus nearly half of those in youth training schools. In the 1970s, John Johnstone found that the family structure of a sample of youthful offenders in Illinois was a much better predictor of how far they went in the criminal-justice system than was the specific behavior that brought them to the attention of authorities to begin with. In Britain, Michael Wadsworth's study of a large sample of boys born in 1946 affirms that, other things being equal, "boys from homes broken by divorce or separation were much more likely" than others to "suffer custodial treatment."

Still, even after the selection biases of the police, courts, and social agencies are taken into account, most studies continue to find some significant overrepresentation of broken homes in the backgrounds of youthful offenders. But the important question is, What is it about broken homes that tends to produce a disproportionate amount of delinquency? The evidence suggests that the problem is not so much that the formal family relationships are disrupted, nor that the home is run by a single parent, nor that the parent happens usually to be a woman, but rather that the broken family has a history of conflict and discord (and sometimes violence) that precedes the break itself, and that the break precipitates a decline in the resources necessary to insure a supportive environment for child development.

The belief that the "brokenness" of the home itself is of crucial importance in creating delinquency derives mainly from a tradition of studies of the supposed pernicious effects of "father absence" or of "maternal deprivation" on the growing child, especially at very early ages. But it has not held up well under the lens of careful research. It is a truism, for example, that families broken by death rather than by separation or divorce do not typically have higher rates of delinquency than intact families— suggesting that it is not the absence of a parent in itself that generates delinquency, but something else about the family dynamic that often leads to breakup. This finding has been confirmed most recently in Donald West's research. Among working-class delinquents in London, about 20 percent—versus 9 percent of nondelinquent youths—came from homes broken by circumstances other than the death of a parent, while a virtually equal proportion of the families of delinquents and of nondelinquents (about 7 percent) had been broken by death.

West's conclusion that "family *discord* is the main reason for the link between broken homes and delinquency" is supported by a long and imposing record of other research. In the United States, Nye's work in the late fifties discovered that parental conflict in *intact* families was more likely to generate delinquency than reasonably harmonious life in "broken" ones, and the finding of high levels of delinquency in "unbroken but unhappy" homes has been repeated many times since. Moreover, that finding apparently applies not only to delinquency and crime but to a wide range of other behavioral problems, all across the social spectrum. Exposure to parental conflict was one important background characteristic of youths who became alcoholics, as well as those who wound up with criminal records, in Joan McCord's follow-up study of children raised in Massachusetts in the late 1930s and early 1940s. In a recent and sophisticated study of early influences on adult behavior, the psychiatrist Stella Chess and her coworkers, following a sample of New York children from infancy to adulthood, found a strong association between parental conflict in childhood and a variety of psychological and social handicaps later on—such as poor performance in school and at work, and alcohol and drug abuse. Once the researchers had controlled for parental conflicts over child-rearing and other matters, separation or divorce had no independent effect on the children's later difficulties.

This isn't to say that family disruption is a benign or neutral event in the lives of children; it usually isn't, and many studies show that it can be damaging, at least in the short run—and for some children, in the long run as well. But as a precursor of delinquency and other developmental problems, it is overshadowed by the effects of family conflict.

It is equally outweighed by the material consequences of family disruption, particularly for women—and especially in America, where supports for single-parent families are much less developed than in most other advanced industrial countries. Attitudes and practices regarding child custody and support are changing, but slowly; it remains true that after separation or divorce, as the sociologist Diana Pearce puts it, "the man becomes single, while the woman becomes a single parent." As Donald West has written, broken homes "stand for a cluster of interacting circumstances": for the children, "added to the emotional stress occasioned by the loss of a parent is the stress caused by consequential loss of income and the deterioration in standards of child care that may come about through a parent being unexpectedly left to cope alone."

Thus, while it is true that some studies do find an association between family disruption and various developmental problems in children (including aggressiveness and delinquency), it is also true that, as the psychologist E. Mavis Hetherington points out, these results "do not seem to be attributable mainly to father absence but to stresses and a lack of support systems that result in changed family functioning for the single mother and her children." Hetherington's conclusion is affirmed by studies showing the extraordinary resilience of single-mother families with above-average social and economic supports; a recent study by Marsha Weinraub and Barbara M. Wolf of a group of single mothers who were generally better educated, older, and better employed found no clear differences in family functioning between their families and a group of two-parent families.

As in the case of women's employment, in short, whether single parenthood leads to problems within the family depends on forces that originate well beyond the family itself. And it cannot reasonably be argued that those forces are altogether beyond our control. It is not written in stone that a woman who winds up as the sole support of her family must therefore be poor, or that the loss of one parent must necessarily condemn a child to intermittent, inadequate, or grudging care. If we wish seriously to address the ways in which the stresses upon single-parent families may generate behavioral problems, we will need to start by acknowledging that such stresses are not part of the natural order of things. We will accomplish more by way of preventing delinquency if we worry less about the decline of traditional family forms and more about the quality of work and public supports available to parents, in whatever sort of family they may be found.

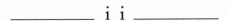

i i

It is over specific techniques of child-rearing, however, that conservative writers have recently become most exercised. For it is here that they see the "moral decay" occasioned by the spread of permissiveness and tolerance wreaking the most havoc. But it is here, too, that the conservative analysis becomes most perilously detached from the useful discipline of experience and evidence.

To be sure, few of us would seriously disagree that "upbringing"—the Gluecks' "under-the-roof culture"—has a great deal to do with whether a child will turn out to be delinquent or not, and I think this commonsense observation has sometimes been unduly neglected by liberal criminology. Criminologists who probably take enormous care in bringing up their own children have nevertheless sometimes disparaged the idea that less careful or less concerned parents might do things to hurt *their* children's chances of growing up as compassionate and cooperative human beings. But recognizing this general connection is one thing; attributing American rates of crime and delinquency to the rising tide of destructive "toleration" within the family, as many conservatives now do, is another.

Not many students of human development would quarrel with the observation that parents who persistently fail to discipline their children when it's needed are likely to run into trouble; and capricious or erratic discipline has often been found to be a fairly predictable precursor of delinquency.* If these mundane findings were all that was at issue, there would be little disagreement. But the recent critics of American "permissiveness" are not pleading for balanced and consistent guidance of children, but for a greater emphasis on punishment, physical or otherwise.

Most call for a return to a regime of heightened scrutiny and punitive discipline in the pursuit of a kind of regimented, unques-

---

* Here again, it is important to view parental behavior in its larger social setting. Much research shows that poor supervision is associated with higher rates of delinquency. But why do some parents seem to have more trouble supervising their children than others? One obvious explanation—that parents' capacity to supervise is affected by their social situation—is affirmed in a study by Harriett Wilson in an English city. She compared a group of families in the inner city with another from the suburbs. Both were mainly low-income, working-class families, but those living in the inner city had a much greater likelihood of what Wilson called "severe social handicap"—including poor jobs and large families. Wilson found that children from "lax" families, in which there were few rules about coming home at night and where parents often didn't know where to find their children, were more likely to be delinquent (and to be recidivists once delinquent). At the same time, families burdened with "severe social handicap" were far more likely to produce delinquent children. What complicates all this, however, is that parental laxness is also closely associated with social handicap. The "inner-city severes" showed by far the greatest degree of "lax" supervision. Wilson concludes, however, that her findings should not be used to blame poor parents for their children's problems: "Lax parenting methods are often the results of chronic stress, situations arising from frequent or prolonged spells of unemployment, physical or mental disabilities among members of the family, and an often permanent condition of poverty. If these factors are ignored and parental laxness is seen instead as an 'attitude' which can be shifted by education or by punitive measures, then our findings are being misinterpreted."

tioning obedience they imagine was widely enforced by "middle-class" families in the past. "Parents successful in crime prevention," writes Travis Hirschi, "seem inclined to err in the direction of over-control, to see seeds of trouble in laziness, unreliability, disrespect for adults, and lack of concern for property," while "unsuccessful parents" are "considerably more tolerant." Some conservatives go so far as to argue that corporal punishment should be "restored" in American schools and homes —as if it had ever disappeared. (Edward Wynne, for one, thinks that encouraging regular corporal punishment for young people would constitute a "real experiment" in the control of youth crime. That this "experiment" has been going on continuously for decades in some of the most violent regions of the United States seems not to faze Mr. Wynne unduly.)

All of this, however, is not only wrong but dangerous. For the evidence consistently points to a very different conclusion. Punitive, harsh discipline does not prevent crime: it *breeds* crime. There is, first of all, only a thin and not easily discernible line between rigid, punitive styles of parenting and serious child abuse —itself a violent crime of shocking dimensions in the United States. In turn, abuse and neglect in childhood all too often lead to later violence in those who experience them. They are indeed among the most powerful sources of serious criminal violence in America today.

Comparative evidence, once again, is illuminating. The most obvious difficulty with linking "tolerant" child-rearing to criminal violence is that it not only fails to come to terms with cross-national differences in violence, but indeed makes precisely the wrong prediction about where the worst levels of criminal violence should be expected. American attitudes and practices regarding the rearing and discipline of children tend to be *more* punitive, not less, than those of many other advanced societies with much less violent crime. Sweden, for example, has progressively moved to outlaw corporal punishment in schools and homes since the 1920s, and it could reasonably be argued that this policy and the public attitudes underlying it are related to Sweden's low levels of major violent crime compared to the United States—where the legal right of school officials to beat children was still upheld by the Supreme Court in the late seventies and is permitted to this day. On the other side, it is unlikely to be simply accidental that societies in which severe physical punishment is considered a normal feature of child-rearing—like some Caribbean countries—are also among those with violent crime rates even higher than our own.

A look at the social distribution of attitudes toward punishment and discipline of children *within* the United States leads to a similar conclusion. It is virtually a truism that parents' repertoires of child-rearing techniques tend to narrow as you go down the income scale. The emphasis on instant obedience and on punishment rather than encouragement and reward, the fundamental view of children as little bundles of bad impulses who are in constant peril of being spoiled and therefore in constant need of correction, is not—as Hirschi or Wilson would have it—really a "middle-class value," for middle-class parents typically encourage a certain amount of independence and initiative in their children. It is much more characteristic of some *lower-class* families —or of parents trapped in jobs that require rote conformity and discourage initiative. And it is from poor families, not the families of the permissive academic and professional upper-middle class, that most violent criminals come.

These commonsense observations are supported by a formidable body of research in child development suggesting that punitive and authoritarian child-rearing is poor ground for the development of competent, cooperative children. "The kind of parenting that appears to promote optimal child functioning" at very early ages, according to one recent and comprehensive review of the evidence, is "attentive, warm, stimulating, responsive, and nonrestrictive caregiving." As children grow older, "parental use of induction or reasoning, consistent discipline, and expression of warmth have been found to relate positively to self-esteem, internalized controls, prosocial orientation, and intellectual achievement." Parents who are capable of rearing cooperative and effective children, far from "erring on the side of over-control," are able to understand and empathize with the perspectives and limitations of their children and to adopt a "nurturant orientation."

The link between punitive, harsh, or rejecting discipline and a variety of later behavioral problems has been apparent for decades. The classic studies of the social psychologists Albert Bandura and Richard Walters in the 1950s found that parents of aggressively destructive boys relied much more often than other parents on ridicule, physical punishment, and deprivation of privileges to control their sons, and less on praise and rewards for good behavior; and the finding has held up well since. The sociologist Joan McCord, following the development of a group of Massachusetts men who were first studied when they were boys during the early 1940s, found that punitive parental discipline was unusually common among those who had become either adult criminals or alcoholics. In Donald West's London studies, the parental practices most consistently associated with later delinquency included "attitudes of indifference, positive rejection or neglect, over-strict or erratically varying discipline and harsh methods of enforcement."

There are several ways in which punitive parental discipline may generate these results—some relatively subtle, others painfully glaring. On the less obvious side, rigid and punitive parenting hinders children's ability to do well in school. Parents who exact obedience through fear do not prepare their children well for educational and occupational settings that reward a certain amount of independence, initiative, and self-direction. How this works to undermine the chances of poor children in school has been detailed in a fascinating study of ghetto child-rearing patterns and school achievement by Daniel Scheinfeld of Chicago's Institute for Juvenile Research.

Scheinfeld found that mothers' attitudes about how their children should relate to the outside world were one of the most important factors distinguishing youths from urban ghettos who managed to achieve highly in school from similar youths who did not. Mothers of *high* achievers from these otherwise unpromising backgrounds tended to emphasize the desirability of the child's developing an inner sense of self-direction and motivation; to trust in the child's judgment, rather than assuming that children are incapable of self-guidance and in need of unremitting control; and in general to emphasize "cooperation, consideration, and sharing responsibilities" in raising their children. Mothers of *low* achievers, on the other hand, were mainly concerned with "controlling [the child's] behavior." They saw the child's role as simply one of obeying the authority of adults; were preoccupied with defending their children against outside threats; and in general defined their goals for their children negatively or "aversively"— that is, exclusively in terms of meeting life's burdens and staying out of trouble, rather than striving toward personal growth. A mother with this orientation, according to Scheinfeld, may actually "take comfort in her son's constraint, withdrawal, nonengagement with others or, in some cases, his aggressive alienation of others." Sons, in turn, may internalize their mothers' negation of their sense of efficacy and "competence-gaining activity"; they soon develop a crippling hesitancy to take on difficult learning tasks, are "easily discouraged," and perform badly in school. Scheinfeld emphasizes that these parental attitudes do not come from nowhere; they are fostered by the larger social context in which these families must function. The real external threats and daily dangers confronting lower-class blacks encourage the aversive, negative, and controlling strategy adopted by many ghetto mothers, a strategy that in turn undermines their children's ability to surmount those conditions. And thus a cycle of failure and defeat is perpetuated—one that, all too frequently, culminates in delinquency and crime.

But it is in their close connection with child abuse that punitive child-rearing practices are most directly linked to crime and delinquency—and particularly to the kind of severe criminal violence we rightly fear the most. Not too surprisingly, parents who place an unduly high value on punishment and instant obedience tend also to be abusive and neglectful of their children. They often hold exaggerated expectations of children's ability to stay out of trouble (to avoid breaking things, for example); they are likely to have "significant misconceptions about children and fear of spoiling them," along with "a strong belief in the value of punishment" and a "serious lack of ability to be emphatically aware of a child's condition and needs." Parents at *high risk* for abuse are characterized, in a recent review by the developmental psychologist James Garbarino and his colleagues, as "less supportive and more punishing"; they have "positive values and attitudes concerning coercion," while *low-risk* families are characterized by "a disavowal of coercion and a more supportive, less punitive style of parenting." Similarly, Carolyn Newberger and

Susan Cook describe abusing parents as more likely to approach child-rearing according to their *own* needs and comfort, not those of their children, and to rely for guidance on traditional authority or conventional wisdom about how children as a class *ought* to behave, rather than how children as individual human beings *do* behave. These connections are important in understanding criminal violence not only because child abuse is itself a common and serious form of violent crime, but also because abused children have a disturbingly high chance of becoming violent themselves.

That violent homes breed violent children has been driven home over and over again by recent studies. To be sure, not every abused child becomes delinquent or aggressive; and tracing clear and unequivocal links between abuse and later violence is a complicated and difficult problem for researchers. But the evidence is much too strong to ignore.

Some of the most striking—and troubling—evidence comes from clinical studies of institutionalized violent delinquents or of children referred to child-abuse treatment programs. In a study of delinquent boys in a youth institution in Connecticut, for example, Dorothy Lewis and her coworkers compared the "extremely violent" ones with those who were less violent or aggressive. Of the more violent delinquents, 75 percent had a "history of abuse by parents or parent substitutes," versus 33 percent of the less violent. Among the most violent, the level of abuse they had suffered "was often extraordinary":

> One parent broke her son's legs with a broom; another broke his fingers and his sister's arm; another chained and burned his son; and yet another threw his son downstairs, injuring his head, following which the boy developed epilepsy.

In addition, nearly four-fifths of the more seriously violent youth, versus only a fifth of the less violent, had witnessed extreme violence; as the researchers note dryly, this "went beyond mere fist-fights":

> Several children witnessed their fathers, stepfathers, or mothers' boyfriends slash their mothers with knives. They saw their siblings tortured with cigarette butts, chained to beds, and thrown into walls. They saw their relatives—male and

female—arm themselves with guns, knives, and other sharp instruments and, at times, use these weapons against each other.

Lewis and her colleagues argue that the mechanisms by which the experience of this level of violence breeds further violence are multiple and complex. Severe physical abuse may cause damage to the central nervous system that contributes to "impulsivity, attention disorders, and learning disabilities," which can lead to delinquency through school failure and alienation; it may provide a role model that children all too quickly learn to follow; and it may engender deep, long-lasting rage that they learn to displace onto others.

Similarly, the psychiatrist Arthur H. Green of New York's Downstate Medical Center concludes that for severely abused children "aggressive and assaultive behavior become the primary vehicles" for establishing ties with others. "One can envision these children," Green says, as "miniature editions of the angry parents." By attacking a "real or imagined adversary" and thus "identifying with the aggressor," the abused child can "express in displaced form some of his original rage toward his abusive parents." Green illustrates this mechanism with the case history of an eleven-year-old who

> was referred for psychiatric treatment after he persuaded his three-year-old half-brother to drink some lye. One year prior to this incident, Juan had returned to live with his mother and her boyfriend after having spent the past seven years with his physically abusive father and stepmother in Puerto Rico. Juan had been subjected to chronic physical abuse during this period which consisted of beatings on the head and burns on his body inflicted with a hot iron. Since living with his mother, Juan displayed hyperactive, aggressive behavior in school, frequently hitting and kicking his classmates. . . . Juan disclosed to his therapist that he enjoyed catching mice and smashing their heads with a hammer. He would then flush them down the toilet. When asked to explain the reasons for this behavior, Juan pointed to the scars and ridges on his scalp, exclaiming "This is what my father did to me. . . ."

Other studies illustrate with special force how early these violent responses may appear in the lives of severely abused children. Following their study of incarcerated delinquents, Dorothy Lewis and her coworkers investigated "homicidally aggressive" young children in New York. From among a group of children —all under twelve and disproportionately (86 percent) black or Hispanic—who had been admitted to an in-patient child psychiatry ward in a New York hospital, Lewis and her colleagues sorted out those who had either committed (or threatened to commit) at least one act that, if done by an adult, would have resulted in the death or serious injury of the victim. The violent acts that these children committed—remember, they were under twelve— were astounding:

> Strangled sister until she turned red; tried to choke cousin; says witch's voice told her to do this.
> Set fire to couch where mother was sleeping.
> Tried twice to kill mother, stood over her with hammer and turned on gas jets in house; wanted to kill boy with kitchen knife.
> Tried to immolate a classmate; tried to hit another boy over head with heavy equipment.
> Set fires in trash can, igniting entire apartment.

It's from children like these that we can expect some of the most serious, repetitive, violent criminality later on, with even more devastating results. What set them apart from the other seriously disturbed—but not violent—children in the ward?

Lewis and her coworkers discovered that the homicidally aggressive children couldn't be reliably distinguished from the others by specific psychiatric diagnosis or psychological symptoms. They had a number of severe emotional and neurological problems—hallucinations, seizures, learning disabilities—but so did the rest of the children in this ward. Most of the children in both groups came from low-income, single-parent families. What most distinguished the homicidally violent children was that the households in which they were raised were "filled with violence."

Among the families of the violent children, the fathers, when they were present, were unusually likely to have been violent to the children's *mothers* as well as to the children themselves (62 percent of the fathers of violent children, versus just 13 percent of the others, had a history of violence toward the mothers). Nearly two-fifths of the fathers of homicidally violent children had *themselves* engaged in homicidal behavior in the past. Among twenty-one fathers, two were currently in jail for manslaughter, one was wanted for murder, one had been deported for stabbing a man, one attempted to drown his son, one threw his infant daughter against a crib, and one beat his wife so severely that she was hospitalized for two weeks. Even some of the *mothers* were extremely violent; two had "stabbed their mates in the chest."

The single most important factor, then, distinguishing the families of violent children from the others was the father's severe violence against the mother. Again, Lewis and her colleagues argue that this may breed violence in the children in several ways: the children may "model" their own behavior on the pattern set by their fathers, or—since "witnessing and being the victim of irrational violence engenders a kind of rage and frustration"—the children may direct these powerful feelings both inward (they also had extraordinarily high suicidal tendencies) and outward.

The fact that not only suffering violence and abuse in the home but also merely *witnessing* it may lead to behavioral problems in children is a repeated finding in recent research. A University of North Carolina study of a sample of children referred to child-protective services found that the most serious psychological disturbance was found among those who had been abused physically both by their mothers and by their fathers or stepfathers; many such children had experienced "a family climate of total parental rejection." But even those who had been "bystanders" while their mothers suffered abuse had a number of serious emotional problems, and "their behavior mirrors the adult violence which they observe."

The clinical evidence is backed by long-term research. Joan McCord's forty-year follow-up of Massachusetts youths, for example, found that—after controlling for such factors as income level and the absence of a parent—rates of delinquency were much higher for abused and neglected children.

. . .

Yet in the face of the strong connections between harsh childhood punishment and abuse and later delinquency, conservative criminologists have sometimes become uncharacteristically inarticulate. Hirschi, for example, acknowledges that the "gross correlates" of both child abuse and delinquency are the same and that there is probably truth in the assertion that child abuse causes criminality. Since abuse and punishment "have elements in common," he recognizes that it might therefore appear "that punishment is conducive to delinquency," in which case "our argument would be in serious trouble, to say the least." Hirschi is certainly right about that; how does he respond? "One way to reconcile the abuse/delinquency results," he tells us,

> is to recognize that abuse does not occur in a vacuum. It is more likely the less the parent cares for the child and the fewer the resources the parent is able to devote to childrearing. Recall that delinquency is also more likely under these circumstances. But before delinquency is possible, there exists the potentially delinquent child. This child has not yet been introduced properly. He or she is more likely to be "demanding, stubborn, negativistic," "aggressive," and "troublesome." When the uncaring or overburdened parent faces such behavior, he is unlikely to see it as his own creation. But if our analysis is correct, it is—at least to some extent. If so, the abuse that follows should not be confused with "correction."

Even after several tries, I'm not sure I understand exactly what this means. Hirschi appears to be saying that parents first create delinquency by failing to punish children sufficiently and then respond to it with the wrong *kind* of punishment. But this simply begs the question of whether reliance on punishment is the appropriate strategy for rearing capable and cooperative children in the first place; and it ignores the demonstrable fact that parents who adopt that approach are often precisely the ones who are most likely to abuse their children.

To be fair, most conservative writers would surely not encourage physically abusive punishment of children as a first line of defense against delinquency. But some, as we've seen, do call for a "return" to corporal punishment, despite the fact that such

punishment has long been specifically implicated in aggressiveness and violence. (A recent Harvard investigation by Jessica
Daniel, Robert Hampton, and Eli Newberger illustrates how this
process becomes self-perpetuating; among inner-city black parents involved in serious child abuse, both mothers and fathers had
been severely punished as children and adolescents themselves.)
And they are both disturbingly imprecise in their language about
the necessity for greater punishment of children and very much
inclined to sidestep the connections between the punitive, obedi-
ence-centered values they do clearly espouse and the abusive
violence toward children that most of them probably genuinely
abhor. They ignore the fact that many of the "traditional" families that embody these punitive and rigid attitudes about child-
rearing have been—and are—fraught with brutality and fear.

They also fail to acknowledge that the same "traditional"
values frequently go hand in hand with norms about male authority and female subordination within the family that at the very
least fail to discourage, and may explicitly encourage, the use of
violence against women. Indeed, conservative criminologists
have, with few exceptions, been oddly silent on the entire issue
of domestic violence. Violence against women is, after all, one of
the most serious and deadly forms of criminal violence in America. Furthermore, as the research we've just examined makes
clear, it wreaks its havoc on the next generation as well, for the
children of mothers who are abused by husbands or lovers are
themselves at high risk for criminal violence. Given the emphasis
on the integrity of family life to be found in conservative writers,
we might logically expect them to be particularly concerned
about the kind of behavior that most dramatically threatens it.
That such concern isn't usually evident in conservative writing
on crime and the family leads us to suspect that these thinkers
may be more concerned with upholding "traditional" norms, at
whatever cost, than with reducing violence, inside or outside the
family. But the evidence suggests that one of the most significant
things we can do to reduce criminal violence over the long run
will be to move—as a number of more civilized advanced societies
have already begun to do—away from that "traditional" acceptance of punitive and violent behavior within the family toward
an ethos of tolerance, mutuality, and care.

There is a similar illogic in the conservatives' simultaneous insistence on the importance of "under-the-roof culture" and their curious lack of interest in confronting the social conditions that are routinely associated with child abuse. Here again, as with the issues of family disruption and overlarge families, we have another instance of the fallacy of autonomy—the belief that what happens inside the family can be understood in isolation from what goes on outside it.

Virtually every study in recent years shows that severe child abuse is predictable, with depressing regularity, from several interlocking disadvantages that afflict certain families far more than others. To be sure, there is child abuse in all strata of society, and —like other forms of criminal violence—it is subject to biases in reporting that may exaggerate its concentration among some groups. But the evidence is clear that those biases, though real enough, cannot explain away the sharp differences that turn up over and over again. The parents *most* at risk for serious child abuse have low incomes and are most often poorly educated; they are typically subject to a greater than ordinary barrage of social stresses, including frequent unemployment and excessive geographical mobility; where there are men in the home, they are disproportionately often out of work or employed in low-level jobs; the families are often very large, with at least some of the children unplanned and unwanted; the parents are likely to be very young, frequently under twenty; they have few parenting skills and are generally unprepared for the complexities and frustrations of child-rearing; and they are unusually isolated from sources of social support—extended family, friends, community organizations, or adequate public social services.

Not all parents who face this syndrome of difficulties, of course, end up abusing their children. Nor does the importance of these environmental conditions rule out the influence of individual psychological problems among parents. But the predictable recurrence of these conditions in the histories of abusive families warns us that we will not understand either child abuse or its results in isolation from their social setting. Most importantly, these factors help explain why severe child abuse is much more common in the United States than in most other developed societies, as recent studies make clear (an American child aged one to four is about eleven times more likely to die of injuries "purposely inflicted by another person" than a Dutch child). These differences cannot be explained simply as the result of individual difficulties among American parents; rather, they reflect a social environment—an "ecology," as many researchers now define it—characterized by unusual extremes of stress, deprivation, and neglect.

_____ i i i _____

All of this, as the developmental psychologist Urie Bronfenbrenner reminds us, suggests the great potential of public policies that can "create additional settings and societal roles conductive to family life." Yet oddly enough, those conservative writers who have made the most of the connections between family practices and crime have also been the most insistent that there is little that can be done about them through deliberate social action. For Travis Hirschi, the only acceptable role for public policy in this area is to encourage school classes in the "technology" of child-rearing. James Q. Wilson, while insisting on the decisive influence of "character-forming processes within the family," nevertheless argued in *Thinking About Crime* that nothing much could be done to enhance them: "What agency do we create, what budget do we allocate, that will supply the missing 'parental affection' and restore to the child consistent discipline by a stable and loving family?"*

In part, this reluctance to intervene in the social conditions affecting family life reflects the stock conservative distaste for most forms of government action, supported in this case by the fallacy of autonomy: if family problems are internal, in the sense of being largely unaffected by external conditions, then efforts to

---

*Professor Wilson has more recently expressed some support for certain programs that attempt to teach parents how to better "monitor and punish" their children through "behavior modification" techniques, but seems no more inclined than before to favor either more supportive or comprehensive family programs or the larger social interventions that could reduce the stresses and deprivations faced by so many American families. See, for example, *Crime and Human Nature*, p. 343.

enhance family life by changing those conditions are by definition likely to be fruitless. In much conservative writing on crime
and the family, moreover, this argument is often merged with
another, related one—that *both* crime and family problems reflect
deeper psychological or biological proclivities, which may be
innate and are in any case extraordinarily difficult to change. This
view—what I have called the fallacy of intractability—has a long
heritage; it came to dominate both European and American criminology around the turn of the century. It has reappeared with
a vengeance in some recent and influential work on the childhood
roots of aggressive or "antisocial" behavior.

The argument is based on the important truth that the developmental problems that foreshadow delinquency often appear
early in life: children who are troubled or aggressive, do badly in
school, or frequently are truants are more likely than others to
become serious delinquents or adult criminals. On this level, there
is little disagreement. But some contemporary writers on "antisocial" behavior have gone much further, virtually insisting that
certain children are predestined to lives of failure, delinquency,
and crime. "Third-grade bullies," according to a newspaper account of one recent study, "are likely to become tomorrow's
hard-core criminals." According to the psychiatrist Lee Robins,
the "syndrome of antisocial behavior" in childhood "presents a
remarkably stable and ominous picture for the future." Unlike
some other disorders of early childhood, Robins argues, it is not
transient, but often worsens as the child grows older. Moreover,
its effects "may extend into virtually every aspect of adult life;
marital, parental, occupational, legal, interpersonal and substance
abuse." Furthermore, when these antisocial children become parents themselves, they "are likely to neglect the supervision of
their children, fail to support them, and subject them to broken
homes when their own marriages fail, thus setting the scene for
a renewal of the same pattern in the next generation." In this
perspective, "antisocial personality" is a kind of malevolent entity
that sits inside certain children, rather like a disease with several
manifestations; the appearance of any of them is a portent of
worse to come.

At its extreme, this argument suggests that the syndrome is
constitutionally or genetically determined; in the American con-

text, this comes perilously close, as we shall see, to being an argument for the inherent inferiority of blacks. In less extreme versions, the argument still helps to legitimize a sort of malign neglect of the social and personal needs of the disadvantaged. What should we make of it?

It is important to separate the element of truth in this argument from the unfortunate ideological uses to which the relevant research is often put. There is good evidence that criminals and delinquents often have troubled childhoods (and some evidence suggests that aggression and delinquency may be more *stable* in this respect—more likely to continue into adulthood—than many other behavioral problems). No data, however, exist to support the assertion of an iron link between childhood difficulties and later criminality. In Lyle Shannon's study of youths in Racine, Wisconsin, early delinquency in fact turned out to be a relatively *poor* predictor of later criminality. In one group, for example, 43 percent of the young men who had trouble with the police after age eighteen had had no earlier contacts with them at all. The idea that early trouble represents a relatively intractable "syndrome" that persists stubbornly into later life is undercut even more decisively by the fact that the relationship doesn't work well in the opposite direction: that is, a very substantial proportion of children who are rated as "antisocial" or even "aggressive" at an early age do *not* go on to become delinquents or serious criminals —or, indeed, to have serious behavioral problems of any kind.

In an important study of the continuities between early childhood aggression and later criminality, Leonard Eron of the University of Illinois and his coworkers surveyed all the third-grade children in a semirural county of New York in 1960. The subjects were followed periodically until 1981, through interviews and official records. In general, boys who were rated by their schoolmates as being "highly aggressive" at age eight turned out, by a variety of measures, to be more aggressive at age thirty as well. They rated themselves, in interviews, as being more aggressive; were judged by their wives to be so; and had more criminal convictions and more serious crimes, as well as more traffic violations and more convictions for drunken driving. But this doesn't mean that early aggressive behavior necessarily evolved into later criminality. Only 23 percent of the boys who were rated as highly aggressive as eight-year-olds by their peers were ever convicted of a crime in New York state. That is significantly more than the proportion convicted of a crime whose aggression had been rated "moderate" (15 percent) or "low" (9 percent), but the fact that the vast majority of aggressive children did *not* become criminals does not speak well for the contention that aggression represents an intractable syndrome. (Nor do Eron and his coworkers argue that it is; they are more inclined to view aggression as a form of *learned* behavior that, presumably, can also be unlearned.) Similarly, Stella Chess and her colleagues, in their study of New York children, found some continuity in behavioral problems from early childhood to young adulthood, but also considerable change and unpredictability. Early behavior problems explained only a fraction of the differences among young adults, and in many of their subjects "striking and even dramatic psychological changes . . . occurred—changes that appear fundamental and not superficial, and changes which could not have been predicted from earlier life data." Even in Robins's own work, for that matter, no more than half of any group of children studied, however extreme their childhood behavior, exhibited the antisocial "syndrome" as adults.

Yet Robins and some other writers have managed to use the finding of some continuity between childhood and adult problems as ammunition in a larger argument denying that social or economic conditions have much impact on delinquency or antisocial behavior in general. But the evidence offered for that argument turns out to be inadequate at best, and sometimes verges on the bizarre. Robins's studies are worth examining in detail in this regard, both because they have been among the most widely influential efforts to minimize the importance of social and economic factors in delinquency and because they illustrate with special clarity the fallacies in this line of reasoning.

A fundamental concern in all of Robins's work on the so-called antisocial personality syndrome has been to engage "the controversy between those who regard antisocial behavior in adults as the product of low status and racism," on the one hand, and "those who regard it as symptomatic of underlying psychopathology induced genetically or by pathological family environments or by an interaction between the two," on the other.

Robins's own conclusion leans decidedly in the latter direction, for she argues that it is likely that "severely antisocial behavior, as indicated by failure to conform over a broad range of functioning—job failure, illegal activities, excessive drinking, heavy drug use, failure to maintain stable interpersonal relationships, and financial dependency"—has its origins "chiefly within the person and his family."

There are several striking aspects of this stance. One is the artificial separation of matters such as "low status and racism" from the presumably more "internal" issues of what goes on "within the person and his family." This is the fallacy of autonomy again, the insistence that family life and individual personality somehow manage to remain virginally unstained by the social settings in which individuals and families exist and make do, for better or for worse. We may, of course, reasonably disagree about the relative balance of these elements in shaping the course of individual lives or about exactly how they do so, but this stark separation of one realm from the other is suspect, for it suggests an underlying ideological agenda.

Other themes add to our suspicion. It's noteworthy that Robins's description of the syndrome that is said to lie deeply lodged within certain of her subjects includes several different kinds of behavior, of which some are more plausibly understood as reflections of individual personality deficiencies than others. Her list includes both things that are often (though not always) beyond any imaginable control by individuals, like unemployment and financial dependency, and things that are arguably much more within their control, like illegal activities or drug use. In Robins's perspective, they're all pretty much the same problem. This is crucial to her analysis (and to this line of reasoning generally), because it enables her to ignore the possibility that some of the phenomena she describes as behavioral manifestations of a defective personality syndrome might better be understood as *causes* of other problems in the syndrome. Having poor job prospects outside the unstable secondary labor market, for instance, might be conducive to drug abuse or heavy drinking, rather than simply being one more indication of an underlying—perhaps "genetically induced"—personality syndrome.

Robins is aware of this possibility, but dismisses it. "When we try to see how [the sociopath's] economic and social environment might cause his problems," she tells us, "we cannot separate its effect from the fact that his problems have largely created that environment." While no one would deny that there is an *interaction* between individuals' behavior and the environment in which they wind up, Robins's insistence that the relationship runs for all practical purposes in only one direction is extraordinary: "The sociopath lives in a depressed neighborhood because his early behavior has kept him from completing school and his current behavior patterns make it very hard for him to hold a job or to pay his rent even when he has money." He is divorced or separated "because he has been non-supporting, abusive to his spouse, and unfaithful." And so on. We are not given a shred of empirical evidence to support these assertions; apparently we are simply to take it on faith that people who are divorced or who live in bad neighborhoods have brought their suffering upon themselves. Robins's "sociopaths" live in a world strangely devoid of social or economic consequences, even of history—a world where circumstances are never beyond the individual's control, in which nothing untoward ever seems simply to *happen* to people.

Another example of this attitude in Robins's work borders on the ludicrous. She argues that the substantial continuity between adult social problems and childhood personality difficulties means that the "immediate situation" of individuals is irrelevant in understanding their behavior: "The absence (or extreme rarity) of adult onset has aetiological importance because it is often believed that the kinds of behavior typifying antisocial personality could be elicited by the immediate situation." What does this mean in less abstract terms? It isn't "hard to imagine," Robins acknowledges, that poverty and racial discrimination may be "sufficiently demoralizing" to explain adult problems like poor work histories, unstable relationships, and criminal activities. But she doubts it. The only way to find out, she argues, would be to "expose a large number of persons to such an environment for the first time as adults and see whether antisocial personality does emerge in any of them." She guesses it would not. On what evidence? "I base this guess," Robins tells us in all seriousness, "on the few anecdotal accounts of upper-class African students or embassy attachés who, on coming to the United States, have been treated like any other black by their suburban neighbors, and who then become indignant but not in the least sociopathic."

Robins's single-minded effort to rule out the importance of factors other than the child's own antisocial tendencies can lead to an astonishing tendency to ignore the contrary evidence of her own results. One of her studies involved the histories of a sample of black men drawn from inner-city schools in St. Louis. Again, the results showed that most of those who suffered from a variety of social problems as adults had shown considerable evidence of "antisocial personality" at an early age. (Very importantly, though—and a point quickly passed over in Robins's reports of this research—arrests for crimes of *violence* were actually *less* common among men with a history of antisocial personality in childhood than among men who had *not* shown evidence of the "disorder"!) Robins then goes on to show, however, that what most distinguished those antisocial children who went on to exhibit high levels of antisocial behavior as adults were three features of their early childhood environments: growing up in severe poverty; having been removed from the parental home; and having lived in a home with parent figures of both sexes for only a few years. In other words, a variety of *environmental* circumstances, including severe economic disadvantage, were apparently what most often accounted for the fact that *some* of these antisocial children grew up with severe problems while others did not. This is an important finding, and one with promising implications for social policy, for it suggests that what might seem on the surface to be a fatally determined progression from childhood problems to adult crime may often be deflected by improving the living conditions of poor families and the supports available to them.

Robins nevertheless proceeds to dodge the implications of her own evidence. Despite her stark findings on the role of poverty, she insists that antisocial behavior among adults in this sample "has its origins chiefly within the person and his family" as opposed to their "social class of rearing," which is "*not* an important predictor of severely antisocial behavior in adults." How is this extraordinary leap accomplished? What happened to the strong connection between childhood poverty and adult problems? Robins has simply explained it away by a definitional sleight-of-hand.

Poverty, ingeniously enough, is defined as irrelevant to the larger issue of the child's "social class of rearing"—and, for reasons that are far from clear, is then dropped altogether from the analysis. Robins acknowledges that poverty is "associated with lower class status," but represents "an extreme measure"; if we measure "lower class status" instead by the occupation of the children's parents or guardians, the relationship between class and later behavior is much diminished. Why we should ignore the evidence on poverty and focus instead on parental occupation is never made explicit.

But that is by no means the whole problem with this line of thought. More subtly, Robins has here engaged in a bit of fallacious reasoning that has served as an essential prop of this type of argument for decades. The Gluecks, for example, also contended in some of their work that there was little relation between social status and youthful delinquency. But as numerous critics have since pointed out, the Gluecks' result was virtually assured from the start, because all their subjects were drawn from roughly the *same* social stratum! This happens again in Robins's study: all these men were drawn from similar inner-city minority neighborhoods, most were (at best) blue-collar workers, and indeed, of the few white-collar workers in the sample, very few turned out to be severely antisocial. Common sense suggests that this is in itself fairly good evidence for the significance of social inequality in the explanation of "antisocial" behavior. Robins seeks to escape the testimony of common sense essentially by comparing poor black men with each other.

As has become obvious, the central failing of this kind of research is that it stacks the deck in favor of "individual" explanations by simply choosing to ignore the implications of variations in "antisocial" behavior across different social strata, racial and ethnic groups, or countries. It is all very well to look for whatever factors may distinguish particular inner-city black men who become criminals or drop out of school from those who do not; but this cannot be an *alternative* to explaining these outcomes in terms of the corrosive effects of racial or economic inequality, since it cannot tell us why inner-city black men as a *group* have much higher crime rates than *other* groups.

Likewise, the notion of "antisocial personality" may give us a name for what is wrong with particular individuals who hurt others. But it cannot legitimately *substitute* for an explanation of why these individuals appear where they do. Why should severe personality disorders be so much more common here than elsewhere in the developed world? Why so much more common in the inner cities of Baltimore or Cleveland than in the suburbs of Minneapolis or Boston?

This is where the implications of Robins's argument become most troubling. For to the extent that she confronts these questions at all, her answer consists of the suggestion that the prevalence of antisocial behavior among blacks may be genetically determined—a suggestion that seems gratuitously tacked on without anything resembling solid evidence. Consider her analysis of the factors that cause *some* black children to fail in school while others succeed. Using the same sample of St. Louis black men, Robins investigated the possibility that there was some sort of "transmission of a propensity for school problems from one generation to the next." Sure enough, the parents' performance in school—measured by truancy, graduation or nongraduation, and IQ test performance—paralleled similar outcomes in their children. By itself, as Robins acknowledges, this is hardly surprising, and it doesn't serve as evidence for any particular *explanation* of this pattern. But Robins insists that most of the factors affecting these families that might explain the continuity in school problems—from occupational status to mothers' behavior problems—had only limited effects on the correlation between school performance across the generations. When all these were accounted for, there remained a "direct effect" of the parents' school performance on that of their children. What exactly this may mean, Robins is not able to say. But she does think it "at least leaves viable the hypothesis of a genetic factor." What kind of genetic factor might explain this pattern? Robins rules out the hereditary transmission of IQ itself, as promoted by Arthur Jensen and other partisans of genetic theories of intelligence, mainly because IQ was not as strongly transmitted in her sample as the two other problems of truancy and failure to graduate. But what sort of genetic factor, then, could conceivably explain the continuity between the parents' truancy and dropping-out and that of their children? "If there was a gene at work," Robins surmises, "it may have had more to do with ability to conform to rules than with intellectual competence."

The notion that there exists a specific gene responsible for conformity to rules is not simply bad social science, of course, but also bad genetics. That is not how genes work, and the attempt to link specific kinds of social behavior with specific genetic material has a long and unhappy history, much criticized by serious geneticists and social scientists alike. I don't mean to invoke here a simplistic dichotomy between "social" versus "biological" views of human behavior in general or of criminal behavior in particular. After all, two of the most powerful predictors of crime and delinquency are "biological" ones: age and sex. But acknowledging the close association between crime, age, and gender is one thing; attributing the school failure of some poor black children to a genetically predestined difficulty in conforming to rules is quite another.

Ultimately, the issues involved here go far beyond the implausible argument that the school troubles of inner-city children are genetically determined. The real issue is whether we regard the evidence on the persistence of family problems and the continuity of troubling behavior from childhood to adult life as indicative of predispositions that are largely unrelated to their social context and that we are virtually powerless to alter. For many conservative writers, the dark conclusion to be drawn from this evidence—genuine enough, when it is not overstated—is that there are sharp limits to what we can do either for troubled children or the troubled adults they too often become. That conclusion lends support to the ever more intensive search for new methods of screening and incapacitation and to the simultaneous neglect of policies to reduce economic and racial disadvantage.

But the same evidence allows us to draw opposite conclusions. Nothing in it convincingly shows that these childhood problems are intractable; much suggests that improving the living conditions of disadvantaged families and enhancing the social supports available to them can do a lot to deflect the all-too-frequent progression from childhood problems to more serious difficulties in adult life. Moreover, the evidence that the majority of troubled children, even in these unpromising, indeed hostile, settings, do *not* go on to become troubled adults testifies to the great resilience and strength to be found in poor children and their families. If we are not blinded from the start by the ideological conviction that there is little that can or should be done in these communities, we might take heart from that resilience—and perhaps learn how to foster and encourage it. The hopeful conclusions drawn by Alexander Thomas and Stella Chess from their own long-term studies of development from childhood to adulthood are illuminating. "In reviewing the developmental course of our subjects," they write,

> we have been deeply impressed by the human capacity for flexibility, adaptability, and mastery in the face of all kinds of adverse and stressful life situations. . . . We now have to give up the illusion that once we know the young child's psychological history, subsequent personality and functioning is ipso facto predictable. On the other hand, we now have a much more optimistic vision of human development. The emotionally traumatized child is not doomed, the parents' early mistakes are not irrevocable, and our preventative and therapeutic intervention can make a difference at all age-periods.

The increasing popularity of the idea that much if not most crime and delinquency reflect innate and intractable predispositions has more to do, I think, with the larger social and economic trends in America in the last quarter of the twentieth century than it does with the meager and contradictory empirical evidence invoked to support it. As I've already noted, this is not the first time such thinking has become fashionable. Similar ideas flourished in European and American criminology at the close of the nineteenth century. Then as now, deep and stubborn economic crises and the apparent failure of more humane attempts at penal reform bred a rash of theories purporting to explain the inability of great numbers of people to succeed in the competitive "struggle for existence" as an indication of their inferior biological material. The newer, only slightly modified versions of these formulations that have grown up in the past fifteen years are not much more convincing on theoretical or empirical grounds. Nonetheless, they remain attractive to those eager to write off the problems of the urban "underclass" as incapable of constructive resolution.

But is that the only response realistically available to us? Throughout the preceding discussion, I've suggested at several points that it isn't. It's time now to pull those scattered suggestions together into a more coherent discussion of what we might do to confront criminal violence in America.

7

NEW DIRECTIONS

In dealing with social ills, no less than with physical ones, the first step toward cure is an accurate diagnosis. The problem we set out to investigate is why the affliction of criminal violence is so much worse in the United States than in other affluent industrial societies. A hard look at the comparative evidence allows us to dispose of several myths that have hindered our coming to grips with violent crime in America. It is not, for example, unusual leniency with criminals that distinguishes us from less violent nations. On the contrary, as we've seen, we are far more punitive in our response to crime (if often less efficient—two outcomes that are complementary, not contradictory): we rely far more on the formal apparatus of punishment and use it more severely than most other advanced societies. Likewise, the comparative evidence quickly dispenses with the myths that the growth of the welfare state or laxity in the punishment of children are to blame for our crime rate, since the welfare state is distinctly underdeveloped in the United States as compared with other industrial societies and our support for punitive discipline far greater.

On the other hand, we've seen that the United States differs from other industrial societies in several dimensions of social and economic life that are crucial in accounting for our high levels of criminal violence. These include a wider spread of inequality, greater extremes of poverty and insecurity, the relative absence of effective policies to deal with unemployment and subemployment, greater disruption of community and family ties through job destruction and migration, and fewer supports for families and individuals in the face of economic and technological change and material deprivation.

Some of the roots of these differences—particularly our heritage of racial subordination—reach deep into our history in ways that would create profound difficulties for even the most generous and active social policy. Others, however, represent more or less conscious and current choices, for which we pay a steep price in social disintegration and violence. The result has been an unusual degree of erosion of the institutions that bear much of the responsibility for achieving socialization and social cohesion. Like all serious tasks, these require sufficient and appropriate resources—in particular a supportive and nurturing human "ecology" that, among other things, provides for the attentive and undisturbed care of the young and ensures that individuals can contribute to the larger community and in turn be rewarded by it with esteem and respect. Such a supportive ecology does not simply flow automatically from the operation of the economic market. On the contrary, the natural tendency of the marketplace is to put considerable strain on the institutions of family, work, and community that are its chief components. The growth of urban-industrial consumer society has increased those strains throughout the world. In most developed nations, this process has been ameliorated to some extent by countervailing mechanisms of social obligation and support. In the United States, by contrast, this growth has been marked by the relatively unbuffered play of market forces and has been exceptionally disruptive of the institutions essential for the healthy development of character and community. In these differences we may begin to understand why we suffer the worst violent-crime rate among industrial societies—and why we are forced to resort to levels of punishment that sharply distinguish us from all but the most notoriously repressive among them.

The general nature of the remedy is implicit in the diagnosis. If we are serious about attacking the roots of this American affliction, we must build a society that is less unequal, less depriving, less insecure, less disruptive of family and community ties, less corrosive of cooperative values. In short, we must begin to take on the enormous task of creating the conditions of community life in which individuals can live together in compassionate and cooperative ways.

It has recently been fashionable to deny that we can do much about those conditions through deliberate social policy. But the evidence has shown that this, too, is a myth. For we know that many of the conditions that generate criminal violence *are* capable of alteration; other countries have done so. Equally importantly, many of those conditions have been created, in part, by active social policies, conscious or otherwise. Conservatives make much of government's inability to effect significant changes in social institutions. But in fact government is and has been deeply implicated in the decisions—and nondecisions—that have helped to bring about our disastrous level of criminal violence. Government can fairly be said to have adopted a pro-crime policy for decades in America. It subsidized the mechanization of agriculture that pushed masses of the rural poor into the cities, simultaneously encouraging the flight of urban industry and employment. Similarly, it subsidizes the transfer of capital and jobs overseas, and routinely adopts monetary and fiscal policies, in the name of fighting inflation, that create widespread unemployment and its resulting community and family fragmentation. Government then establishes a minimal and inadequate system of support for those whom it has helped deprive of sustaining work, which dictates that many families will have neither the time nor the resources to ensure the healthy development of their children. Far from being a passive bystander whose social role is purely reactive, confined to the operation of the criminal-justice system, government now invokes that system with its right hand to respond after-the-fact to conditions which it helps to create with its left.

Indeed, the proverbial visitor from another planet, coming upon our policies toward crime, would be thoroughly bewildered, for those policies are remarkably contradictory. On the one hand, we have encouraged, either directly or by default, the social and economic forces that undermine social cohesion. We then invoke a grossly outsized penal system to contain the predictable consequences, without notable success. In the homely but accurate metaphor offered by the psychiatrist James P. Comer, we are busily mopping the water off the floor while we let the tub overflow. Mopping harder may make some difference in the level of the flood. It does not, however, do anything about the open faucet. Were this our only course of action, the future would look bleak indeed. Fortunately, we have other alternatives —and recognizing that we have them is the essential first step toward a serious anticrime program for the United States.

To that end, I offer the following discussion. It is not intended as a comprehensive blueprint. In general my aim is to open discussion of what seems essential to an effective anticrime strategy, not close it. Sometimes I will cite specific programs I believe show considerable promise. As often, though, I will draw out more general themes, most of them already implicit in the previous chapters, that can guide the development of such programs in the future.

It may be helpful to mention some of those themes at the outset, in order to make clear how they distinguish the approach I will outline here from what has gone before. By now, the points on which I differ from the recently dominant conservative perspective should be clear. But my approach also differs in important ways from the tradition of what, with severe oversimplification, I have called liberal criminology. These differences center on three shortcomings in much of the liberal view that diminished its credibility and limited its capacity to come to grips with the realities of criminal violence in America. I will call them the problems of *pathology, community,* and *political economy.*

I've already noted the tendency of liberal criminology to shrink from acknowledging the depth of social and personal *pathology* that criminal violence on the American scale represents. This sometimes led liberals to deny the seriousness of the crime problem altogether—more often, to underestimate the resources and energies required to attack it. Too often, liberals responded with poorly conceived, ill-equipped, and superficial programs to problems that cried out for intensive and sustained intervention. In consequence, many such programs were bound to "fail," causing no small delight to those opposed to social programs altogether. This deficiency was closely linked with an inadequate appreciation of *political economy.* For despite considerable—and genuine—concern with opening opportunities for the disadvantaged, liberal criminology typically shied away from confronting the tougher implications of that concern. The liberal support for education and job training, for example, was not matched by a serious commitment to job *creation* or the redirection of public and private investment that it would entail. In general, the liberal strategy toward the disadvantaged amounted to a series of not-always-substantial reactions to the failures of the private market, rather than more active efforts to forestall the market's disruptive and impoverishing consequences. Finally, by an inadequate appreciation of *community* I mean that liberal criminology often couched its approach to crime prevention (and to the rehabilitation of offenders) in individual terms, when a large part of the problem was the weakening of communal institutions that, many criminologists agreed, were the bedrock of social order. Much of the liberal emphasis on rehabilitation, for instance, meant "individual treatment" without regard for the familial and communal networks from which offenders came and to which they would return; much crime "prevention" involved the provision of services to deprived individuals, less often measures to strengthen the resources of their families and neighborhoods. In combination with the inadequate appreciation of political economy, this served to turn liberals' attention (like that of most conservatives) away from the larger forces that were busily ripping apart the institutional infrastructure of American communities and the socializing capacity of American families.

An anti-crime strategy that seeks to move beyond these limitations, therefore, must adopt a more coherent and consistent set of premises. It should take pathology seriously. It should, whenever possible, emphasize prevention rather than reaction. It should address itself to maintaining the integrity of communal institutions of socialization, livelihood, and support. And finally, it must be tough-minded enough to confront unflinchingly the larger social and economic forces that now weaken and strain those institutions. These principles guide the suggestions that follow. The first two sections take up some potentially fruitful shifts in priorities within the criminal-justice system itself and offer encouraging evidence on the rehabilitation of offenders. The following sections consider the three areas for intervention that seem most crucial in preventing criminal violence: the family, the community, and the labor market.

------------ i ------------

Few ideas are more utopian than the belief that we can stop crime by changing the way it is handled within the formal system of criminal justice. Just as we've come slowly to recognize that the hospital and the physician's office are not the only—nor even the most important—sources of physical health, we need to acknowledge the fundamental fact that most of the prevention of crime takes place outside the courts and prisons. This hardly precludes the need for a strong system of criminal justice. It isn't easy today to find people who are "soft" on crime; nonetheless, it is important to be absolutely clear that communities have a fundamental right to the best protection we can offer against the dangerous and predatory—and that this right is worth fighting for in the face of official neglect and indifference. Of course we should "get tough" with brutal people. That is both necessary and proper as far as it goes; it does not, however, go far enough, as an enormous body of accumulated evidence now shows. It is quite easy to appear tough by indignantly declaring that the criminal-justice system is falling down on its job; it is much harder to come up with credible answers as to what, specifically, it should do differently, and still harder to back those answers up with hard evidence that the changes will matter. What is at work here is precisely the same sort of inclination toward instant gratification that conservatives quite rightly deplore when it appears in juvenile delinquents or habitual robbers.

A useful parallel can be drawn with the issue of national defense. In both cases, the public is not well served by vague demands for a tougher stance and a demonstration of will, nor by throwing money at ineffective and expensive programs as if weak commitment or sheer lack of resources was the problem. In both cases, what's required is better targeting of resources to areas of genuine need. In the case of criminal justice, this means focusing on those parts of the system that *are* now weak in ways that seem remediable, where there is good reason to believe that we will gain in effectiveness by the strategic addition of resources.

Three such areas seem especially worth serious exploration: strengthening the system's capacity to deal with domestic violence; exploring ways to increase crime prevention at the stage of apprehension and policing; and encouraging new kinds of *middle-range* sanctions that would help strengthen, rather than tear apart, the ties between offenders and communities and would offer an alternative between doing nothing and the overuse of imprisonment—what Donald West calls "criminal-justice over-kill."

As we've seen, the evidence does not show American criminal justice to be unduly lenient, on the whole, with most serious repeat offenders. But there is at least one major exception: the handling of domestic violence by the courts and police. The research on family violence shows that it is both astonishingly widespread in the United States and also far more serious and repetitive than many people realize. A study by the National Institute of Justice (NIJ) has shown that one in four victims of family violence suffers from repeated incidents involving the same offender, sometimes for years on end; and that serious cases that result in injury or death have usually been preceded by many previous calls to the police. The level of violence involved in such *nonstranger* crime is often staggering; according to the NIJ study, a third of victims of nonstranger crimes typically require medical attention; 40 percent of nonstranger assaults involve guns, knives, or some other deadly weapon. Moreover, as I've shown in Chapter 6, there is substantial evidence that violence in the family is often passed on down the generations. Yet it is a truism that the American justice system has generally taken family violence more lightly than *stranger* crimes. Indeed, much of our conventional imagery of what crime *is* has been tacitly based on the model of the stranger who mugs or rapes in the street. Our institutions of justice have not yet fully absorbed the fundamental truth that some of the most dangerous criminals are in our own homes. To the extent that the criminal-justice system as a whole falls down anywhere along the line in confronting truly serious violence, it is here.

This is tragic, because there is evidence that taking family violence more seriously can make a difference in reducing the risks that it will be repeated. In a recent study of family violence in Minneapolis, Lawrence Sherman and Richard Berk found that victims of assaults by family members were almost twice as likely to be assaulted again if the police made no arrest—an effect that held up in spite of the fact that very few assaulters were *convicted* after arrest. To be sure, as research by Sarah Fenstermaker Berk and Donileen Loseke has shown, the reasons why police don't make arrests in family violence cases often make sense—for example, victims are sometimes unwilling to make complaints—but the evidence that arrest may make a difference is too strong to ignore. This is one of those cases, in short, where a greater investment in formal deterrence may "work" because consistent formal sanctions are now so rare.

Unfortunately, as earlier research by the Berks and their associates have shown, it has been difficult to keep programs designed to take a stronger stand toward family violence on track. The program they studied in Santa Barbara was initially successful in improving police handling of domestic violence cases and boosting the strength of prosecutions, with the result that a greater proportion of batterers were punished, in some fashion, through the justice system. But over time the program's effectiveness deteriorated in a generally "unsupportive environment"; few people at any stage of the justice system, from police officers to prosecutors and judges, considered family violence a major priority. The authors conclude that keeping such programs working at high levels of commitment requires "constant vigilance" and substantial organizing efforts. They are worth it.

Another useful redirection in criminal justice priorities would be to shift our emphasis away from overreliance on incarceration and toward innovative approaches to policing. In Chapter 3, I showed that by far the most problematic stage of the criminal-justice process is apprehension. How much it's possible to improve the ability of the police to catch offenders or to deter street crime is still an open question—but one eminently worth continued investigation. For if ways can be found to do it, we will have achieved the most important possible breakthrough in the ability of the justice system itself to prevent crime. Unlike the courts and prisons, the police have the supreme advantage, in terms of efficiency, of being able to stop crime before it happens, rather than merely dealing with offenders after the fact. And if we can do it, preventing crime through increasing the chances of apprehension is also cheaper and less disruptive of personal and community life than incarceration.

The evidence is sparse at best that simply adding more police to the payroll or throwing money at police departments for technological gadgetry affects the crime rate, but there are glimmers of evidence that certain specific police strategies *might* do so— especially increased foot patrol. Though some studies—including one conducted by the Police Foundation in Newark, New Jersey —have found no relationship between putting more police on foot patrol and crime rates, others—including a study of foot patrol in Flint, Michigan—have found that it may indeed reduce street crime. At the very least, closer linking of patrol officers with the daily life of the community can reduce the *fear* of crime and provide a greater sense of community security and cohesion —a position now shared by a diverse spectrum of supporters ranging from radical community activists to James Q. Wilson. Freeing more police officers for this kind of work by hiring people to do other things—as police auxiliaries, for example, as in Santa Ana, California—*may* affect crime rates and almost certainly will affect community satisfaction. (It is also likely to be popular; in a recent *New York Times* poll, three out of five respondents said that more foot police would "help reduce crime a lot.")

Because policing is a relatively labor-intensive enterprise, moreover, this strategy can serve a second and complementary social purpose. There are few more meaningful things for young and relatively unskilled people to do than to help secure the safety of their communities. Putting them to work doing so with public funds, it seems to me, is a better approach than expecting local communities to create and sustain voluntary, unpaid citizen patrols (an alternative sometimes suggested), for it can put money in their pockets and offer them serious training—training that, ideally, could lead upward into rewarding permanent jobs in policing or other kinds of public service. (In this regard, the proposal launched by Adam Walinsky and Jonathan Rubinstein to fund a "Police Corps"—providing college scholarships to young people in exchange for a commitment to serve at least three years as police officers—seems another intelligent step in the right direction.)

Finally, we should make much greater use of middle-range sanctions for offenders that are consequential, but not necessarily severe. The absence of credible sanctions short of incarceration is one of the most crucial limitations of contemporary criminal justice in America. On the whole, we either lock offenders up for unusually (and often unnecessarily) long periods or we do virtually nothing at all, oscillating between alienating harshness and sheer neglect. But this exclusion of the middle ground is grossly unsatisfactory. Both the community and the offenders themselves often need something to happen other than the futile formality of an appearance in court; but neither is well served by putting less dangerous people behind bars. What we most need in this regard are alternative sanctions that provide tangible consequences for offenders—thus letting them know that their conduct is not considered tolerable by the community —but that simultaneously strive to integrate them into community life rather than severing their connections with it.

Two programs, often related and currently being explored, seem especially promising. Both are alternatives to incarceration, but unlike some earlier ones, they are not alternatives in the sense of mere *nonintervention,* of simply setting offenders loose to flounder by themselves.

One is community-service sentencing for offenders who would otherwise be sent to prison. A particularly interesting program has been developed in New York City by the Vera Institute of Justice. Offenders are sentenced to do useful work— for example, in housing rehabilitation—for a specified number of hours under the auspices of a nonprofit local community-development corporation. There is no compelling evidence that such programs reduce crime directly, but they accomplish two other goals at once: linking offenders to the community through work that the community needs, and relieving the crowding of the prisons.

A second middle-range approach (which could be combined with community service) is intensive probation. Through it is now our standard alternative to prison, conventional probation has lost much of its credibility as a meaningful sanction. This is not the fault of probation workers themselves. In an age of systematic starvation of the public sector, many probation departments have such ludicrously high caseloads that they can provide only minimal supervision. Under current conditions, almost nothing happens to the offender on probation—no credible sanctions are imposed, no serious services offered, no social or personal problems addressed. The widespread belief that this neglect results in increased danger to the community has been supported by recent Rand Corporation research, which shows that substantial numbers of serious crimes are routinely committed by offenders on probation. By default, this can make institutionalization seem more attractive. But recently several states—including Georgia, Texas, and New York—have experimented with smaller caseloads, intensive supervision of offenders in the community, and placement in some kind of program that offers alternative sanctions—like community service. Intensive probation, not surprisingly, costs more than the conventional variety. But it adds teeth to it and is still cheaper than incarceration (in Georgia, intensive probation cost $4.50 per offender per day in 1983, versus $0.75 for regular probation and $24.50 for state prison).*

---

*I've said little so far in this book about another criminal-justice-related preventive approach: handgun control. The omission isn't for lack of interest. Rather, gun control is an issue whose complexities have been treated well by others—and I have little new to add. But given the importance of the issue, I don't think it will be out of place to register a strong opinion. I've argued (in Chapter 1) that the easy availability of handguns in America doesn't suffice to explain the difference in levels of lethal violence between the United States and other advanced societies. I do think it explains *some* of it, though precisely how much is a question we cannot yet answer. My own reading of the evidence is that the presence of guns can have a substantial effect on the likelihood that a violent encounter will result in serious injury or death, especially for some crimes

————————— i i —————————

Some of the same considerations that prompt greater attention to middle-range sanctions also suggest a related point: that an effective anticrime program must reconsider the recently fashionable rejection of rehabilitating offenders. Again, one of the most unfortunate aspects of the conservative approach to crime is that it provides no middle ground—nothing that we can do with offenders short of either warehousing them in prisons or simply letting them go, to cope with their problems on their own. There are times when either of those options is doubtless the right one. Some criminals surely cannot be much helped by anything we know how to do; others pose no real danger to the rest of society and would be better off with a minimum of interference. But those are extremes. In the middle are vast numbers of people who appear before the courts suffering from a wide variety of personal and social problems. Our current practice is generally to let them go until they do something bad enough or often enough to justify imprisoning them. Once they are behind bars, little or nothing is done with them before they get out, at which point they are either resolutely neglected by the larger society or, if they cause enough further damage, are thrown back behind bars

—such as domestic violence—where there may rarely be a clear intent to kill the victim and where the sheer presence of a gun makes the difference between an assault and a murder. Especially because of its potential to reduce the deadliness of domestic violence, then, handgun control should have an important place in an anticrime strategy. There is much debate, of course, over which approaches to gun control show the most promise, particularly between those who favor a strategy of stiffer penalties for gun carrying or use and those who lean toward restricting *availability* through tougher requirements for buying and selling handguns or measures to ban them altogether. In Chapter 3, I argue that mandatory sentences for carrying or using guns have had uncertain success at best; my own sense is that taking the first steps down the long road to domestic disarmament through restricting availability is the more promising direction. But no one can reasonably argue that the issue is settled. For readers who wish to follow these issues in more detail, I'd suggest two recent sources in particular: Philip J. Cook, "The Role of Firearms in Violent Crime," in *Criminal Violence*, ed. Marvin Wolfgang and Neil Alan Weiner (Beverley Hills: Sage Publications, 1982); Franklin E. Zimring, "Violence and Firearms Policy," in *American Violence and Public Policy*, ed. Lynn A. Curtis (New Haven, Conn.: Yale University Press, 1985).

with much self-righteous headshaking. This is one tragic consequence of a world-view that cannot envision a significant role for
public authorities other than the reactive power to coerce and
punish.

But liberal criminology, too, has had a hand in creating this
situation. The liberal wariness about the claims and motives of
many programs obstensibly designed to rehabilitate offenders was
often well founded. But it is one thing to criticize the oppressive
or trivial character of so much of what has passed for treatment
of criminals and delinquents, another to throw out the idea of
rehabilitation altogether. For doing the latter requires us to believe either that criminal offenders (unlike most of the rest of us)
do not have problems deep enough to require help in overcoming
them, or that the larger society has no responsibility for seeing to
it that they get such help if they need it. This is a clear instance
of what I've called the liberal failure to acknowledge pathology
—the unwillingness to confront the fact that people who do
violent things to others often have a great deal wrong with them.

There is scattered evidence that doing nothing at all may even
be the worst course of all for some violent offenders. This was one
conclusion of a Harvard University evaluation of the well-known
experiment in closing the youth training schools in Massachusetts
in the seventies. The study did show that even very dangerous
youths could be safely treated in smaller, community-based facilities, and that the need for conventional youth prisons had been
much exaggerated. But it also found that to leave these youths
without *any* services was likely to increase their rates of delinquency.

The ideological attack on the concept of rehabilitation has
usually been accompanied by the argument that nothing more
constructive can be done anyway—that we have "tried" rehabilitation and discovered that it "doesn't work." But the reality is
considerably more complicated, and also considerably less discouraging. To begin with, while it was true that rehabilitation
carried far more rhetorical weight in the sixties than it did in the
next decade, in practice serious rehabilitation programs, either
inside or outside the prisons, were even then attempted only
sporadically, and never on a scale that could remotely be said to
have tested the potential of rehabilitation itself. In the sixties, for

example, the youth prisons of the District of Columbia were widely thought to be among the most advanced in the country in terms of their commitment to rehabilitating rather than simply warehousing the youth under their care. But as the President's Commission on Crime in the District of Columbia pointed out at the time, the resources they actually devoted to that task were minuscule; the youth facilities "lacked even the rudiments of essential diagnostic and clinical services"; there was "little time for individual counseling and no group therapy" in the juvenile institutions. The District of Columbia Children's Center had one full-time psychiatric staff member and one part-timer to serve over two thousand youths.

The conclusion that rehabilitation had failed was based in part on a series of studies reviewing the scattered evaluations of rehabilitation programs up through the mid-sixties, of which the best known was done by Robert Martinson and his colleagues at the City University of New York. Summarizing that research in 1974, Martinson concluded that "with few and isolated exceptions, the rehabilitative efforts that have been reported so far have had no appreciable impact on recidivism." Martinson's conclusion, already gloomy enough, was amplified considerably in the less careful accounts of his work by the media, which quickly began to proclaim that, when it came to rehabilitating criminals, "nothing works."

Similar conclusions had been offered by earlier reviews of the evidence, such as it was, on rehabilitation programs before the sixties. But these conclusions were much stronger than the data warranted, and their enthusiastic reception had at least as much to do with ideology as with evidence. For the critique of rehabilitation, in this sweeping and categorical form, was attractive to both ends of the political spectrum. To the criminological Right, it offered further testimony that the only feasible response to criminal offenders was increased efforts at deterrence and incapacitation, and it served in a deeper sense to confirm the view that crime reflected fundamental flaws in human nature or in the constitution of offenders. In spite of all our best efforts, the research seemed to say, you can't do anything with these people after all, so you shouldn't try. For the Left, on the other hand, the apparent failure of rehabilitation frequently supported a very different argument: that given the deep social and economic sources of crime in the United States, little could be gained (and much abuse would be encouraged) by tinkering with offenders in the name of "individual treatment."

But both of these extreme views strained credibility. As Donald West remarks, "Fashionable as it has become, there is a certain implausibility" about the conclusion that "nothing works"; for "it seems to imply that nothing one does to delinquents, however kind or however nasty, makes the slightest difference." By the late seventies, there was already some fragmentary but significant evidence for a more encouraging view, and it has grown since. In 1979 the criminologists Paul Gendreau and Bob Ross published a survey of more recent evaluations of rehabilitative programs, arguing that some of them had indeed worked, at least for some offenders. In the same year, the National Academy of Sciences came to similar conclusions, only a bit more restrained. A Rand Corporation report in 1976 had already suggested that the "nothing works" verdict had been too hasty, and cited several programs whose positive results seemed to have survived hard scrutiny. Moreover, Charles Murray and Louis Cox's evaluation of the UDIS program in Illinois, noted in Chapter 3, seemed to suggest —although this was not necessarily their intention—that indeed everything worked: that programs ranging from community-based counseling services to residential camps and intensive psychiatric care all reduced delinquency among hardened young offenders. And by the end of the seventies, Martinson himself had changed his mind dramatically; on the basis of new evidence, he "withdrew" his earlier conclusion that "rehabilitative efforts have no appreciable effect on recidivism."

These more positive assessments center on two points. They find considerably more evidence of success in some kinds of programs, under some conditions, than the earlier studies—in part, because they examine more recent programs that are more intensive and more carefully evaluated. But even more importantly, they also suggest that we know something about *why* rehabilitation "fails," when it does; and that the reasons don't lie solely with the unregenerate human material with which the programs must contend, but also with intrinsic limitations in the programs themselves and in the larger community to which offenders must return.

To begin with, many rehabilitation programs simply didn't do what they were designed on paper to do. Most lacked what Gendreau and Ross call *therapeutic integrity;* that is, they failed to follow through on their theoretical assumptions about what rehabilitation would actually require (if they had theoretical assumptions at all). The programs cited by Martinson and other critics as evidence that rehabilitation did not work were often not only underfunded and understaffed, but typically staffed by poorly trained and often unmotivated people. The early critics of rehabilitation made little effort to separate reasonably serious and intensive programs from those—vastly more common—that at best offered minimal counseling or tutoring to people who were otherwise allowed to languish in the enforced bleakness of institutions or in the shattered, dead-end communities from which they had come. This led a National Academy of Sciences (NAS) panel, in their 1979 review, to conclude that "when it is asserted that 'nothing works,' the Panel is uncertain as to just what has even been given a fair trial."

By the same token, however, the rather unsurprising failures of most conventional rehabilitation programs suggest some of the requirements for success. From the scattered evidence collected by Gendreau and Ross, by the NAS panel, by the supported-work experiments, and by others, it's possible to piece together some of the characteristics of those programs that are likely to be successful, and which, therefore, seem worthy of serious further exploration.

Interestingly, most of the positive assessments of rehabilitation suggest that what distinguishes promising from unpromising approaches is not so much any specific program or therapeutic technique. Robert Martinson argued in 1979 that "the most interesting general conclusion is that no treatment program now used in criminal justice is inherently either substantially helpful or harmful." The "critical fact seems to be the *conditions* under which the program is delivered." More concretely, the evidence suggests that the "strength and integrity of treatments," as the NAS panel put it, is crucial; whatever the specific technique used in treatment programs, the most important issue is whether it is implemented intensively, seriously, and for a reasonable length of time. When these conditions are met, the results can be impressive. We've seen this already in the case of supported work for addicted offenders. And the principle is affirmed in Murray and Cox's evaluation of the UDIS program. For what's striking about the various alternatives to imprisonment UDIS offered is how mild and short-range most of them—even those defined as most "restrictive" or "intensive"—really were in practice. One of the most effective programs, according to Murray and Cox, was the out-of-town residential camps. These camps were hardly regimented, intrusive, "total institutions." In one of them, youths were put to work at construction and painting; they attended classes in an alternative school and went on overnight camping trips, hikes, and riding excursions, along with swimming and other sports. Another camp was designed around the theme of exploring rural life: hiking, camping, talking with farmers, and observing farm life. It also had an urban component along the same lines, which included exploring city neighborhoods and going to museums. In the first camp, the average youth stayed two to four months; in the second, about six weeks. Yet these relatively limited experiences were superior, measured by their effects on later delinquency, to traditional imprisonment—even for very serious delinquents.

The "strength and integrity" of the programs, then, is clearly one factor in whether rehabilitation "works" or not. Another is whether the program is closely linked with other community resources—schools, employers, social-service agencies, networks of relatives, and neighborhood organizations. This finding makes considerable sense in light of the clear importance of "informal" communal institutions in crime prevention, a finding we've encountered at several points. Linking delinquents with the range of available services in the community was a central principle of the UDIS program and a major ingredient in its success. Similarly, in evaluating the sources of success or failure in programs developed in Massachusetts, Robert Coates argues that the more successful programs were those that closely involved the surrounding community and the delinquents' families on a day-to-day basis, rather than being "community" programs only in the sense of being located in a neighborhood rather than an institution. As Coates puts it, what is important is "working with youth in the context of their networks":

> The youngster is a participant in numerous networks (family, peer groups, school, work) that influence his or her behavior and at times compete for his or her allegiance. To expect that directing short-term treatment only at the individual will dramatically alter those network relationships that have been shaped over many years is unrealistic at best and foolhardy at worst.

Thus it is important to think of rehabilitation not so much as something that takes place only within the minds of individual offenders, but also as a process of strengthening their relationships with the communal and familial institutions that most influence their lives.

Communities, however, cannot function well in this capacity unless they can offer a modicum of stability and the means for a decent and dignified life as the fruit of respectable and cooperative behavior. And it is this problem, as I've argued in Chapter 4, that bedevils even truly serious rehabilitative programs and that most tellingly reminds us that what appears to be "failure" on the surface is often less a failure of the programs themselves than of the institutions of the larger community. This obvious but often overlooked reality is illustrated most dramatically in a recent study by William McCord and Jose Sanchez of the careers of 1950s graduates of New York's Wiltwyck School for delinquents. This research is worth examining in some detail, because it offers a compelling look at both the genuine potential of serious efforts at rehabilitation and the roots of their frequent failure.

McCord and Sanchez compared two groups of men who had been institutionalized as adolescents either at Massachusetts's Lyman School—a conventional, punitive, regimented youth prison—or at Wiltwyck, a school for severely disturbed boys that offered an intensive and supportive therapeutic environment. The two institutions were about as far apart in philosophy and practice as they could be.

Wiltwyck offered its residents what its founders called "disciplined love." It emphasized the avoidance of punitive discipline, the encouragement of self-government, and the development of a "community of understanding." The school's basic aim was "to increase the child's understanding of the consequences of his behavior, to enhance his self-esteem, and to offer him a degree of emotional security." As McCord and Sanchez note, "Since the children usually came from brutal urban environments, the unwalled school provided a totally new milieu." Wiltwyck's departure from conventional prison practice won it considerable liberal support in the state, including that of Eleanor Roosevelt; its graduates included Claude Brown and Floyd Patterson.

On the other hand, at Lyman—the first American reform school and one of the most typical—"the slightest deviation from the rules—such as talking when not allowed, 'stubbornness,' or disobedience—resulted in physical punishment and a sentence to the 'disciplinary cottage,' " in which "the master maintained absolute silence." "Those children who avoided harsher discipline," McCord and Sanchez write, "typically spent their time in a silent classroom or in a field where they shovelled manure." In this respect, Lyman was "neither better nor worse" than the average youth prison in America. As in most of them, the aim was "to mold children through punitive discipline and rudimentary education," emphasizing the principles of "punishment, incapacitation, and severity" over the "therapeutic milieu" attempted at Wiltwyck.

McCord and Sanchez traced the histories of all 175 boys who had been at Wiltwyck for eighteen months or longer between 1952 and 1955, as well as a random sample of 165 boys who had graduated from Lyman in the same years. By the beginning of the 1980s, they were in their late thirties or early forties. How had they fared in the meantime? The results, as measured by commitments for serious criminal offenses, were at first quite confusing. For the first five years after release, the Wiltwyck graduates had very low rates of recidivism, particularly as compared with the Lyman youths. At earlier and more crime-prone ages, McCord and Sanchez point out, the Wiltwyck approach seemed "significantly effective in preventing felonies." Wiltwyck's policies appeared to work—at first—even for the most troubled youths, those who had been defined as "psychopathic" and were often "violent, impulsive, and aggressive." At ages fifteen to nineteen, for example, the Wiltwyck graduates diagnosed as "psycho-pathic" were rearrested for felonies after graduation at a rate of just 11 percent; the Lyman graduates, 79 percent. But though the Wiltwyck boys never reached as high a level of recidivism as the Lyman youths had at the beginning, their troubles with the law, *after* the first five years beyond graduation, increased steadily with age. Those of the Lyman graduates, on the other hand, generally *decreased* with age and, by the late twenties, were lower than those of the Wiltwyck group.

What accounted for the curious pattern of early success and later declines among the Wiltwyck graduates? Only one differ-ence in the characteristics of the two groups seemed to matter: "the person's ethnic background." The increases in recidivism in the Wiltwyck boys took place entirely among black and Hispanic graduates; with increasing age, the rates for *white* graduates de-clined. And this ethnic difference explained much of the variance in the patterns of recidivism over time between Wiltwyck and Lyman, because the Wiltwyck boys were more often black and Hispanic, the Lyman boys more often of European descent—Irish, Italian, or French-Canadian. It was this ethnic mix, McCord and Sanchez argue on the basis of official records as well as interviews with some of the graduates, that largely accounted for the fact that "in contrast to the Wiltwyck group, many of the men from Lyman found it relatively easy to deal with life on the outside." They quote one Lyman graduate of Irish descent, a retired policeman, to the effect that "I fooled around a lot when I was a kid. . . . But then I got an uncle on the force. When I was twenty, he got me my first job as a traffic man. And look at me now—sitting on this porch and enjoying life. It helps to have the Irish connection." By contrast, the positive effects of the Wilt-wyck experience for the school's heavily minority graduates deteriorated because of the deprivation and discrimination they encountered in their communities of origin. They had nothing comparable to the "Irish connection." Interviews with these men in later life

> suggested that all of the men remembered Wiltwyck fondly
> —perhaps, in a sense, too fondly. The sojourn at Wiltwyck
> offered a welcome relief from "real" society. As the years

passed, experiences at Wiltwyck became largely irrelevant. The blacks and Hispanics encountered discrimination in education, jobs, and housing—a feeling of frustration which dashed the hopes Wiltwyck had engendered.

"In fact," the authors conclude, "Wiltwyck rehabilitated most of its boys." But by ten years after graduation, they "faced the all-too-tangible barriers of prejudice and lost the advantages given them by the treatment at Wiltwyck." And the lesson that McCord and Sanchez draw is surely the correct one: not that rehabilitation is doomed to fail, even for severely troubled youths, but that "effective treatment in childhood must be accompanied by a fundamental change in opportunities and intergroup relations."

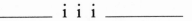

iii

Rehabilitative programs, then, can indeed work—but their best efforts are often overcome by the larger forces that impinge on the lives of offenders. As Robert Coates puts it, "What a youngster brought into the program, and the situation to which he or she returned," are much better predictors of how they ultimately fare than the specifics of the program itself. This necessarily focuses our attention on the broad conditions of community life into which offenders must return and on the conditions of early life that helped propel them into the justice system in the first place.

The evidence that what goes on inside the family is important in understanding violent crime is substantial. Yet as we've seen in Chapter 6, that understanding hasn't led to much sustained interest among criminologists in thinking through what might be done to improve the conditions of family life in America. For some criminological liberals, any concern with the family's role in delinquency and crime smacks of self-righteous middle-class values; programs to aid families, especially with child-rearing problems, seem intrusive and likely to subject those families— especially the families of the poor—to the uncomprehending or manipulative mentality of middle-class professionals. For conservatives, many policies designed to help families are also seen as unwarranted intrusions by the state into what ought to be private matters (not an entirely consistent position for people who often simultaneously advocate the most zealous governmental regulation of private life in the service of what they imagine to be "traditional" family values). Sometimes, too, the lack of interest in improving family life reflects a belief that public policy is powerless to do anything for families that might have a bearing on delinquency and crime. A revealing example of this attitude appears in an exchange during recent congressional testimony on violent juvenile crime by the noted criminologist Marvin Wolfgang. Wolfgang presented illuminating commentary on the dimensions of youth violence and its starkly disproportionate racial distribution in the United States. But pressed by the committee's chair, Senator Arlen Specter of Pennsylvania, for suggestions on what might be done in response, Wolfgang seemed at a loss. He finally allowed that, like the Gluecks, he believed that "under-the-roof culture" held the key to much that went wrong in young people's lives. But he was pessimistic indeed about what anyone could do about it; "the federal government," he declared, "cannot legislate love."

Of course it cannot; but the statement is a non sequitur, and Wolfgang should know better. For there are many things government can do to improve family life and functioning in ways that should—at least in the long run—reduce crime. Even more fundamentally, government is *already* inextricably involved in promoting policies that affect families—all too often, however, in ways that undercut their capacity to serve as compassionate and nurturing agencies of child-rearing and guidance. "No government," wrote the Swedish social theorist Alva Myrdal, "whatever its wishes, can avoid doing things that profoundly influence family relationships. These patterns of activity add up to family policy." When the federal government subsidizes the elimination of livelihoods through technological change, and simultaneously fails to generate new ones for those family heads it has displaced, it is affecting the quality of life "under the roof." When it transfers public resources to defense at the expense of the support and care of future generations, it is affecting the character of family life. When it subsidizes "boomtown" growth in some regions at the cost of unemployment in others, thus forcing families to move and rupturing networks of social support, it is profoundly influencing the prospects for nurturing and loving relations in the affected families. We may legitimately argue about the relative costs and benefits of such policies; we cannot credibly pretend that they are irrelevant to family life.

Hence the real issue is not *whether* government will involve itself in policies that affect the character of family life—but how. Failure to understand this leads inexorably to the kind of self-righteous blaming of parents for the transgressions of their children that so pervades the conservative literature on the family and crime. The issue is whether government will continue to encourage the social forces that so often split, stress, and isolate families, or whether it will work to create a protective and supportive framework of public policies that can cushion families against those undercutting forces and—more actively—help develop the conditions under which patterns of tolerance, reciprocity, and understanding can flourish "under the roof."

To begin with, we can forcefully encourage policies to minimize the conflict between the demands of child-rearing and paid work. As I've argued in Chapter 6, one of the most glaring deficiencies of the rudimentary American welfare state, in stark contrast to its counterparts in many European countries, is the relative absence of those key entitlements that respond to a fundamental fact of life among most modern families: that women, whether heads of households or not, are in the labor force to stay. These international differences have been detailed before, especially in a series of studies by Sheila Kamerman and Alfred Kahn at the Columbia University School of Social Work. Virtually every other advanced industrial society offers more accessible child care, especially for young children. Many also provide, as a matter of right, flexible work schedules and leaves that give parents the option of spending time with their children at home (or, as in Sweden, at day-care centers). As Barbara Ehrenreich and Frances Fox Piven have pointed out, these options are frequently available in the United States—but only to the affluent. Swedish social policy has been especially sensitive to these issues; we could profit from their example. Sweden provides not only lengthy childbirth leaves, but also generous leaves to care for sick children. Even more significantly, recent legislation entitles either parent to a six-hour workday, with income supplements, until the child is eight years old.

We also need to maintain and strengthen our commitment to family planning. As I've shown in Chapter 6, unplanned and unwanted children, and families that are too large for their resources, are routinely associated with both child abuse and delinquency. Even where it doesn't translate into severe abuse, the combination of too young parents and unwanted children is likely to foster neglectful and apathetic child-rearing. In the ideological furor over family planning, its concrete achievements in preventing unwanted children are usually ignored. But they are impressive. One recent study estimates that during the seventies, well over 5 million unwanted pregnancies were averted through enrollment in family-planning programs. Of those pregnancies, about 2.3 million would have eventuated in the birth of an unwanted child; about an equal number would have been aborted, and nearly 700,000 would have ended in miscarriage. Half of the unwanted births would have been among adolescents—roughly a *million* to women under seventeen. (Well over half of all births to women aged fifteen to nineteen are unintended, according to studies based on data from the early seventies.) About 90 percent of these women were not only young but also poor or "near-poor," with family incomes less than twice the poverty level.

The apparent stabilization of crime rates in the past few years is often attributed, in part, to the maturing of the "baby boom" generation and the resulting lower proportion of youth of the most volatile ages in the population. Those who point out the significance of this phenomenon for the crime rate, however, often describe it as if it fell from the sky. But the truth, of course, is that the declining birth rate represents, in good part, conscious decisions made by American families—decisions made possible by the provision of family-planning services that increased their ability to exercise choices in the number and timing of their children. Conservatives do not approve of those choices and want them restricted. They are entitled to that attitude. But they should then be willing cheerfully to shoulder responsibility for the consequences of removing from the young, poor, and ill-prepared the option of avoiding children they do not want and cannot provide for.

Family planning is one line of approach to the link between large families, unwanted births, and delinquency; another is the development of programs to mitigate the *consequences* of early childbearing by keeping adolescent parents in school or at work. One such program is Project Redirection, developed in four cities for teenaged parents by the Manpower Demonstration Research Corporation. This program provides adolescent parents with help in staying in school, finding jobs, and getting adequate health care; it also offers classes in parenting and peer-support groups. Evaluations of the first year of the program showed important successes. More recent ones find the same phenomenon that turns up in supported work and other job-training programs: the positive effects wear off once the participants leave the program. As with job training, however, this is less a clear repudiation of the potentials of the program than a reminder that much else needs changing in the larger community.

Overly large families and unprepared parents are deeply implicated in child abuse and neglect, as well as later delinquency and violence. So, too, are a wide variety of severe family stresses and the neglectful or brutal patterns of child-rearing they often foster. But there is encouraging evidence that some kinds of careful intervention with "high-risk" families can help forestall these patterns. Of particular interest are the results of recent, experimental *family-support* programs that help hard-pressed families cope, both with child-rearing problems and with the whole gamut of stresses that undermine family stability and functioning.

These programs are an outgrowth of the 1960s emphasis on early-childhood intervention as one way of preventing later social pathology—itself an offshoot of the antipoverty efforts of the Great Society. At that time, the idea that children's early educational and social development could be directly enhanced was stimulated by studies that seemed to show that the first few years of development were critical in shaping a child's later functioning. This premise was accordingly built into a range of programs developed largely under the umbrella of Head Start. From the beginning, these efforts attracted much dispute, not least because they touch on the volatile ideological issue of the relative influence of constitutional versus environmental forces in child development. Some fairly discouraging *early* evaluations of Head Start programs helped brand the whole idea as misguided—and provided a starting point for the claims of Arthur Jensen and others in the seventies that genetic inadequacy substantially explained the school failure of poor black children. Critics on the Left, for their part, have sometimes attacked family-support programs as Band-Aid approaches that, by "focusing on the failures of parents and suggesting educational solutions . . . drew attention away from the social and economic causes of child-rearing problems and substituted a notion of the 'happy home,' adjusted to the conditions of poverty, as the goal of social policy."

But both critiques are simplistic. It's true that the hopes for early-childhood intervention were often overstated and therefore easily deflated; it's also true that some "parenting" programs have had a disturbing tendency to blame parents for problems beyond their control. But a growing body of evidence suggests that some family-support programs have had encouraging successes. And the most successful ones have not been nearly as narrow in their approach to family problems as the critique from the Left suggests.

One of the most important experiments along these lines was the Child and Family Resource Programs (CFRP) inaugurated by the Department of Health and Human Services in the 1970s. These programs, established in eleven sites across the country, were based on the premise that "the family's ability to foster child development depends on its own cohesiveness, economic security, and social ties." Accordingly, they offered both training in child-rearing methods and a comprehensive range of social services, from job counseling and medical and nutritional care to help in dealing with housing problems and the welfare system. CFRP "family advocates," most of whom were local mothers, engaged in an "almost endless" array of efforts on behalf of the families.

The programs' ability to provide specific help in child-rearing —including instructions on parenting offered either in home visits or at neighborhood centers—was more limited, in part because so many other more pressing problems needed to be attended to. "Crises were common," the project's evaluators note, "and when they occurred, parent education and activities with children took a back seat. As one family worker commented, 'It's difficult to tell parents that your child should be at this or that stage of development when they're worried about having enough money to pay the rent or buy food.' " The home visits, moreover, took place only on an average of once a month—partly because the family workers had high caseloads of twenty or more families.

These strengths and weaknesses help explain the programs' substantial but uneven results. CFRP considerably improved families' capacity to function effectively in the community and with their children. Compared with similar families not enrolled in the program, there was a "dramatic" increase in the proportion of CFRP mothers working or in school or training programs. CFRP also substantially strengthened what the program called "parental coping skills"; "Perhaps the most important finding," the evaluation reports, "was that CFRP increased parents' feelings of efficacy." More subtly, the program brought "intangible but crucial shifts in attitude" in parents "who were often badly demoralized at the start." Moreover, despite the relatively small amount of time the programs were able to invest in parent training, CFRP "led to significant changes in parents and promoted child-rearing practices associated with positive social and cognitive development of children." CFRP mothers, for example, were less frustrated and irritated with their children and more willing to encourage initiative and independence. On the other hand, it was not clear that the program had much effect, at least after eighteen months, on the children's cognitive or social development. But this was fairly predictable, as the evaluators noted, given the amount of time and effort actually devoted to child-development activities themselves.

This may help explain why stronger developmental results were achieved by another federally sponsored family program launched in the seventies. The Parent-Child Development Centers (PCDC) were demonstration projects, established in six cities, designed to improve the child-rearing practices of low-income parents. Children were enrolled shortly after birth and "graduated" at thirty-six months. Like CFRP, PCDC offered families a wide range of services, including medical care, help in using community services, and classes in nutrition, family budgeting, and community political issues. They provided parent support groups and, sometimes, material support—including transportation, meals, and emergency funds. A particular effort was made to recruit staff of the same cultural and ethnic backgrounds as the participating parents.

The core of the PCDC program was to teach parents effective child-rearing practices, which the parents would then teach to others. In Birmingham, Alabama, for example, low-income mothers cared for their children in a neighborhood nursery, assisted by "teaching mothers" who had come up through the ranks of the programs. After several months, the new mothers served as understudies to the "teaching mothers," and later went on to become teaching mothers themselves. By the end of twenty-four months, according to a careful evaluation by Susan Ring Andrews and her colleagues at the Bank Street College of Education, there were already signs of significant improvement in the way these parents related to their children, and by the children's "graduation" at thirty-six months, "evidence of the programs' effects on both mothers and children was clear and convincing." As compared with carefully matched control groups, the PCDC parents were much more inclined to adopt a nurturing, unrestrictive, and nonpunitive approach to their children; they gave them more guidance, praise, affection, and encouragement. A year after graduation, these improvements still held—as did gains in the children's IQ scores. As in CFRP, one of the most important results was a sense of increased competence and social support among the parents.

It's important to put these successes in perspective. No one is suggesting that family-support programs can overcome a legacy of destructive attitudes toward child-rearing overnight, or that they can by themselves compensate for the larger stresses and deprivations faced by low-income families. But with these reservations, it remains true that the best-designed programs have shown encouraging results. To expect too much of them is a mistake, but so is ignoring their potential. Some families do need help; we ought to be willing to offer it.

The exact form in which that kind of help can best be delivered is open for experimentation. We might, for example, learn much from the experience of the Danish Family Guidance service, which, unlike the American programs I've just described, was deliberately designed to be universally available to *all* families, rather than oriented specifically toward poor or "problem" families. This strategy helps reduce the potential stigma associated with asking for help and encourages a high level of participation. The Danish family services are decentralized, with neighborhood centers staffed by people—many of them paraprofessionals—who are familiar with local conditions and cultures. Whatever the specifics, as a National Institute of Mental Health study of the Danish service argues, "perhaps the single most important lesson to be learned from the Danish experience is that a nationwide support system for families with children is feasible—it can be done and it works."

Before leaving the subject of early intervention, one further program should be noted. I have touched on the relationships between schooling and crime at several points in this book. In particular, the association between school failure and delinquency has emerged as both important and closely intertwined with broader conditions of social and economic disadvantage in childhood. In the past, the general idea of attacking delinquency through some sort of educational reform was often a conspicuous part of the vision of liberal criminology. Yet the impulse to educational reform was rarely based on a clear understanding of just what it was about the schools that contributed to failure and delinquency, and what, therefore, ought to be done about it. In consequence, as I noted in Chapter 1, the liberal approach often translated into a simple demand for more schooling or more money for schools, with only vague conceptions of how this would help.

A more focused approach was embodied in Head Start and some other early-education programs for the disadvantaged, for these were based on the fundamental understanding that much school failure was rooted in the learning disadvantages carried into schools from the beginning by many children growing up in severely deprived families. Until recently, however, there was not much strong evidence one way or another on the effectiveness of early education in breaking this pattern.

But we now have better-designed studies, and their results are encouraging. Especially so are the results of an experimental intensive preschool education program in Ypsilanti, Michigan, called the Perry Preschool Project. The project involved a group of poor black children, half of whom lived in single-parent homes and less than a fifth of whom had parents who had completed high school. The children were divided into an experimental group receiving high-quality preschool attention from age three onwards and a control group without the special education services. The experimentals attended preschool for two and a half hours, five mornings a week. The pupil-adult ratio was intensive —one adult for every five or six children. Preschool teachers, moreover, visited each child and its family at home once a week. The two groups have been studied from 1962 onward.

And the results? By age nineteen, three-fifths of the experimental group were employed, versus less than a third of the control group. More than two-thirds of the experimentals, versus less than half the controls, had graduated from high school; two-fifths, versus one-fifth of the controls, were enrolled in college or a postsecondary vocational program. Less than a third of the experimentals, moreover, had been arrested or detained by police; over half of the controls had. A third of the controls, versus a fifth of the experimentals, were on welfare; the rate of teenage pregnancy was twice as high among the controls. According to the evaluation, the program—which cost about $4,800 per child in 1981 dollars—nevertheless paid off at a rate of seven to one because of the community's gain in reduced welfare dependency and increased earnings later on.

To be sure, the relatively high rates of social pathology even among the preschool graduates tell us that such intervention is not *enough,* in many cases, to combat the effects of early deprivation. But the sharp differences in outcome nevertheless tell us that it makes a difference. And this counters the fashionably gloomy interpretation that the transmission of school failure across the generations in poor families reflects constitutional or genetic predispositions over which we have little or no control. This research, as the program's evaluators argue, "demands prompt action to benefit the common good. We must get about the task."

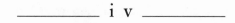

i v

As with rehabilitation, the evidence on the character of successful family programs points up the importance of wider community ties in crime prevention. As I've shown, we have considerable evidence that strong social networks play a large part in preventing crime and, for that matter, provide the context for administering effective "informal" social sanctions. Indeed, the recognition of the importance of local communal institutions in social and personal well-being—in mental and physical health, for example, as well as crime and delinquency—has become a kind of quiet revolution in recent social thought. By now, nearly everyone agrees that the "community" is important in preventing crime. But this surface consensus masks considerable disagreement over what "community" crime prevention means or should mean—and who should pay for it.

Most "community crime-prevention" programs since the early seventies have fallen within the categories that a recent National Institute of Justice (NIJ) survey calls the "Big Three" —neighborhood block watches, "Operation Identification" programs that engrave identification numbers on valuables, and home-security surveys. More elaborate, but less common, programs also include public education campaigns, perhaps citizens' patrols, and efforts to bring community residents closer to the police. Because so many different kinds of programs are typically lumped together under the rubric of community prevention, sorting out their overall effects is difficult—more so, I think, than their supporters often acknowledge. There are few consistent findings in evaluations of Operation Identification, education programs, or citizens' patrols. Neighborhood watches have been studied more often, but the results are conflicting. It seems clear, for example, that in some cases neighborhood-watch programs can bring otherwise atomized community residents together and, like police foot patrols, help reduce the *fear* of crime. These are not insignificant results, and they are surely worth encouraging. But the evidence that these programs have a substantial effect on serious criminal violence is ambiguous, though it may be less so for some property crime, especially household burglary. There have been occasional reports of dramatic reductions in crime in cities that have adopted neighborhood-watch programs, but few that are backed by solid evidence.

One key limitation of these programs is that they are oriented much more to "stranger" crime—and especially to property crimes like burglary—than to nonstranger violence. Indeed, some of the writing on community crime prevention has a disturbing tendency to describe the world as divided into "the community" on the one hand and "strangers" on the other; as the NIJ pamphlet on community crime prevention says of neighborhood watches: "Residents get to know their neighbors and so learn to distinguish strangers and recognize when the activity in the next yard or down the corridor may not be legitimate." But in many badly violence-ridden communities, the problem in the neighbor's yard or home, as often as not, is not a stranger, but the neighbor. Moreover, as a number of studies have pointed out, what often accounts for any apparent success of some neighborhood prevention programs, when it can be measured at all, is the disheartening fact that crime has merely been displaced from one neighborhood to others less organized (and often from those neighborhoods back into the original ones when interest in the program wanes). In response, some partisans of such programs argue that this simply means that *every* neighborhood should get itself better organized. But that betrays an insensitivity to the obstacles that make it difficult for many neighborhoods to do so —especially on anything like the long-term basis necessary to make much of a dent in the local crime rate. For those neighborhoods often lack the resources of time, money, and energy required to maintain effective anticrime organizations for long.

In this form, the notion of community prevention appeals to the quintessentially American penchant for self-help and an equally traditional visceral distaste for "government." At its best, it is a useful corrective to the unreflective belief that the formal criminal-justice system can insure public order without the backing of cohesive communities. The danger arises when these principles are taken too far, to the point of encouraging a nostalgic vision of individual self-reliance that fails to come to grips with the larger structural reasons why the sort of community concern evident in the New England village of the last century no longer holds in Houston.

Something similar happens in the case of another often-promoted approach to crime prevention of the late sixties and seventies—what was called "crime prevention through environmental design." The aim was to design the physical structure of neighborhoods—particularly public housing projects—in order to create more "defensible" residential space. Most often, this meant redesigning entryways or making corridors and yards more accessible to the scrutiny of residents. But again the results were not impressive. The "environmental design" approach frequently shared the unfortunate predilection in American social policy for the quick technical solution that could erase what decades of social neglect and economic disruption had put into place. But as the urban anthropologist Sally Engle Merry has shown on the basis of a careful ethnographic study of one housing project, even if such places are designed architecturally to be "defensible," they cannot really be defended against crime if the social organization of the community is fragmented, atomized, and without solid networks of social support and concern.

What this suggests is not that community crime prevention is a mistaken concept, but that it needs to encompass a much broader range of potential community activities. We've seen some examples already. The most effective rehabilitation and family-support programs are decentralized, involve the participation of local people, and link their clients to other community institutions.

How these themes might be drawn together in an effective delinquency *prevention* program is suggested in a recent study by the historian Steven Schlossman of one of the most innovative of such programs: the Chicago Area Project (CAP). CAP, begun in the 1930s by the noted criminologist Clifford R. Shaw, differed from a number of less serious and less successful "delinquency prevention" programs, then and now, in two crucial ways. First, it rigorously pursued the genuine involvement of indigenous community organizations—notably the churches—in a "bottom up" process of decision-making. Through an elected or appointed board of directors, local residents took most of the responsibility for analyzing community problems that seemed related to delinquency and for carrying out programs to confront them. Equally crucial was CAP's commitment to working closely and untiringly with "high-risk" neighborhood youth—including the most difficult youngsters and those who had already tangled with the criminal-justice system. CAP pioneered what it called "curbstone counseling": the use of street workers, mostly local young adults, whose job was to stay in close contact with these young people at all times, advising them on how to stay out of trouble, how to handle problems at school and work, and more generally trying to "*be* with them as much as possible." CAP closely followed young parolees as they reentered the community, linking them with new friends, getting them to participate in CAP-sponsored community projects, and trying—as much as possible in Depression-era Chicago—to place them in jobs, often ones funded by the WPA and other Depression work programs. Schlossman describes CAP's approach as an "aggressive, omnipresent caring and monitoring of youth at risk in their natural, criminogenic habitats." In an important sense, the community took on a real commitment to troubled youths and never let go: "For both child and community, the CAP was an advocate for all time." Did CAP's efforts reduce delinquency? The difficulties of interpreting the data are formidable, but Schlossman argues that the evidence generally supports the view that "CAP has long been effective in reducing rates of reported juvenile delinquency."

It's precisely that kind of close, hands-on concern with youths in trouble, especially those with serious problems, that has been most lacking in conventional programs for delinquency prevention programs—and in American communities generally. Despite the often bewildering profusion of social agencies, few communities possess a single, comprehensive, indigenous institution charged with just that task of "aggressive caring" that CAP seems to have accomplished to an encouraging degree. The result is that "high-risk" youths most often simply fall through the cracks, or are fruitlessly bounced from one harried social agency to another and ultimately into the hands of the juvenile-justice system. The CAP model is not the only one we might wish to investigate, but its fundamental principles are sound, important, and well worth exploring.

Another crucial role for the community lies in the realm of what we might call preventive conflict reduction. Two programs in particular illustrate this function: community dispute resolution and shelters for victims of domestic violence.

The conventional judicial process can be both alienating and superficial, and the courts are often clogged with minor disputes between neighbors, kin, or other community members that could be better handled outside the formal system. One way of doing this is through mediation or dispute resolution, an idea that has recently gained considerable support. There are many possible variations. Some, like San Francisco's Community Boards Program, avoid the formal justice system altogether by having disputants appear before a special board of community residents. Others, like the Community Arbitration Program in Anne Arundel County, Maryland, use paid arbitrators in an informal setting to handle minor offenses committed by young people. The result may be an "informal adjustment" requiring the youth to participate in community service or victim-restitution efforts, or referral to appropriate community agencies to deal with specific problems. According to some evaluations, the Anne Arundel program reduced repeat offenses among youths while simultaneously freeing courts and police from some of the time and paperwork typically devoted to minor offenses. Whether or not they reduce crime in the short run, moreover, such programs can often allow more serious attention to the social and personal problems underlying the youths' offenses than is possible in the congested courts. And they have a still more important long-range effect of contributing to community identification and cohesion.

Given the importance of family violence as both a large component of the overall problem of violent crime in a community and a frequent precursor of yet more violence in the future, the significance of programs for its victims in a strategy of community crime prevention should be self-evident. I've already suggested the need for greater attention to family violence within the criminal-justice system. But there is a simultaneous need for immediate relief from the threat of further attacks, and this is a role that local communities can fill admirably. The establishment of adequate programs for victims of family violence in every community would be an important—and rapid—step toward the reduction of violence in America. During the 1970s, with the growing concern for violence against women in the home, a number of innovative programs began to combine short-term shelter and emergency assistance to battered women with more extensive services: employment and housing assistance, programs for children of abused women, and even for batterers themselves. Every one of these programs makes eminent sense in the light of what we know about the stubbornness and the long-term effects of family violence. Yet practically every shelter program in the country has been jeopardized by the reduction in public funding in the past few years. These programs depended in good part on the energy and enthusiasm of volunteers, but the majority also drew vital support from several much-maligned government programs that have since been abolished or cut back, including the Comprehensive Employment and Training Act, the Law Enforcement Assistance Administration, and the antipoverty agency ACTION. Some have managed to continue with private funding; many have not.

The fate of such programs in recent years suggests the chief danger lurking in the idea of "community crime prevention": it may become a sort of code phrase for reducing public funding for local programs in the name of an ideologically and fiscally attractive "voluntarism." This possibility helps explain why the appeal of community crime prevention has crossed conventional political boundaries. Some of the most suggestive ideas, indeed, have come from a highly conservative source—a series of studies sponsored by the American Enterprise Institute (AEI) on what it calls *mediating structures*: the institutions of kinship, ethnic and religious organizations, and other bodies that lie between the individual and what these theorists regard as an inevitably distant and bureaucratic state. In a well-known analysis of the importance of mediating structures in preventing youth crime, Robert Woodson argues that nonprofessional, community-based agencies that share a common culture with violence-prone youth and stay resolutely clear of entanglements with government bureaucracies offer the best hope for dealing with youth crime in the face of the failure of more traditional juvenile institutions. One of Woodson's most prominent examples is Philadelphia's House of Umoja, a residential program for black youth-gang members. Umoja's approach is to create a "family" atmosphere for the youths, to instill a sense of ethnic pride, and to encourage the youths' participation in decision-making.

There are no careful evaluations of Umoja's effect; some observers believe the program has indeed reduced gang-related violence in the city over the past decade. It certainly provides something that more traditional programs for young offenders usually do not—a sense of being part of a cohesive community of people with shared concerns and common needs. This makes a great deal of sense and is a principle well worth pursuing.

In the conservative reading of this principle, however, there is another, less justifiable agenda. Programs like Umoja have recently become fodder for a larger conservative argument in support of the further dismantling of the American welfare state and the replacement of our rudimentary sense of public responsibility for community wellbeing, especially in the inner cities, with a reliance on voluntarism and on the uncertain good-will of private corporations. Ronald Reagan himself, for example, lavishly praised the House of Umoja in the fall of 1981 as a prime example of how voluntarism could substitute for wasteful government spending on social programs for minorities and the poor. The people who actually ran the House of Umoja saw things a bit differently, however. According to a report by Howell Raines in the *New York Times*, Reagan cited Umoja as a vibrant example of the "kind of volunteer effort he believes can replace government funded programs."

> However, a founder of the House of Umoja, Falaka Fattah, said in a telephone interview Monday that courts and local government social agencies paid $46 daily tuition for a majority of the 500 boys sheltered by the home. Fattah said that the

House of Umoja, founded in 1968 by her and her husband, has also received Federal grants totalling $400,000. She said the Reagan budget cuts have set back plans to build an "urban Boys' Town" for black teenagers—a project praised Monday by Reagan in his speech. "Already $100,000 that was committed for that project will not be coming," she said, because of reductions proposed by Reagan in community-aid projects under the Comprehensive Employment and Training Act.

In 1980, AEI sponsored a conference in Washington attended by the Fattahs and other leaders of community-based youth organizations, several of them former youth-gang leaders. The conservative pundits lavished praise on the community leaders as exemplars of the principles of voluntarism and rejection of government aid and the demoralizing lures of the bureaucracy. The community leaders had few kind words for the bureaucracy either, but even fewer for the noted conservative theorists' argument that they were better off without government jobs or grants. Thus, the sociologist Peter Berger chastised the community leaders for emphasizing the need for sufficient political clout to bring employment and funding to their hard-pressed clientele: they should forego those "soft-money" jobs, Berger admonished them, and instead seek jobs in the private sector. V. G. Guinses, a black community leader from Los Angeles, had this to say in response:

> Always there are three sides to a story, my side, yours, and the real truth. We are beating around the bush. . . . The jobs you are talking about are limited. Every company I went to, we talked about jobs. What kind of jobs? Peanut money, $2.10 an hour, $2.90 an hour, $3.10 an hour.

The conference participants also let it be known that they did not share the devotion to voluntarism that the scholars considered to be their most distinctive contribution. Indeed, they thought it was high time someone took them seriously enough to offer them something more tangible than pats on the back. David Fattah of the House of Umoja told the AEI staffers, "We're doing this for love, but whoever is here from a foundation or whatever else should reciprocate. Each of these groups should be able to get some benefit. . . . Each group sitting here has proved it has the right to be funded." A bit taken aback, Woodson told the participants, "The role and the function of this conference have to be clear. This conference is not to give you immediate payoffs other than a trip to Washington and an opportunity to sit and learn from one another and share." Woodson then asked the participants for "brief answers" stating the "two most pressing needs of your organization and the needs of the people you serve." The responses included these:

> Funding and education . . . education in the sense of training. . . . Jobs and training money. . . . Funding, because without that you can't do much. . . . We're three months behind on our rent. We need general operating expenses. . . . Money programs. . . . What we need is jobs; that's what we need, more work. . . . More work, that's right.

As it turned out, most of the organizations represented had been the recipients of public funds—and all desperately wanted more in order to keep doing their jobs. The passion for voluntarism was lodged almost entirely in the minds of the AEI staff, a breed sufficiently comfortable materially to feel deeply moved by the lures of unpaid community efforts, albeit at a distance.

Shorn of its ideological posturing about voluntarism and its gratuitous critique of the role of the public sector, the emphasis on mediating structures touches on an important set of issues that are truly relevant for an effective strategy of crime control. But the conservative version of this idea both misreads the nature of community and substitutes a kind of middle-class nostalgia for a hard-headed understanding of the conditions that make or break real communities. The vision of community it encourages is that of the idealized small town thought to have characterized an earlier and simpler America, when everyone pitched in to rebuild the neighbors' barn. It is an appealing picture, but hardly a workable conception of contemporary urban life. For to the degree that such communities existed, they were held together by ties of livelihood, common purpose, and reciprocity. Where those ties have been broken—by disruptive economic growth, extremes of inequality, and the separation of youths and adults from stable occupational roles—the appeal to the traditional community virtues is hollow and often hypocritical. The emphasis on the reconstruction of community responsibility is not wrong; it must be central to any serious strategy against crime. But it needs to be broadened and deepened—to be grounded in a more adequate sense of what a community really is and what is required to nourish and sustain it. This means that community crime prevention cannot become a substitute for public spending; instead, we need to couple the genuinely useful ideas of decentralization of services and local participation with an equal insistence on adequate public funding for effective programs. A strategy of community-oriented crime prevention must also address the question of how people can be given the stable livelihoods without which their participation in the community cannot be other than marginal.

V

In the long run, a commitment to full and decent employment remains the keystone of any successful anticrime policy.

To be sure, there are many steps we can take against crime even in the absence of that commitment; I've just outlined some of them. They will help, and we cannot wait for full employment before we take them. But without a simultaneous move toward an effective employment policy they will not be enough; nor, for that matter, will they fulfill their own potential. Serious rehabilitation, community service and intensive supervision, family-support programs, and the rest all depend for their effectiveness on the existence of stable work roles in the larger community. Without them, the society cannot make good on its side of the social contract: it cannot credibly promise that being good will result in doing well.

We've explored the reasons for this in Chapter 4. To begin with, work constitutes one of the most central bonds through which individuals are integrated into the purposes and values of their society; when work is long inadequate or unavailable, that bond is correspondingly weakened. But this is not all, for in our society what happens to individuals in the labor market decisively shapes virtually everything else in their lives. Inadequate work deprives individuals of a livelihood—the essential material resources that enable them to achieve the standard of living to which their culture bids them aspire. In consequence, it is also a root source of extreme economic inequality. The principal reason why the spread of inequality in the United States is so wide is that the bottom is so far down—primarily because we perpetuate unusually high rates of persistent unemployment and an extensive sector of poorly paid, unstable jobs (as well as stingier income supports—two phenomena that, as we'll see shortly, are closely related). Inadequate work, moreover, ensures that families will be perennially afflicted by economic insecurity and insufficient resources to support their capacity to nurture and socialize. It is also a main cause of the rootless mobility that undermines the efficacy of local networks of kinship, social support, and informal sanctioning.

So it is hardly accidental that every advanced industrial society with a far lower level of violent crime than ours has also developed much more humane and effective employment policies. Usually they include both substantial public expenditure for job training and retraining of the work force and active policies to ensure high levels of employment—including, where necessary, creation of public jobs. In the United States, as I've shown, such measures have always been comparatively underdeveloped; this left us thoroughly unprepared to cope with the wrenching technological and economic changes of the postwar era. Today the situation is even worse, for many of the useful efforts we *did* make in employment and training policy since the sixties have been sharply reduced or eliminated.

Few strategies could be more wrongheaded if the reduction of violence is seriously on our agenda. It is undoubtedly true, as critics have contended, that many employment and training programs in the sixties and seventies were insubstantial and ineffective. But we've seen that others, more carefully conceived and seriously implemented, were successful to an encouraging degree, both in providing real training and useful work and in reducing social pathology. Programs like the Job Corps and, especially, supported work can make a difference, if not for all of their clientele, certainly for enough of them to make the programs eminently worth defending and expanding.

Moreover, as I've suggested, we also know a good deal about what limits the success of even these more serious programs. In our country, in contrast to many others, such programs have typically been launched on a narrow, usually uncoordinated basis, with precarious and inadequate funding. Most important, even the best training programs must inevitably be crippled when there are no solid jobs available for those trained. Where training works well, it does so partly because it is taken more seriously (the proportion of the labor force enrolled in training programs in Sweden, Germany, and Japan in the seventies ranged from ten to twenty times that in the United States) and partly because it is just one component of a set of policies designed to maintain full employment through public intervention.

On the desirability of full employment in the abstract, there is likely to be little disagreement. But an effective anticrime policy requires a sharper and more focused conception of what we *mean* by full employment. It is not enough to call for "more jobs"; what are required are *good* jobs. Nothing will be gained by attempting to force the poor and the young into employment that cannot provide either an adequate living or a sense of dignity and self-respect. The point should be obvious. But in fact much recent employment policy is based on precisely the opposite principle. It seeks to encourage employment through the ominous trade-off of diminishing its rewards—reducing or eliminating the minimum wage, removing restrictions on hours of work for teenagers and establishing special "subminimum" wages for them, or forcing cities to compete with the low-wage countries of the Third World in order to attract private investment and jobs. Yet everything we know about the relationships between work and crime tells us that these are at best fruitless, at worst destructive ways to think about job creation.

There may indeed be developmental costs associated with working in poor jobs, especially for the young, as a recent study by Ellen Greenberger, Lawrence Steinberg, and their colleagues at the University of California at Irvine has shown. Among the youths they studied, long hours of work meant less "quality" time spent with their families and on homework, less enjoyment of school, and a probable decline in school performance—as well as increased use of cigarettes, alcohol, and marijuana. The Irvine researchers put the blame for these results squarely on the character of the low-quality jobs teenagers usually hold. "Youngsters, like adults, often work under stressful conditions—at tasks that are perceived to be meaningless, under poor environmental conditions, in an impersonal organization, with an autocratic supervisor, for low wages." In these jobs, little of lasting value is learned, few skills are needed or imparted, and there is virtually no chance to advance into more challenging roles (The Irvine group suggests that, in many typical jobs in the youth labor market, it takes more skill to fill out a job application than to do the work itself.)

Under these conditions, many of the jobs for youth in the burgeoning service economy represent a downward extension of some of the worst features of the poorest jobs for adults more than they do stepping-stones into stable adult livelihoods. Hence an anticrime employment policy should focus on ways of linking young people with stable adult work roles, rather than on providing stop-gap, temporary work designed mainly to keep kids off the streets. It is less important that young people have a "job" at sixteen than that they have the expectation of a genuine livelihood at twenty-five—and therefore a compelling reason for staying in school at sixteen. What most clearly separates the experience of inner-city black adolescents from their better-off contemporaries, as much research has shown, is not their initial work experience —*most* young people move rapidly in and out of the labor market before they settle down; usually, it doesn't matter. But for many urban blacks, the opportunity to settle down never comes: for them, the solid adult jobs are simply not there.

An extended discussion of strategies to upgrade the quality of jobs would take us beyond the reasonable boundaries of this book. But two general points are in order. A strong public commitment to full employment is itself the single most effective device for upgrading poor jobs, for it means that workers who would otherwise be forced to accept poor jobs in a shrunken labor market would have a wider and more promising variety of options. But strategies that directly seek to raise the pay and quality of what are now poor jobs should also have a prominent place in an anticrime employment policy. Few such approaches hold more promise than the growing movement for pay equity between "women's" and "men's" jobs of comparable worth. Trapping women—especially single women—in the ghetto of low-wage work is one of the surest ways to perpetuate the severe family stresses that contribute so heavily to child abuse and later crime. Raising the rewards of these typically women's jobs, in turn, may be one of the surest ways to begin to break those tragic links.

The need for good jobs rather than just *any* job is one central theme in any employment policy that fits what we know about the relations between work and crime. A second is that such a policy should be geared to what the economists Gar Alperovitz and Jeff Faux call *community full employment.* By this, they mean to distinguish between policies that merely seek to boost the national level of employment and those that take on the tougher but more fruitful task of maintaining jobs in local communities —jobs that will enable those communities to achieve long-term stability and a sense of communal identity. Again, there is considerable evidence that the stability of long-established social networks and community supports can be a strong bulwark against serious crime—even in communities that are otherwise deprived. Conversely, their breakdown may lead to crime and other social pathologies even in communities otherwise well endowed. This helps explain the appearance of high rates of crime in the midst of rapid economic development—why, for example, crime in boomtowns is often as high as it is in more depressed areas. To an important extent, as I've argued in Chapter 5, it is just this sort of uneven, uncontrolled "growth"—what the French social theorist Jacques Attali calls *explosive development*—that helps account for the otherwise perplexing rise in crime amidst the statistical "prosperity" of the sixties.

This suggests a more general, and crucial, point: economic growth, that core icon in the secular belief system of the modern industrial era, will not by itself provide the kinds of livelihoods that reliably inhibit criminal violence. The reasons are systemic and fundamental. For the very logic of the private economy runs counter to all of the elements of what I've called an anticrime employment policy. Left to its own devices, the private economy tends to disrupt local communities, to eliminate vast numbers of jobs, and, even though it may create new ones in great numbers, it leaves a drastic mismatch between workless people and available opportunities for work. We've seen how these tendencies helped create the urban crisis of the sixties and seventies; the outlook for the near future, in the absence of more effective public direction of the economy, seems little better. The disturbing trends have often been described. Increasingly, the American economy is eliminating many of the kinds of jobs that once provided a solid middle-range income. And though the long-range trends are difficult to predict with certainty, there is evidence that the job structure is shifting toward both extremes of the occupational continuum—but mainly toward the bottom. (Roughly three-fourths of those moving out of the middle class are falling downward.) The jobs we are losing in the middle are not likely to be replaced by new ones in the "high-tech" industries. The newer industries provide far fewer total jobs than we once expected, and, faced with international competition, the new industries, like the old, have moved toward greater automation and increased shipment of jobs overseas. Finally, the distribution of work and wages within those industries is even more unequal than it has been in the rest of the economy—creating a broad base of poorly paid workers at the bottom and a relative handful of highly skilled, highly paid workers at the top.

This, most emphatically, does not mean that growth in the private economy is irrelevant to the purposes of an anticrime employment policy. But the mix of private and public in the determination of how work and its rewards are distributed must necessarily be approached more flexibly if we are to attack effectively the patterns of development that have helped create our devastating crime rate. There is, of course, substantial ideological resistance to public job creation in America. But in an economy where the private sector has in fact been heavily underwritten by public expenditure for decades, the public-private distinction has lost its salience, if not its meaning, for all but the most ideologically stalwart.

To describe in detail exactly what an appropriate combination of public and private employment efforts might be is, of course, beyond the purview of a book on crime. But since others have carefully examined this issue in recent years, there is no shortage of concrete suggestions. It seems clear that the mechanisms required to achieve community full employment include: a national public planning mechanism, which can set broad priorities for investment and growth in ways explicitly designed to create livelihoods and stabilize local communities; corresponding, decentralized, local planning agencies that involve community residents in defining their employment needs and in creating an inventory of local economic-development projects that need doing (what Alperovitz and Faux call a *community investment agenda*); finally, to make both of these mechanisms meaningful in practice, a federally enforced job guarantee for all those willing and able to work.

Linking anticrime programs to these strategies for local economic development would dramatically enhance their effectiveness. If we had a serious mandate for local public job creation, for example, the potential of an intensive training program like supported work could be realized to its limits, since the program would no longer be stymied by the meager offerings of the outside labor market. The potential of other effective rehabilitation programs, like the one at Wiltwyck, would be transformed if there were realistic opportunities for steady work in the community for their graduates.

Surely, there is no lack of useful work to be done in American communities. What kinds of work seem most worth emphasizing in an anticrime program? Almost by definition, this question is not well answered in the abstract, since it depends to a great extent on particular local conditions and needs. But in a book on criminal violence it will not be out of place to argue for particular attention to some areas of job creation that might be especially fruitful in crime prevention. I've already suggested one of the most obvious: hiring young people for entry-level positions in public safety, as police auxiliaries, escorts for the elderly, and so on.

One promising effort along these lines has been developed by the Eisenhower Foundation for the Prevention of Violence in Washington, D.C. The foundation gives funding and technical assistance to community organizations that are trying to integrate anticrime programs with local economic development. Neighborhood-based community development corporations create jobs in security services for neighborhood businesses (as well as in housing rehabilitation and other services designed to promote local economic development and stability). The emphasis is on long-term employment for youth—jobs that, as Lynn Curtis of the Eisenhower Foundation puts it, "are not make-work, but hold the promise for careers and a decent, stable personal future" in employment that not only "develops the individual, but also enriches the neighborhood" and helps create a "personal stake in a common turf."

Within the context of a comprehensive local economic program, we could also put substantial numbers of people to work in family-violence shelters, in rape-crisis centers, and as counselors and group leaders in expanded programs for delinquents, abused children, and spouse-batterers. I've already argued that we badly need more of these programs; if they are to work well, we also need more people to work in them, and we need to train them well enough and pay them well enough to do the kind of serious and intensive job that is required to make the programs effective. The same principle, of course, holds for family-support programs as well. In addition, there are other services that we have substantial reason to believe can have a crucial indirect role in reducing criminal violence. We've seen, for example, that the paucity of public services for families helps explain the susceptibility of low-income families to child abuse and delinquency. One obvious answer is more accessible child care, a commodity notoriously scarcer in the United States than in other industrial societies. Why not hire young people as child-care workers and pay them decently to do the job?

Anyone can surely add to this list, or make another. The general point is that hiring people to do work that directly or indirectly aids public safety, promotes the reintegration of offenders, or provides support for family life and child development nicely kills two birds with one stone. We know that we can train even some of the most troubled people in America to do that work. And we know, with reasonable certainly, that if we link the people with the work, many of them will be much less likely to commit serious crimes. Beyond that, we have every reason to believe that their children will benefit even more. For by choosing to create and maintain rewarding occupational roles, we will strengthen the family and intervene positively in what is now too often a downward spiral of pathology and violence. Similarly, by keeping those livelihoods in local communities, we will strengthen networks of kinship, friendship, and social support that play such a crucial role in preventing criminal violence. Over time—though not overnight—we may begin to replace the atomized and brutal character of all too many American communities with a culture of care, cooperation, and productivity.

Finally, a concerted strategy of community full employment will also make it possible to pursue another dimension of an effective anticrime policy: the generous support of *non*employment. I've already argued that what happens to people who are not working has much to do with whether being out of work leads to crime. To be sure, the subsidization of sheer dependency in place of sustaining work has no place in an anticrime policy. But effective cushions against the vagaries of the labor market do. Moreover, there are times when being out of the paid labor force is good not only for those involved but for the larger society as well, and particularly for the generations following; it is past time that this fact be recognized in our social policies.

This is especially true for those who wish to devote more time to child-rearing. Today, of course, that responsibility still falls primarily on women; and the fact that we do not regard what they do outside the paid labor force as legitimate work has a great deal to do with why women who head households are so often poor. Acknowledging that the work of rearing children is a centrally valued social task, and ensuring that no one performing it should be without generous and effective support, would simultaneously accomplish several things that might reduce crime. For one thing, it would substantially diminish the extremes of economic inequality in the United States, by significantly increasing the income available to some of the poorest people in America. This, in turn, would mean that heads of households who are not in the labor force could afford better services for themselves and their children, including improved health care and nutrition. And it could help provide the supportive and unharried environment, undisturbed by the stresses of juggling paid labor and child care, in which nurturing and competent child-rearing can take place. Given what we know about the familial sources of delinquency and child abuse, I think the importance of adequate income supports for families in a strategy of crime prevention is obvious.

How might we do this specifically? Several models exist that seem far more attractive than our current, demeaning welfare system. Many European countries provide some form of family allowances, for example, that offer fixed benefits for the support of each child and are given as a matter of right. Another approach is the Swedish system I've already mentioned, where parents of both sexes are eligible for a shortened workday coupled with guaranteed, no-strings income transfers to raise their income to the full-workday level. Recently, the economist Robert Kuttner has proposed a variant of this approach; that "every parent, male and female, living with a minor child shall be entitled to five years of full-time pay for half-time work." As a result, Kuttner argues, "parents would be able to be less frantically job-obsessed during the years when their children need them most"; the proposal would simultaneously address the larger problem of unemployment by freeing "millions of person-years of jobs for people who are now unemployed."

For our present purposes, the specifics are less important than the general idea—that no child in America should be condemned to grow up in a pinched, deprived, and stressful home simply because of its parents' experience of the vagaries of the labor market. This principle, to be sure, violates the ideological belief that those who do not work in the paid labor force, for whatever reason, ought to suffer. But conservatives will at some point have to decide whether their penchant for righteous suffering outweighs their support for family life; whether enforcing the "spur" of the market should take precedence over defending family cohesion and childhood nurturance. One or the other has to give. Without a simultaneous commitment to full employment, however, adequate income support for those outside the labor market becomes utopian—for it will be widely regarded as both impossibly expensive and likely to draw able-bodied people out of the labor force.

The evidence for the crucial importance of a comprehensive

employment policy in a long-range strategy against crime is abundant. What, then, prevents us from taking that path?

As we've seen, conservatives have downplayed the significance of employment strategies in crime prevention—on the ground partly that unemployment is only peripherally related to crime, and partly that there is not much to be done about the problem in any case. "Job creation," James Q. Wilson writes, "takes a long time, when it can be accomplished at all." But our own experience both during the Depression and since, as well as the evidence from other countries, shows that job creation is neither technically difficult nor particularly time-consuming—especially when compared to Professor Wilson's alternative of choice, the construction of new prisons. (One Depression-era job program, the Civil Works Administration, put over four million people to work at public jobs during 1933–34 alone; Minnesota's new prison at Red Oak took two years to plan and four more to build.)

The issue is not whether we *can* create good jobs—but whether we are willing to. What the conservative argument fails to acknowledge is that America's longstanding difficulty in creating full and stable employment has not been the result of fate or even exclusively of the iron logic of market forces. To an important extent, it reflects deliberate and calculated opposition. Twice in our recent history we have put legislation on the agenda mandating the federal government to guarantee full and equitable employment—in the Employment Act of 1946 and the Humphrey-Hawkins Full Employment and Balanced Growth Act of the seventies. Both times, what began as legislation with an unequivocal commitment to reducing joblessness to low and clearly specified levels wound up either stripped of specific employment targets and a clear role for public job creation or, in the case of Humphrey-Hawkins, consigned (as Robert Lekachman puts it) to the "national memory hole." Both initially called for a strong government role as the "employer of last resort" if the private economy failed to meet specific employment targets for both youth and adults. In each case, these provisions were bitterly—and effectively—fought by private employers. In neither case was this opposition based on the contention that government *could not* create useful jobs—but that it *shouldn't,* because doing so would interfere with the right of private employers to determine the structure of employment and wages.

The resistance, therefore, is only partly because public job creation is expensive. Certainly, all this costs money. But so do the alternatives. We already spend upwards of thirty billion a year on labor-market-related programs, not to mention public assistance. Most of this goes for unemployment compensation—which, like public welfare, represents a reactive response to labor-market failure, not an active expenditure to keep workers employed in the first place. To the expenditure on unemployment insurance and welfare must be added the cost of compensatory programs in mental health and corrections that exist in part to mop up the consequences of worklessness. Our resistance to the public provision of useful work in American communities, then, is more ideological than strictly fiscal. But the burden of proof is on those opposed to such measures to show how paying people good wages to do socially useful work will decisively harm the social fabric or bring the economy to its knees, and why idleness, dependence, and predation are to be preferred to gainful labor.

It is important to realize, moreover, that opposition to a stronger public role in job creation is a minority position. Most Americans believe that the provision of jobs and training will help stop crime, and that if the private economy does not provide them, the government should. A poll sponsored in the early 1980s by the National Council on Crime and Delinquency found that three-fourths of the California public believed that "more jobs" would help stop crime; more recently, a *New York Times* poll found a similar proportion agreeing that more youth job training would "help reduce crime a lot." And for years the polls have found that upwards of seven out of ten Americans think that "government should see that everyone who wants to work has a job."

Hence, insisting on a more serious employment policy for America is far from utopian. What *is* fanciful is the belief that we can enjoy social peace while great numbers of Americans are systematically deprived of a rewarding place in their society. In practice, that belief is already forcing us into a different and dangerous response—one that reinvokes the language of the Social Darwinism of the last century to justify the exclusion and isolation, the marginality and waste of lives, that our pattern of disruptive ecomonic development fosters. If we do not find new ways of including the displaced within the bonds of a supportive and enriching social life, we are likely to see ever more elaborate theories justifying their exclusion and ever harsher efforts to contain the consequences of their anger and demoralization.

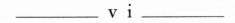

As this chapter has shown, however, this is not the only course available to us. There are alternatives.

"In social argument," John Kenneth Galbraith has warned, "one must never press a strong case too far." I do not wish to overstate the claims for any of the individual programs I've described. But they add up to a fairly imposing list. To recapitulate briefly, they include, first of all, these three changes in the priorities of American criminal justice:

- A stronger response to domestic violence by police and courts.
- Increased attention to innovative police strategies, including more use of foot patrol and hiring youth for auxiliary police work.
- Much greater use of middle-range sanctions, including intensive probation and community service.

In addition, the list of promising alternatives includes greatly expanded public and private support for the following measures:

- Exploration and development of intensive rehabilitation programs for youthful offenders, preferably in the local community or in a supportive institutional milieu.
- Community-based, comprehensive family support programs, emphasizing local participation and respect for cultural diversity.
- Improved family planning services and support for teenaged parents.

- Paid work leaves and more accessible child care for parents with young children, to ease the conflicts between child-rearing and work.
- High-quality early-education programs for disadvantaged children.
- Expanded community dispute-resolution programs.
- Comprehensive, locally based services for victims of domestic violence.
- Intensive job training, perhaps modeled along the lines of supported work, designed to prepare the young and the displaced for stable careers.
- Strong support for equity in pay and conditions, aimed at upgrading the quality of low-paying jobs.
- Substantial, *permanent* public or public-private job creation in local communities, at wages sufficient to support a family breadwinner, especially in areas of clear and pressing social need like public safety, rehabilitation, child care, and family support.
- Universal—and generous—income support for families headed by individuals outside the paid labor force.

Adopting these measures would not eliminate criminal violence from American life. But taken together, they would provide an impressive start toward bringing our crime rates closer, at least, to those of other advanced societies. And it is crucial to understand that these are practical measures, not simply idealistic wishes. Every one of them not only has been tried before, but has *succeeded*—either in this country or in other countries not too different from ours. All of them cost money; some are fairly expensive. But so—as we've seen over and over again—are the alternatives. The difference is that these measures pay off in the long run in a more humane and constructive use of our human resources, the reduction of sheerly wasteful expenditure, the enhancement of community life—and the saving of lives.

But, as is always the case in social policy, it is much easier to describe what *should* be done than to predict whether it *will* be done. Taking this road will not be easy. For it means not only interfering with the prerogatives of those who benefit from our current social and economic arrangements, but also challenging some of the deepest cultural and political tendencies of contemporary American life.

As I've argued earlier, I think it is simplistic and misleading to blame our crime rate on a creeping cultural permissiveness that has eroded the stern but beneficent influence of market values. If anything, the cultural roots of crime in American must be sought in the opposite direction—in the spread throughout so much of our social and economic life of a distorted emphasis on the values of the economic marketplace at the expense of all others.

Seventy years ago, the noted Dutch criminologist Willem Bonger warned that a single-minded emphasis on market values breeds crime because it "weakens the social instincts of man." The United States has always been distinctive, even among other societies based on market capitalism, for the intensity of that emphasis, the absence of countervailing traditions and institutions to mediate and humanize it. That difference, moreover, has intensified in the political climate of the past decade. This affects the whole tenor of social life in America; its impact on crime and violence is hard to measure, but the connection is difficult to ignore. In a society that values its people for what they can acquire rather than what they can contribute and that encourages predatory and manipulative behavior in the service of immediate gain as the guiding principle of economic life, we should not be altogether surprised if more explosive forms of the same ethos are expressed among the most deprived. As R. H. Tawney once wrote, the quality in our social life "which causes it to demoralize a few by excessive riches is also the quality which causes it to demoralize many by excessive poverty."

But I do not believe that this is the *only* direction in which the American political culture is moving. If there has been a resurgence of the harsh and irresponsible themes of a resuscitated Social Darwinism, there has also been a counterdevelopment, perhaps less visible, but nonetheless crucially significant. It involves a growing understanding of the importance of maintaining the integrity of communal life, of providing cooperatively for human needs, and of integrating citizens into membership in a productive and purposive community.

No one, at this point, can predict the outcome of the struggle between these views of the American purpose. But it is profoundly important to engage in that struggle, for what we do in the coming years will have decisive consequences for the future character of American social life, and not least for the security of our communities. Given what we've seen of the evidence on the roots of criminal violence, it is disturbingly clear that much of the thrust of our recent social policy bodes ill for the possibilities of enduring social peace.

If we wanted to sketch a hypothetical portrait of an especially violent society, it would surely contain these elements: It would separate large numbers of people, especially the young, from the kind of work that could include them securely in community life. It would encourage policies of economic development and income distribution that sharply increased inequalities between sectors of the population. It would rapidly shift vast amounts of capital from place to place without regard for the impact on local communities, causing massive movements of population away from family and neighborhood supports in search of livelihood. It would avoid providing new mechanisms of care and support for those uprooted, perhaps in the name of preserving incentives to work and paring government spending. It would promote a culture of intense interpersonal competition and spur its citizens to a level of material consumption many could not lawfully sustain.

Does that model fit any societies in the real world? I think it does. It closely resembles some of the developing countries of the Third World—Brazil, the Philippines, parts of Mexico—which have among the worst rates of criminal violence in the world. But we don't have to go that far: It looks uncomfortably like the United States in the eighties—and like one version of our own future.

NOTES

CHAPTER I: RETHINKING CRIMINAL VIOLENCE

PAGE

4   Incidents: "Two Cars Attacked by Marauders on a U.S. Highway," San Francisco *Chronicle,* December 28, 1983; "Woman Saved from Mob," San Francisco *Chronicle,* September 20, 1983; "New York City Is Re-examining Use of Central Park After Thefts," New York *Times,* April 30, 1985; "Church Bandit Subdued by Worshipers, Dies," San Francisco *Chronicle,* January 17, 1984; "Armed Intruder Robs Inmate in Prison," San Francisco *Chronicle,* March 27, 1984; "I'm from Connecticut but I Love New York," *Newsweek,* September 19, 1983; "Death Toll Rises to 5 in Shooting at L.A. Party," San Jose *Mercury-News,* October 14, 1984; "Burglars Hit Top L.A. Cop—Again," San Francisco *Chronicle,* October 15, 1983.

4 – 5   Vigilante survey: Gallup/*Newsweek* poll, cited in San Francisco *Chronicle,* March 4, 1985. In addition to the 57 percent "support" for Mr. Goetz's action, more than 25 percent of respondents said they would use deadly force to protect themselves in similar situations; about half kept a gun or other weapon to defend themselves against crime.

5   "Embattled population": Roger Starr, "Crime: How It Destroys, What Can Be Done." *New York Times Magazine,* January 27, 1985, p. 19.

5   Homicide risks: World Health Organization data for 1976–1981, in U.S. Bureau of the Census, *Statistical Abstract of the United States, 1984* (Washington, D.C., 1983), p. 181 (hereafter cited as *Statistical Abstract*).

5   California comparisons: calculated from State of California, Office of Criminal Justice Planning, *Crime in California, 1971–1981* (Sacramento, 1983), p. A-6; and *Statistical Abstract,* p. 181. The frontier explanation is also of little help in explaining why violent crime in former "frontier" areas has often grown so much *worse* in recent years, as we move farther from frontier times—why the 1983 murder rate in Dallas was half again that of 1959, and in Houston double. Nor, for that matter, does it explain why some of the cities of the old "Wild West" have quite low levels of violence today—like Laramie, Wyoming, which had no murders in 1983. Finally,

the "old frontier" turns out on close inspection to have been less violent than we've traditionally believed. "Serious juvenile offenses, crimes against the elderly and weak, rape, robbery, burglary and theft were either nonexistent or of little significance" in a California frontier community in the nineteenth century studied by Roger D. McGrath; see *Gunfighters, Highwaymen, and Vigilantes: Violence on the Frontier* (Berkeley: University of California Press, 1984).

5 – 6   Germany–U.S. comparisons: Raymond Teske and Harald Arnold, "Comparison of the Criminal Statistics of the United States and the Federal Republic of Germany," *Journal of Criminal Justice* 10 (1982).

6   Home Office study: Mike Hough and Pat Mayhew, *The British Crime Survey: First Report* (London: Her Majesty's Stationery Office, 1983), pp. 16–21. U.S. figures from U.S. Bureau of Justice Statistics, *Criminal Victimization in the United States, 1973–82 Trends* (Washington, D.C.: U.S. Department of Justice, 1983), p. 2. The difference in rate between the two countries is actually understated in this comparison, since the American sample includes everyone over twelve and hence spreads the rate over a less intensively victimized population.

6   Other countries: see, for example, Ragnar Hauge and Preben Wolf, "Criminal Violence in Three Scandinavian Countries," *Scandinavian Studies in Criminology* 5 (1974); Marshall B. Clinard, *Cities with Little Crime* (Cambridge: Cambridge University Press, 1978); and J. J. M. van Dijk, et al., *The Burden of Crime on Dutch Society* (The Hague: Ministry of Justice Research and Documentation Center, 1980).

6   Third World rates: see, for example, Dane Archer et al., "Cities and Homicide: A New Look at an Old Paradox," *Comparative Studies in Sociology* 1 (1978).

6 – 7   Reported crime rates: calculated from Neil Alan Weiner and Marvin B. Wolfgang, "Violent Crime in America, 1969–1982," in *American Violence and Public Policy*, ed. Lynn A. Curtis (New Haven, Conn.: Yale University Press, 1985), p. 23; and Federal Bureau of Investigation, *Uniform Crime Reports, 1983* (Washington, D.C.: U.S. Government Printing Office, 1984), p. 43 (hereafter cited as *Uniform Crime Reports*).

6 – 7   Victim study rates: U.S. Bureau of Justice Statistics, *Criminal Victimization 1983* (Washington, D.C.: U.S. Department of Justice, 1984), p. 3.

7   State figures: *Uniform Crime Reports, 1983*, pp. 46–47. Detroit and East St. Louis rates: *Uniform Crime Reports, 1981*, pp. 69–78; and *Uniform Crime Reports, 1983*, pp. 75, 85. Oakland rates: data from state attorney general's office, cited San Francisco *Chronicle*, March 6, 1985. In California as a whole, homicide rose about 4 percent during 1984.

7 – 8   Prison inmates: U.S. Department of Justice data, cited in New York *Times*, August 28, 1984. Jail population: U.S. Bureau of Justice Statistics,

Jail Inmates, 1982 (Washington, D.C.: U.S. Department of Justice, 1983). On juvenile detention populations, see Thomas R. Hughes and Nicholas A. Reuterman, "Juvenile Detention Facilities: Summary Report of a Second National Survey," *Juvenile and Family Court Journal* 33, no. 4 (1982). On military prisons: between 1978 and 1981 alone, the combined population of Army, Navy, Air Force, and Marine Corps prisons rose by 49 percent. Philip B. Taft, "Corrections, Military Style," *Corrections* 7, no. 6 (1981).

8   Violence Commission quotation: National Commission on the Causes and Prevention of Violence, *To Establish Justice, to Ensure Domestic Tranquility: Final Report* (Washington, D.C.: U.S. Government Printing Office, 1969), pp. 44–45.

8   Los Angeles armored personnel carrier: San Francisco *Chronicle*, January 1985.

8 – 9   Murphy quotation: New York *Times*, April 23, 1984.

9   Electronic security: Milton Moskowitz, "Crime Control and Gambling Look Good," San Francisco *Chronicle*, May 30, 1984. This article finds booming investment opportunities in firms selling electronic security devices.

9   Youth population: calculated from *Statistical Abstract*, 1984, p. 31, and U.S. Bureau of the Census, *Estimates of the Population of the United States, by Age, Sex, and Race, 1980–83* (Washington, D.C.: U.S. Government Printing Office, 1984).

9 – 10   Prescriptions—Corporal punishment: Edward Wynne, letter in *Working Papers*, September–October 1982, p. 6. Penal colonies: Tom J. Farer, "Innovating Policies," *Society*, July–August 1982; Sweaty palms: research proposal submitted to the U.S. Department of Justice, cited in Jack Anderson, "Sweaty Palms and Crime," San Francisco *Chronicle*, March 6, 1984. "Uplift": James Q. Wilson, "Thinking About Crime," *Atlantic*, September 1983, p. 88.

10   *Newsweek:* "The Epidemic of Violent Crime," March 23, 1981.

10   Task force: Attorney General's Task Force on Violent Crime, *Final Report* (Washington, D.C.: U.S. Government Printing Office, 1981), p. 2 (hereafter cited as *Final Report*).

11 – 12   Murphy quotation: New York *Times*, April 23, 1984.

12   "Six dollars' worth of meat": an Atlantic City, N.J., case, cited in San Francisco *Chronicle*, March 12, 1984.

15   Violence Commission quotation: *Final Report*, p. 46.

15 "Warring on Poverty": cited in *Final Report,* p. 55.

19 Tawney quotation: R. H. Tawney, *The Acquisitive Society* (New York: Harcourt, Brace & World, 1948), p. 4.

CHAPTER 2: THE CONSERVATIVE MODEL

22 Wilson quotation: James Q. Wilson, *Thinking About Crime* (New York: Random House, 1975), p. xv.

23 "Wicked people exist": Wilson, *Thinking About Crime,* p. 235.

24 Wilson quotation: *Thinking About Crime,* p. xiii.

24 "Several countries": see Marshall B. Clinard, *Cities with Little Crime* (Cambridge: Cambridge University Press, 1978); David Downes, "The Origins and Consequences of Dutch Penal Policy Since 1945," *British Journal of Criminology* 22, no. 4 (October 1982); Robert J. Smith, *Japanese Society: Tradition, Self, and the Social Order* (Cambridge: Cambridge University Press, 1983); and Luis Salas, *Social Control and Deviance in Cuba* (New York: Praeger, 1979).

24 Denmark and Norway: Hauge and Wolf, "Criminal Victimization in Three Scandinavian Countries." A more recent Swedish study similarly found little change in criminality among cohorts of Swedish youth who entered the most crime-prone age groups between the late sixties and the late seventies. "The most striking aspect" of this study, the researchers conclude, "is the *stability* of criminal activity among the cohorts." Hans von Hofer, Leif Lenke, and Ulf Thorsson, "Criminality Among Thirteen Swedish Birth Cohorts," *British Journal of Criminology* 23, no.3 (July 1983).

25 "Twenty for every Dane": calculated from *Statistical Abstract, 1980,* p. 187.

25 "Sober view of man": *Thinking About Crime,* p. 223.

25 – 26 Wilson quotation: "Crime and American Culture," *Public Interest,* Winter 1983, pp. 38–39.

26 Becker quotation: cited in James Thompson et al., *Employment and Crime: A Review of Theories and Research* (Washington, D.C.: National Institute of Justice, 1981), pp. 31–32.

26 Tullock quotation: Gordon Tullock, "Does Punishment Deter Crime?" *Public Interest,* Summer 1974, p. 105.

26 – 27 Van den Haag quotations: Ernest van den Haag, "Could Successful Rehabilitation Reduce the Crime Rate?" *Journal of Criminal Law and Criminology* 73 no. 3 (Fall 1982): 1025, 1035.

27 Vera quotation: Thompson et al., *Employment and Crime,* p. 37.

PAGE

28 Wall Street *Journal:* quoted in Bureau of Justice Statistics Newsletter, February 1983, p. 14.

28 – 29 International incarceration rates: Eugene Doleschal and Anne New-ton, *International Rates of Imprisonment* (Hackensack, N.J.: National Council on Crime and Delinquency, 1981).

29 Dutch sentences: Downes, "Dutch Penal Policy," pp. 330–334; see also D. W. Steenhuis et al., "The Penal Climate in the Netherlands: Sunny or Cloudy?" *British Journal of Criminology* 23, no. 1 (January 1983). Ameri-can sentences: U.S. Bureau of Justice Statistics, *Prison Admissions and Releases, 1981* (Washington, D.C.: Department of Justice, 1984). Average time served for robbery in the early eighties was 61.5 months in Maryland, 40.8 in North Carolina, and 33.5 in Pennsylvania; these figures, moreover, do not include the time prisoners spent in local jails before sentencing—which, for robbers, averaged nearly 8 months in Illinois. Herbert Koppel, *Time Served in Prison* (Washington, D.C.: U.S. Bureau of Justice Statis-tics, 1984).

29 – 30 Wilson quotation: James Q. Wilson, "Dealing with the High-Rate Offender," *Public Interest,* Fall 1982, p. 68.

30 – 31 Wolpin study: Kenneth I. Wolpin, "An Economic Analysis of Crime and Punishment in England and Wales, 1894–1967," *Journal of Political Economy* 86, no. 5 (October 1975).

31 Second Wolpin study: "A Time-Series Cross-Sectional Analysis of Inter-national Variations in Crime and Punishment," *Review of Economics and Statistics* 62, no. 3 (August 1980).

32 Incarceration figures: *Statistical Abstract, 1982–83,* p. 193; and Bureau of Justice Statistics communication.

33 – 34 New York study: Correctional Association of New York, *The Prison Population Explosion in New York State: A Study of Its Causes and Conse-quences with Recommendations for Change* (New York, 1982), pp. 10–118.

35 – 36 Wilson quotation: *Thinking About Crime,* p. 236. "Ethos of self-expression": James Q. Wilson, "Thinking About Crime," *Atlantic,* Sep-tember 1983, p. 88.

36 – 40 "Moral uplift": the following is based on Wilson, "Crime and American Culture," pp. 32–38.

41 American versus English students: H. Wesley Perkins and James L. Spates, "American and English Student Values," in *Comparative Social Research,* vol. 5, ed. Richard F. Tomasson (Greenwich, Conn.: JAI Press, 1982), p. 251.

NOTES

41 Dutch tolerance: see, for example, Netherlands Justice Ministry, "Research on Public Attitudes Toward Crime Policy in Holland" (The Hague, 1981), which finds most Dutch citizens support their country's generally mild penal policies and favor preventive rather than repressive strategies of crime control.

41 Death penalty: see David Bruck, "Decisions of Death," in *Crisis in American Institutions*, 6th ed., ed. Jerome H. Skolnick and Elliott Currie (Boston: Little, Brown & Co., 1985).

41 Hirschi quotations: "Crime and Family Policy," *Journal of Contemporary Studies* 6, no. 1 (Winter 1983): 10, 13. Corporal punishment support: Joan Senzek Solheim, "A Cross-Cultural Examination of the Use of Corporal Punishment on Children," *Child Abuse and Neglect* 6 (1982): 147–154; Teuvo Peltoniemi, "Child Abuse and Physical Punishment of Children in Finland," *Child Abuse and Neglect* 7 (1983): 33–36; and Elaine Arnold, "The Use of Corporal Punishment in Child Rearing in the West Indies," *Child Abuse and Neglect* 6 (1982): 141–145.

42 – 43 Wynne quotations: Edward A. Wynne, "What Are the Courts Doing to Our Children?" *Public Interest*, Summer 1981.

43 – 44 Toby article: Jackson Toby, "Crime in American Public Schools," *Public Interest*, Winter 1980.

44 Violent outside the school: see Joan McDermott, "Crime in the School and in the Community: Offenders, Victims, and Fearful Youths," *Crime and Delinquency*, April 1983.

44 – 45 School characteristics: Michael Rutter, *Changing Youth in a Changing Society* (Cambridge: Harvard University Press, 1980), pp. 168–169; Richard A. Kulka et al., "Aggression, Deviance, and Personality Adaptation as Antecedents and Consequences of Alienation and Involvement in High School," *Journal of Youth and Adolescence* 11, no. 3 (June 1982): 273.

45 "On the streets with nothing to do": McDermott, "Crime in the School," p. 281.

45 – 47 Bayley article: David H. Bayley, "Learning About Crime: The Japanese Experience," *Public Interest*, Summer 1976, p. 68.

46 Smith quotations: *Japanese Society*, pp. 6, 126–127.

48 Steinfels quotations: Peter Steinfels, *The Neoconservatives* (New York: Simon & Schuster, 1980), pp. 92, 246.

PAGE

49   Bell quotation: Daniel Bell, "The Cultural Contradictions of Capitalism," in *Capitalism Today*, ed. Daniel Bell and Irving Kristol (New York: New American Library, 1971), p. 53.

CHAPTER 3: THE LIMITS OF IMPRISONMENT

55   "Rational planning is the exception": see especially Edna Erez, "Planning of Crime and the Criminal Career: Official and Hidden Offenses," *Journal of Criminal Law and Criminology* 71, no. 11 (Spring 1980). Interviewing Philadelphia delinquents now in their twenties, Erez found that only 21 percent of all offenses had been planned rather than essentially "impulsive," according to the respondents; the "impulsive" offenders, moreover, committed twice as many crimes as the "planners." Other research supports this point. A Rand Corporation survey of California prison inmates found that their perceptions of the certainty of arrest had little bearing on the amount of crime they committed; Mark A. Peterson, Harriet B. Braiker, and Suzanne Polich, *Doing Crime: A Study of California Prison Inmates* (Washington, D.C.: National Institute of Justice, 1980), p. xii.

55   "Influence of alcohol or drugs": almost a third of state prison inmates reported having had four or more ounces of alcohol just before committing the crime that put them in prison. The use of alcohol was especially heavy among repeat offenders and inmates convicted of rape, assault, and burglary; U.S. Bureau of Justice Statistics, *Prisoners and Alcohol* (Washington, D.C., 1983). The same survey found that a third of inmates were under the influence of some illegal drug while committing the crime for which they'd most recently been convicted; drug use was particularly common among robbers, burglars, and repeat offenders. *Justice Assistance News*, April 1983.

56   Deterrence quotations: Charles Tittle, *Sanctions and Social Deviance* (New York: Praeger, 1980), p. 4; Alfred Blumstein, Jacqueline Cohen, and Daniel Nagin, eds., *Deterrence and Incapacitation: Estimating the Effects of Criminal Sanctions on Crime Rates* (Washington, D.C.: National Academy of Sciences, 1978), p. 9; and Jack P. Gibbs, *Norms, Deviance, and Social Control* (New York: Elsevier, 1981), p. 143.

56 – 57   Tittle quotation: *Sanctions and Social Deviance*, p. 320. Paternoster et al. quotation: Raymond Paternoster, Linda Saltzman, Gordon Waldo, and Theodore Chiricos, "Perceived Risk and Social Control: Do Sanctions Really Deter?" *Law and Society Review* 17, no. 3 (1983): 478. A good general review of recent deterrence research is Sheldon Ekland-Olson, William Kelly, and Michael Supancic, "Sanction Severity, Feedback, and Deterrence," in *Evaluating Performance of Criminal Justice Agencies*, ed. Gordon P. Whitaker and Charles David Phillips (Beverly Hills: Sage Publications, 1983), pp. 129–164.

PAGE

57 Tittle quotation: *Sanctions and Social Deviance,* p. 320. Drug dealers: Ekland-Olson et al., "Sanction Severity," p. 155.

57 Shannon study: Lyle W. Shannon, *Assessing the Relationship of Adult Criminal Careers to Juvenile Careers: A Summary* (Washington, D.C.: U.S. Office of Juvenile Justice and Delinquency Prevention, 1982), p. 10.

57 "Unduly neglected implications for social policy": it should be noted that the tendency of conservative writers in particular to support formal deterrence—despite the paucity of supporting evidence—seems especially peculiar given the traditional emphasis in conservative thought on the integrative role of smaller-scale social institutions in achieving social order. In theory, that emphasis ought to lead neoconservatives to promote sanctions at the level of family and local community. With some exceptions (to be taken up in Chapter 7), many conservatives instead push for precisely those sanctions that most decisively separate individuals from their surrounding communities and lodge the most power in the hands of that arch-villain of conservative rhetoric, the state.

58 – 59 Bowker study: Lee H. Bowker, "Crime and the Use of Prisons in the United States: A Time-Series Analysis," *Crime and Delinquency,* April 1981, p. 211.

59 Biles study: David Biles, "Crime and Imprisonment: A Two-Decade Comparison Between England and Wales and Australia," *British Journal of Criminology* 23, no. 2 (April 1983): quotation at 171.

59 Econometric studies: see especially Isaac Ehrlich, "Participation in Illegitimate Activities: A Theoretical and Empirical Investigation," *Journal of Political Economy* 81, no. 3 (May–June 1973). For an excellent discussion of the difficulties of this research generally, see Thompson et al., *Employment and Crime,* chap. 2.

59 – 60 Biles study: David Biles, "Crime and the Use of Prisons," *Federal Probation* 43, no.2 (1979).

60 – 61 Problems in "cross-sectional" research: for discussion, see especially Blumstein et al., *Deterrence and Incapacitation;* and Alfred Blumstein, "Research on Sentencing," *Justice System Journal* 7, no. 3 (1982): 314–315.

61 – 63 Drug Law findings: Kenneth Carlson, *Mandatory Sentencing: The Experience of Two States* (Washington, D.C.: National Institute of Justice, 1982); and Prison Association of New York, *The Prison Population Explosion in New York State* (New York, 1982), pp. 59, 114–119.

63 Carlson quotation: *Mandatory Sentencing,* p. 8.

PAGE

64 – 65   "Tough law": Milton Heumann, Colin Loftin, and David McDowall, "Federal Firearms Policy and Mandatory Sentencing," *Journal of
Criminal Law and Criminology* 73, no.3 (Fall 1982): 1055.

66   Rand survey: Joan Petersilia, Peter Greenwood, and Marvin Lavin, *Crim-
inal Careers of Habitual Felons* (Washington, D.C.: National Institute of
Law Enforcement and Criminal Justice, 1978), p. 38. For similar findings,
see Peter Greenwood, "The Violent Offender in the Criminal Justice
System," in *Criminal Violence*, ed. Marvin Wolfgang and Neil Alan
Weiner (Beverly Hills: Sage Publications, 1982), pp. 325–330.

66   "Critics argue": for example, Edwin Meese, "Improving the Criminal
Justice System," *Christian Science Monitor*, December 2, 1982.

66 – 67   Studies of exclusionary rule: cited in Thomas Y. Davies, "A Hard
Look at What We Know (and Still Need to Learn) About the 'Costs' of
the Exclusionary Rule," *American Bar Foundation Research Journal* (Summer 1983): 611–624. Cf. Shirley Melnicoe et al., *The Effects of the Exclusionary Rule: A Study in California* (Washington, D.C.: National Institute of
Justice, 1982).

67   Vera study: Vera Institute of Justice, *Felony Arrests: Their Prosecution and
Disposition in New York City's Courts* (New York: Vera Institute, 1977).
See also Hans Zeisel, *The Limits of Law Enforcement* (Chicago: University
of Chicago Press, 1982).

67   "Rational and consistent guidelines": Joan E. Jacoby et al., *Prosecutorial
Decisionmaking: A National Study* (Washington, D.C.: National Institute
of Justice, 1982).

67   "Increase the courts' efficiency": for example, though the evidence so far
is mixed, many feel that the "Career Criminal" programs inaugurated in
recent years, which provide greater resources to prosecutors to try the
most hardened repeat offenders, have made a difference in conviction rates
—and hence, presumably, to deterrence. For a less sanguine evaluation,
see E. Chelimsky and J. Damaan, *Career Criminal Program National Evaluation, Final Report* (Washington, D.C.: National Institute of Justice,
1981); for a positive one, California Office of Criminal Justice Planning,
*Career Criminal Prosecution Program: Second Annual Report to the Legisla-
ture* (Sacramento: Office of Criminal Justice Planning, 1980).

68   Drunken driving evidence: see, for example, the review in Ekland-Olson
et al., "Sanction Severity," p. 139; Harold L. Votey, "Control of Drunken
Driving Accidents in Norway," *Journal of Criminal Justice* 11, no.2 (1983);
and H. Laurence Ross, "Interrupted Time Series Studies of Deterrence
of Drinking and Driving," in *Deterrence Reconsidered*, ed. John Hagan
(Beverly Hills: Sage Publications, 1982).

68   Vera quotation: *Felony Arrests*, p. 134.

68   Chances of arrest: Petersilia et al., *Criminal Careers*, pp. 36–37.

69   Clearance rates: see especially John Burrows and Roger Tarling, *Clearing Up Crime* (London: Home Office Research Unit, 1982); also John M. Stevens and Brian Stipak, "Factors Associated with Police Apprehension Productivity," *Journal of Police Science and Administration* 10, no. 1 (1982). Note that the crucial relation of apprehension to deterrence is well understood by offenders themselves. The Rand survey of California repeaters found that half those inmates said that *nothing* could deter them from further crimes after release; the remaining half reported that certainty of apprehension, not the threat of longer sentences, would have the most deterrent influence. As the researchers note, this "reflects their awareness of a fairly high probability of conviction and incarceration once arrested." Petersilia et al., *Criminal Careers*, p. xiii.

70   Department of Justice recidivism data: cited New York *Times*, December 3, 1984.

70   Youth Authority figures: Rudy Hapaanen and Carl F. Jesness, *Early Identification of the Chronic Offender* (Sacramento: California Youth Authority, 1982), pp. iii, 35.

70   Ball figures: John C. Ball et al., "Lifetime Criminality of Heroin Addicts in the United States," *Journal of Drug Issues* 12, no.3 (Fall 1982).

71   Chaiken quotation: Jan M. Chaiken and Marcia R. Chaiken, *Varieties of Criminal Behavior: Summary and Policy Implications* (Santa Monica, Calif.: Rand Corporation, 1982), p. 21.

71   "High rate" offender histories: Peter Greenwood and Allan Abrahamse, *Selective Incapacitation* (Santa Monica, Calif.: Rand Corporation, 1982), pp. xv, xvi.

71   Violence Commission findings: National Commission on the Causes and Prevention of Violence, *Crimes of Violence*, vol. 13 (Washington D.C.: U.S. Government Printing Office, 1969), pp. 561–567. More recent evidence is abundant. See, for example, Petersilia et al., *Criminal Careers*, p. 58.

71   Myers study: Samuel L. Myers, Jr., "The Incidence of Justice," in *The Costs of Crime*, ed. Charles M. Gray (Beverly Hills: Sage Publications, 1979), especially p. 76. Berecochea and Jaman study: John E. Berecochea and Dorothy R. Jaman, *Time Served in Prison and Parole Outcome: An Experimental Study* (Sacramento: California Department of Corrections, 1981).

72 – 73   Murray and Cox study: Charles A. Murray and Louis A. Cox, *Beyond Probation: Juvenile Corrections and the Chronic Offender* (Beverly Hills: Sage Publications, 1979).

73 "Get-tough side": Kevin Krajick, "A Blow for the 'Get Tough' Side," *Corrections*, September 1978.

73 – 74 "Critics pointed out": Michael Maltz, Andrew Gordon, David McDowall, and Richard McCleary, "An Artifact in Pre-test–Post-test Designs: How It Can Make Delinquency Programs Look Effective," *Evaluation Review* 4, no. 2 (April 1980).

74 "Two years after . . . discharge": Murray and Cox, *Beyond Probation*, pp. 118–119.

74 "Three months or less": Murray and Cox, *Beyond Probation*, p. 130. It should be noted that, like most investigators, Murray and Cox found no evidence to suggest that *longer* prison sentences were more effective deterrents than shorter ones.

76 Commission quotation: President's Commission on Law Enforcement and Administration of Justice, *The Challenge of Crime in a Free Society* (Washington D.C.: U.S. Government Printing Office, 1967), p. 159.

77 Shannon quotation: Shannon, *Assessing the Relationship*, p. 8.

77 – 78 Wolfgang study: Marvin Wolfgang, Robert M. Figlio, and Thorsten Sellin, *Delinquency in a Birth Cohort* (Chicago: University of Chicago Press, 1972), p. 252.

78 Dinitz/Conrad quotation: Simon Dinitz and John P. Conrad, "The Dangerous Two Per Cent," in *Critical Issues in Juvenile Delinquency*, ed. David Shichor and Delos H. Kelly (Lexington, Mass.: Lexington Books, 1980), p. 149.

78 "With all else controlled": John P. Conrad, "The Quandary of Dangerousness," *British Journal of Criminology* 22, no.3 (July 1982): 261. Similarly, controlling for personal characteristics of Colorado offenders, their criminal histories, and the nature of the offense, Scott Menard and Herbert Covey found that offenders sentenced to prison were more likely to be rearrested than those sentenced to a community-based correctional institution, who in turn were more likely to be rearrested than those given probation. "Community Alternatives and Rearrest in Colorado," *Criminal Justice and Behavior* 10, no.1 (1983).

79 "As many crimes as it prevents": Charles David Phillips, Bruce W. McCleary, and Simon Dinitz, "The Special Deterrent Effect of Incarceration," in Whitaker and Phillips, *Evaluating Performance of Criminal Justice Agencies*, p. 261.

80 West study: Donald West, *Delinquency: Its Roots, Careers, and Prospects* (Cambridge: Harvard University Press, 1982), pp. 104–108.

81 "What the boy didn't know": Dinitz and Conrad, "Dangerous Two Per Cent," p. 151.

PAGE

81   "Myriad . . . disabilities": in a recent study of the impact of incarceration on Mexican-American men in California, Joan Moore writes that the institutional forces of the prison create "dependency, uncertainty, and the loss of important social skills (such as vocabulary) and a style that permits self-confident communication with squares and particularly with women. Convicts are trained into an incapacity to deal with the routines of normal street life and with real money. . . ." *Homeboys* (New York: Free Press, 1977), p. 108.

81   Crime in prison: during 1981, eighty-eight inmates and seven staff members were killed by inmates in the state and federal prison systems, according to the journal *Corrections Compendium* (cited in *Criminal Justice Abstracts*, September 1983, p. 7). The inmate deaths alone yield a murder rate of about 27 per 100,000, a rate that ranked the prisons above every metropolitan area in the United States but one (Miami) in the risk of death by homicide in that year.

82   "Untested assumptions": Blumstein, Cohen, and Nagin, *Deterrence and Incapacitation*, p. 9.

82   Van den Haag quotation: "Successful Rehabilitation," p. 1025. Van den Haag's main target in this article is the effectiveness of rehabilitation, but the point applies equally well to incapacitation. See also Isaac Ehrlich, "On the Usefulness of Controlling Individuals," *American Economic Review* 71 (1981).

82   "Do not require a license": van den Haag, "Successful Rehabilitation," p. 1026.

83   Zimring argument: "Kids, Groups, and Crime: Some Implications of a Well-Known Secret," *Journal of Criminal Law and Criminology* 72, no.3 (Fall 1981): 876–877.

84   "10 percent or even less": Marvin Wolfgang, testimony in U.S. Congress, Senate Committee on the Judiciary, Subcommittee on Juvenile Justice, *Violent Juvenile Crime*, Hearings, 97th Cong., 1st sess., July 1981, p. 132 (hereafter cited as "Testimony").

84   Second Philadelphia study: cited in Wolfgang, "Testimony," p. 133.

84   Shannon findings: *Assessing the Relationship*, p. 3.

86   Youth Authority findings: California Youth Authority, *Delinquency in a Sacramento Birth Cohort* (Sacramento: California Youth Authority, 1981), pp. 10–11.

86 – 87   Blumstein-Graddy study: Alfred Blumstein and Elizabeth Graddy, "Prevalence and Recidivism in Index Arrests: A Feedback Model," *Law and Society Review* 16, no.2 (1981–82): 267–287.

PAGE

87 – 88   Van Dine et al. study: Stephan van Dine, Simon Dinitz, and John Conrad, "The Incapacitation of the Dangerous Offender: A Statistical Experiment," *Journal of Research in Crime and Delinquency* 14, no. 1 (January 1977). A Rand Corporation study using data from Denver calculated that a five-year mandatory sentence for any violent felony would cut the violent crime rate by 6 percent; imposing that sentence for *any* felony, violent or not, would cut it by 31 percent—while increasing the prison population by 450 percent. Greenwood, "Violent Offender," p. 339.

88   Conrad quotation: "Quandary of Dangerousness," p. 262. The Ohio findings generally fit those of several other studies in the United States and abroad. The NAS panel estimated that to achieve a 10 percent reduction in index crimes, California would have to increase its prison population by 157 percent, New York by 263 percent, and Massachusetts by 310 percent. A British Home Office Study comes to broadly similar conclusions: Stephen Brody and Roger Tarling, *Taking Offenders Out of Circulation* (London: Home Office, 1980).

90   Mullen quotations: Joan Mullen et al., *American Prisons and Jails, Vol. 1: Summary and Policy Implications* (Washington, D.C.: National Institute of Justice, 1978), pp. 131, 135.

90   Lower budget level: *Statistical Abstract, 1982–83*, p. 465.

91   Minority community impact: see Scott Christianson, "Our Black Prisons," *Crime and Delinquency* 27, no.3 (July 1981), which shows that the problem is worse in some states than others; in Michigan in 1978, 1.7 out of every 100 black men were in prison. Joan Moore estimates that, well *before* the prison "boom" of the seventies, one in five Los Angeles barrio men had experienced prison. *Homeboys*, p. 98.

92   For a comprehensive general discussion of the difficulties of predicting dangerousness, see Jean Floud and Warren Young, *Dangerousness and Criminal Justice* (London: William Heinemann, 1981), app. C.

92   Rand research: Greenwood and Abrahamse, *Selective Incapacitation*.

92   Supporters and critics: cf. the exchange between Greenwood and Andrew von Hirsch, NIJ *Reports* (Washington, D.C.: National Institute of Justice, January 1984). Interestingly, some of the strongest reservations have come from other Rand researchers: "using the models to identify violent predators," write Jan and Marcia Chaiken, "can potentially result in real injustice. In our opinion, the models would make too many false identifications." *Varieties of Criminal Behavior*, p. 27.

93   Greenwood-Abrahamse quotation: *Selective Incapacitation*, p. xv.

93   Texas "payoff": Greenwood and Abrahamse, *Selective Incapacitation*, p. xix; and Teske and Arnold, "Comparison of the Criminal Statistics of the United States and the Federal Republic of Germany," p. 368.

93 Courts try to predict behavior: guidelines for parole in the federal prison system, for example, include several characteristics of offenders—including prior convictions, previous prison terms, and drug history—that overlap with the Rand criteria.

94 Greenwood-Abrahamse quotation: *Selective Incapacitation*, p. xx.

94 Predictors of high-rate offending: Greenwood and Abrahamse, *Selective Incapacitation*, p. xvi.

95 "Retrospective" prediction: see the similar comments in Blumstein, "Research on Sentencing," p. 318.

95 – 97 CYA quotations: Hapaanen and Jesness, *Early Identification*, pp. 126–131.

98 "Rehabilitation has not worked": Greenwood and Abrahamse, *Selective Incapacitation*, p. 2. This position is especially curious given the evidence that (as we'll see in Chapter 4) it is precisely the kind of offenders to whom selective incapacitation is mainly addressed—drug-abusing property criminals—who may be most amenable to rehabilitative programs.

99 Monahan quotation: John Monahan, "The Prediction of Violent Behavior: Toward a Second Generation of Theory and Policy," *American Journal of Psychiatry* 141, no. 1 (January 1984).

100 "Shouldn't try to change them": compare the response of Murray and Cox to their own findings that fewer than one in four of their sample of incarcerated youths lived with both natural parents, well under half had a parent regularly employed in a legitimate job, and fewer than 2 percent had no serious school-related problems. Murray and Cox had "no argument" with the premise that the causes of crime were embedded in these aspects of the personal histories and "socioeconomic environment" of the youths; what they objected to was the "much more dubious proposition" that "to cure the problem, one must remove the cause." "It is permitted," they wrote, "that solutions not be derived from causes. It is also permitted that solutions be simpler than causes." *Beyond Probation*, p. 174.

CHAPTER 4: UNDERSTANDING CRIME: WORK AND WELFARE

104 Hakluyt quotation: in Carroll D. Wright, "Labor, Pauperism, and Crime," *Proceedings of the 5th Annual Conference of Charities* (Boston, 1878), pp. 154–155.

104 Wright quotation: "Labor, Pauperism, and Crime," p. 161.

105 Inmate statistics: U.S. Bureau of Justice Statistics, *Sourcebook of Criminal Justice Statistics* (Washington, D.C.: U.S. Government Printing Office, 1982), p. 394.

PAGE

105 Rand study: Joan Petersilia et al., *Criminal Careers of Habitual Felons* (Santa Monica, Calif.: Rand, 1978), pp. 86–89.

105 High-rate offenders: Greenwood and Abrahamse, *Selective Incapacitation.*

106 Wilson quotation: "Thinking About Crime" (1983): 81.

107 Sellin quotation: Thorsten Sellin, *Research Memorandum on Crime in the Depression* (New York: Social Science Research Council, 1937), p. 60.

107 Thomas, Winslow studies: cited in Sellin, p. 62.

107 – 108 Brenner research: M. Harvey Brenner, *Estimating the Social Costs of National Economic Policy*, U.S. Congress, Joint Economic Committee, Print (Washington, D.C.: U.S. Government Printing Office, 1976); "Mortality and the National Economy: A Review, and the Experience of England and Wales 1936–76," *The Lancet*, September 15, 1979; and *Assessing the Social Costs of National Unemployment Rates*, in U.S. Congress, House Committee on Banking, Finance, and Urban Affairs, *Hearings*, 97th Cong., 2nd sess., August 12, 1982.

108 "Other studies": see Robert Gillespie, *Economic Factors in Crime and Delinquency: A Critical Review of the Empirical Evidence* (Washington, D.C.: National Institute of Law Enforcement and Criminal Justice, 1975).

108 Orsagh and Witte: "Economic Status and Crime: Implications for Offender Rehabilitation," *Journal of Criminal Law and Criminology* 72, no.3 (Fall 1981): 1069.

108 Methodological difficulties: see Roger Tarling, "Unemployment and Crime," in *Home Office Research Bulletin No. 14* (London: Home Office Research and Planning Unit, 1982).

109 Cohen study: Lawrence Cohen, Marcus Felson, and Kenneth Land, "Property Crime Rates in the U.S.; A Macrodynamic Analysis, 1947–1977," *American Journal of Sociology* 86 (July 1982).

110 Victim study: Robert J. Sampson and Thomas C. Castellano, *Juvenile Criminal Behavior and Its Relation to Neighborhood Characteristics* (Washington, D.C.: National Institute of Justice, 1981).

110 – 111 Phillips-Votey study: Llad Phillips and Harold L. Votey, "Crime Generation and Economic Opportunities for Youth," in *The Economics of Crime Control* (Beverly Hills: Sage Publications, 1981).

112 Witte quotation: Ann Dryden Witte, "Unemployment and Crime: Insights from Research on Individuals," U.S. Congress, Joint Economic Committee, *Hearings on Social Costs of Unemployment*, 96th Cong., 1st sess., 1979, p. 30.

PAGE

112 Wright quotation: "Labor, Pauperism, and Crime," pp. 156–164.

113 – 115 Vera study: Michelle Sviridoff and James W. Thompson, "Links Between Employment and Crime: A Qualitative Study of Riker's Island Releasees," *Crime and Delinquency*, April 1983, pp. 195–212.

115 – 116 URSA study: Jeffrey Fagan, Karen V. Hansen, and Michael Jang, "Profiles of Chronically Violent Juvenile Offenders," in *Evaluating Juvenile Justice*, ed. James R. Kluegel (Beverly Hills: Sage Publications, 1983).

116 Oakland murders: cited in San Francisco *Chronicle*, February 5, 1985.

116 Illegal work and violence: see Margaret Zahn, "Homicide in the Twentieth Century United States," in *History and Crime*, ed. James A. Inciardi and Charles E. Faupel (Beverly Hills: Sage Publications, 1980) for a discussion of the relationship of the peaks of homicide in the late twenties and the late sixties to the illegal alcohol and drug markets. In the same vein, the historian Roger Lane notes that as far back as the nineteenth century, the high homicide rate among American blacks was partly a result of their being disproportionately forced into illegal occupations—which typically required the carrying of weapons as a "survival mechanism." Roger Lane, "Urban Homicide in the Nineteenth Century: Some Lessons for the Twentieth," in Inciardi and Faupel, p. 105.

118 Myrdal quotation: Gunnar Myrdal, *Challenge to Affluence* (New York: Pantheon Books, 1963), p. 53.

118 Subemployment study: cited in Michael Harrington, *Toward a Democratic Left* (Baltimore: Penguin Books, 1969), pp. 55–57.

119 Moynihan quotation: Daniel Patrick Moynihan, *The Politics of a Guaranteed Income* (New York: Random House, 1973), p. 94.

119 European employment policies: see the excellent discussion in Robert Kuttner, *The Economic Illusion* (Boston: Houghton Mifflin Co., 1984), chap. 4.

119 Unemployment rate comparisons: Ira Magaziner and Robert Reich, *Minding America's Business* (New York: Harcourt Brace Jovanovich, 1982), p. 14.

119 Krohn study: Marvin Krohn, "Inequality, Unemployment and Crime: A Cross-National Analysis," *Sociological Quarterly* 17 (Summer 1976).

120 – 121 Lombroso quotation: Cesare Lombroso, *Crime: Its Causes and Remedies* (Montclair, N.J.: Patterson Smith, 1968), pp. 124, 205–208.

121 – 123 Minimum wage effects: see Robert Havemann, "Unemployment in Western Europe and the U.S.," *American Economic Review*, May 1978; and Charles Brown et al., "The Effect of the Minimum Wage on Employment

and Unemployment," *Journal of Economic Literature,* June 20, 1982. Other evidence fuels the skepticism. If overly high minimum wages were pricing youth out of the labor market, we'd expect that subsidizing part of their wages (thus lowering the cost to employers) to ease the problem substantially. But this hasn't been the case. Recent Labor Department studies in Baltimore and Detroit, for example, found that even when the government offered to subsidize half the wages of each low-income youth hired, only 5 percent of employers took them up on it; only 18 percent hired even one low-income youth when offered a *100* percent subsidy. It should be noted, too, that according to the employers surveyed, the problem wasn't poor performance on the youths' part: 80 percent described their young workers as having good work habits, yet only 20 percent of those who hired one said they would keep a youth on the job. See *Employment and Training Report of the President, 1983* (Washington, D.C.: U.S. Government Printing Office, 1983), p. 115.

123 Depression crime data: cf. David Cantor and Lawrence Cohen, "Comparing Measures of Homicide Trends," *Social Science Research* 9, no. 2 (June 1980).

123 Crime among the "mobile" poor: consider this account of survival in the thirties, as recorded by Studs Terkel: "Everybody was a criminal. You stole, you cheated through. Stole clothes off lines, stole milk off back porches, you stole bread. . . . You were a predator. You had to be." Quoted in *Hard Times: An Oral History of the Great Depression* (New York: Pantheon Books, 1977), p. 50.

124 Pandiani quote: John A. Pandiani, "The Crime Control Corps: An Invisible New Deal Program," *British Journal of Sociology* 33, no. 3 (September 1982): 349. Pandiani quotes a 1932 New York *Times* article describing an "alarming increase" in juvenile crime, an increase "in direct proportion to the breakup of homes caused by the Depression."

124 "Why not?": another possible reason for the nonappearance of a Depression crime wave deserves mention: the repeal of Prohibition in 1933. As we've seen, part of the reason for the high crime rates of the late twenties and early thirties was the spread of the illegal markets created by the enforcement of Prohibition laws. As Margaret Zahn's research shows, the reduction in homicide thereafter reflects, in part, a decline in the proportion of homicides associated with those markets. See Zahn, "Homicide in the Twentieth Century," pp. 116–117.

125 Lynds: cited in Sellin, *Research Memorandum,* pp. 57–58. The Dutch criminologist Willem Bonger had suggested in the 1920s that the growth of public relief for the jobless might blunt the expected effects of depression on crime. For an overview of the extent (and the limits) of the changes in relief policy in the thirties, see Frances Fox Piven and Richard A. Cloward, *Regulating the Poor* (New York: Pantheon Books, 1971), chap. 3.

NOTES

125 – 126   Short study: James F. Short, "A Note on Relief Programs and Crime During the Depression of the 1930s," *American Sociological Review* 17, no. 2 (April 1952).

126   DeFronzo study: James deFronzo, "Economic Assistance to Impoverished Americans: Relationship to Incidence of Crime," *Criminology* 21, no.1 (February 1983).

126 – 127   Stipends for inmates: Richard A. Berk, Kenneth J. Lenihan, and Peter H. Rossi, "Crime and Poverty: Some Experimental Evidence from Ex-Offenders," *American Sociological Review* 45 (October 1980); and David Rauma and Richard Berk, "Crime and Poverty in California: Some Quasi-Experimental Evidence," *Social Science Research* 11, no. 4 (December 1982).

127   CCC study: Pandiani, "Crime Control Corps," pp. 351–352.

128   Elder study: cited in Andrew Cherlin, *Marriage, Divorce, Remarriage* (Cambridge: Harvard University Press, 1981), pp. 38–39. Elder also found, however, that the effects of economic hardship on *younger* children were generally negative.

128 – 129   Family life: see, for example, Ruth S. Cavan and Katherine Ranck, *The Family and the Depression* (Chicago: University of Chicago Press, 1938). On economic hardship in the Depression: Jeffrey K. Liker and Glen H. Elder, "Economic Hardship and Marital Relations in the 1930s," *American Sociological Review* 48 (June 1983): 346, point out, "In real earnings, a number of Depression families were actually better off than they had been prior to the Depression."

129 – 130   Unemployment benefits: see Reich and Magaziner, *Minding America's Business*, p. 15.

131   Wilson quotation: "Crime and American Culture," p. 46.

131   Patterson quotation: James T. Patterson, *America's Struggle Against Poverty* (Cambridge: Harvard University Press, 1982), pp. 129–135.

131 – 132   "Theoretical support": for a discussion, see Patterson, *America's Struggle Against Poverty*, chaps. 8 and 9.

132   "Evidence from evaluations of job programs": this discussion draws heavily on Thompson et al., *Employment and Crime*, chap. 4; see also Feeley, *Courts on Trial*, pp. 82–89.

135 – 137   Supported work: Manpower Demonstration Research Corporation, *Summary and Findings of the National Supported Work Demonstration* (Cambridge, Mass.: Ballinger, 1980); and Katherine Dickinson, "Supported Work for Ex-Addicts: An Exploration of Endogenous Tastes," *Journal of Human Resources* 16, no. 4 (Fall 1981). Further evidence that

work provides ex-offenders with benefits beyond the paycheck—self-respect, positive social contacts, structured activity—is offered in Jeffrey K. Liker, "Wage and Status Effects of Employment on Affective Well-Being of Ex-Felons," *American Sociological Review* 47, no. 2 (April 1982).

137 – 138   Danziger research: Sandra Danziger, "Post-program Changes in the Lives of AFDC Supported Work Participants," *Journal of Human Resources* 16, no. 4 (Fall 1981): 646.

138   "Not altogether discouraging": see MDRC, *Summary and Findings,* p. 91.

139   "Overlapping populations": nine-tenths of the addicts had been arrested at least once, three-quarters convicted of some crime; the addict sample had spent an average of two and one-half years behind bars. Likewise, about one-third of the ex-offender sample were regular heroin users. MDRC, *Summary and Findings,* p. 10; and Dickinson, "Supported Work for Ex-Addicts," pp. 554–555.

139   MDRC quotations: MDRC, *Summary and Findings,* pp. 2, 8–9.

139   "Waning steadily": for similar evidence, see also Peter Schmidt and Ann Dryden Witte, "Evaluating Correctional Programs," *Evaluation Review,* October 1980; and Laurence Steinberg, "Jumping off the Work Experience Bandwagon," *Journal of Youth and Adolescence* 11, no.3 (June 1982).

140   Wilson quotation: "Thinking About Crime" (1983), p. 80. To Wilson, this is evidence for the curious position that "rising crime might as easily cause rising unemployment as the other way around." A simpler—and, I think, more plausible—way of putting this connection is that a labor market that limits youths' job opportunities to the car wash will generate both crime and unemployment.

140   Wilson quotations: *Thinking About Crime* (1975), pp. 227–228; "Thinking About Crime" (1983), p. 80.

CHAPTER 5: UNDERSTANDING CRIME: INEQUALITY AND COMMUNITY

144 – 145   City comparisons: crime data from *Uniform Crime Reports, 1983;* demographic data from U.S. Bureau of the Census, *Social and Economic Characteristics of States,* 1980 Census of Population and Housing, volumes for Illinois, California, and Michigan (Washington, D.C.: U.S. Government Printing Office, 1983). Since rates of poverty have risen sharply since these data were collected, the contrasts in affluence and poverty among these cities would now be even greater.

145   Inmate incomes: President's Commission on Crime in the District of Columbia, *Report* (Washington, D.C.: U. S. Government Printing Office, 1966), p.55; U.S. Bureau of Justice Statistics, *Selected Characteristics of State Prison Inmates, 1979,* p.3.

145 Wilson quotation: "Thinking About Crime" (1983), p. 81.

145 Van den Haag quotation: van den Haag, "Successful Rehabilitation," p. 1032.

146 "Appeared . . . for decades": see, for example, the early discussion in Barbara Wootton, *Social Science and Social Pathology* (London: Routledge and Kegan Paul, 1959), pp. 103–106.

146 – 147 Wolfgang study: Wolfgang et al., *Delinquency in a Birth Cohort*, pp. 245–249.

148 Later Wolfgang study: Wolfgang, "Testimony," pp. 143–145.

148 Vera study: Paul Strasburg, *Violent Delinquents* (New York: Monarch, 1978), p. 53.

148 Rand study: Peter Greenwood et al., *Youth Crime and Juvenile Justice in California* (Santa Monica, Calif.: Rand Corporation, 1983), p. 15.

148 – 149 Youth Authority study: Hapaanen and Jesness, *Early Identification of the Chronic Offender.*

149 – 150 Blau study: Judith Blau and Peter Blau, "The Cost of Inequality: Metropolitan Structure and Violent Crime," *American Sociological Review* 47 (February 1982): 121.

150 West findings: West, *Delinquency*, pp. 28, 37, 117. See also Janet Ouston, "Delinquency, Family Background, and Educational Attainment," *British Journal of Criminology* 24, no. 1 (January 1984).

150 Wadsworth study: Michael Wadsworth, *Roots of Delinquency: Infancy, Adolescence, and Crime* (New York: Barnes & Noble, 1979), p. 30.

150 – 151 Denmark findings: Tavs Folmer Anderson, "Persistence of Social and Health Problems in the Welfare State: A Danish Cohort Experience from 1948 to 1979," *Social Science and Medicine* 18, no. 7 (1984). The slum children also suffered much higher rates of hospitalization for a wide variety of psychiatric and physical problems, ranging from genitourinary illness to injuries, poisonings, and schizophrenia and other psychoses.

151 West quotation: West, *Delinquency*, p. 147.

153 "Other things being equal": data from *Uniform Crime Reports* (1981), p. 341.

153 – 154 Homicide death rates: U.S. Public Health Service, *Health-US, 1982* (Washington, D.C.: U.S. Government Printing Office, 1982), p. 20.

PAGE

154 Victim study findings: Michael J. Hindelang, "Variations in Sex-Race-Age-Specific Incidence Rates of Offending," *American Sociological Review* 46 (August 1981): 466.

154 Petersilia study: Joan Petersilia, *Racial Disparities in the Criminal Justice System* (Santa Monica, Calif.: Rand Corporation, 1983).

154 This and other studies": see, for example, Cassia Spohn, et al., "The Effect of Race on Sentencing: A Reexamination of an Unsettled Question," *Law and Society Review* 16, no.1 (1981–82); and Gregory Kowalski and John P. Rickicki, "Determinants of Juvenile Postadjudication Decisions," *Journal of Research in Crime and Delinquency* 19, no. 1 (1982).

155 Blumstein study: Alfred Blumstein, "On the Racial Disproportionality of United States Prison Populations," *Journal of Criminal Law and Criminology* 73, no.3 (1982): 1260–1281.

156 "Studies from the forties and fifties": see especially James Wallerstein and Clement Wyle, "Our Law-Abiding Lawbreakers," *Federal Probation* 25 (April 1947); Austin L. Porterfield, *Youth in Trouble* (Austin, Texas: Leo Potishman Foundation, 1946); and F. Ivan Nye et al., "Socioeconomic Status and Delinquent Behavior," *American Journal of Sociology* 63, no. 3 (1958). A still-interesting study of how the reaction of the criminal-justice system shapes delinquent "careers" is Carl Werthman, "The Function of Social Definitions in the Development of Delinquent Careers," in President's Commission on Law Enforcement and Administration of Justice, *Task Force Report: Juvenile Delinquency and Youth Crime* (Washington, D.C.: U.S. Government Printing Office, 1967); for a mid-sixties overview of the issue, see Stanton Wheeler et al., "Juvenile Delinquency—Its Prevention and Control" in the same volume.

156 – 157 Tittle et al., Hirschi quotations: Charles A. Tittle, Wayne Villemez, and Douglas Smith, "The Myth of Social Class and Criminality," *American Sociological Review* 43, no. 6 (1978); Tittle et al., "One Step Forward, Two Steps Back: More on the Class/Criminality Controversy," *American Sociological Review* 47, no. 3 (June 1982): 437; and Travis Hirschi, Michael Hindelang, and Joseph Weis, "Reply," in the same journal, p. 435.

157 "Many critics": the following discussion relies on John Braithwaite, "The Myth of Social Class and Criminality Reconsidered," *American Sociological Review* 46 (February 1981); Donald Clelland and Timothy J. Carter, "The New Myth of Class and Crime," *Criminology* 18, no.4 (September 1980); Delbert S. Elliott and David Huizinga, "Social Class and Delinquent Behavior in a National Youth Panel," *Criminology* 21, no. 2 (May 1983); and Gary Kleck, "On the Use of Self-Report Data to Determine the Class Distribution of Criminal and Delinquent Behavior," *American Sociological Review* 47, no. 3 (June 1982).

159   Victim data: Robert J. Sampson and Thomas C. Castellano, "Economic Inequality and Personal Victimization," *British Journal of Criminology* 22, no.2 (October 1982). Sampson and Castellano find that the relationship between crime and economic inequality is strongest in urban areas, where what they call "class crystallization"—the differentiation of economic classes—is sharpest.

159   White-collar crime: this point is worth emphasizing. As John Braithwaite puts it, "The nature of the class distribution of crime depends entirely on what form of crime one is talking about" ("The Myth of Social Class and Criminality Reconsidered," p. 47). Predatory behavior is strikingly common at both ends of the economic spectrum in America, a point that I'll take up again in the final chapter. At this stage, however, my argument is focused on "street" crime.

159   "Bad neighborhoods": cf. Braithwaite, "The Myth of Social Class and Criminality Reconsidered," p. 37.

160   "Debate . . . is a long one": a recent summary of the debate may be found in Steven F. Messner, "Regional and Racial Effects on the Urban Homicide Rate: The Subculture of Violence Revisited," *American Journal of Sociology* 88, no.5, (1983).

161   "The argument grew . . .": Robert K. Merton, "Social Structure and Anomie," in *Social Theory and Social Structure* (Glencoe, Ill.: Free Press, 1957); and Richard Cloward and Lloyd Ohlin, *Delinquency and Opportunity* (Glencoe, Ill.: Free Press, 1960).

162   Blau quotation: "The Cost of Inequality," pp. 119, 126. The Blaus' article contains a strong critique of what I have called the "hard" cultural argument; see especially p. 118. There is a second issue involved in this research: whether violent crime is more closely related to *poverty* itself or rather to *inequality* of income. On the whole, criminological theory has emphasized inequality over sheer material poverty as a cause of crime—largely because, in keeping with long-standing sociological concerns, it has looked to the social-psychological impact of a sense of relative deprivation as more salient than "absolute" deprivation. But the issue is complicated. Particularly in the United States, where being at the lower end of the income scale *means* being very poor, the distinction between inequality and poverty is abstract indeed. Some studies—including the Blaus'—find no significant effect of poverty on violent crime once inequality is taken into account, but others do find such an effect (most recently, a study by Kirk Williams of Memphis State University, "Economic Sources of Homicide: Re-estimating the Effects of Poverty and Inequality," *American Sociological Review* 49 [April 1984]). The research problem is complicated by the fact that many of the poor are in sectors of the population that are typically not heavily involved in violent crime: they are disproportionately the old, very young children, and the mothers of those children. Hence correlations between overall rates of poverty and criminal violence probably understate the effects of poverty; other data—like the statistics on the income of prison inmates—may give a truer picture.

PAGE

163 "Burden of background": Richard B. Freeman, "Black Economic Progress Since 1964," *Public Interest*, Summer 1978. Cf. Martin Kilson, "Black
Social Classes and Intergenerational Poverty," *Public Interest*, Summer
1981.

164 "Studies of . . . recent migrants": this evidence was noted by Charles
Silberman in the sixties; *Crisis in Black and White* (New York: Random
House, 1964), p. 46. For more recent work confirming the same point, see
Franco Ferracuti, Simon Dinitz, and Esperanza Acosta de Breines, *Delinquents and Nondelinquents in the Puerto Rican Slum Culture* (Columbus:
Ohio State University Press, 1975), a study of delinquency in San Juan,
Puerto Rico. The parents of delinquents were most often born and raised
in San Juan; the parents of nondelinquents were more likely to have been
born in rural areas or small villages. The highest concentration of delinquency was amomg families "that had been part of the metropolitan
setting for at least a full generation" (p. 132). A look at the figures on
homicide over recent decades in some cities of the American South affirms
the point. Most were tough cities in the fifties, but many became far more
so in the following years; thus, New Orleans's homicide rate tripled
between 1959 and 1983—not a strong argument for the crucial role of a
historic "subculture." Whatever difficulties rural migrants may bring
with them to the cities, it's clear that something in the structure of urban
life itself makes matters worse once they arrive.

165 "Several studies": on the "structural" side, see Colin Loftin and Robert
Hill, "Regional Subculture and Homicide," *American Sociological Review*
39, no. 5 (1974); Robert Nash Parker and M. Dwayne Smith, "Deterrence,
Poverty, and Type of Homicide," *American Journal of Sociology* 85, no.
3 (1979); and Judith and Peter Blau, "The Cost of Inequality." On the
"subcultural" side, Raymond D. Gastil, "Homicide and a Regional Culture of Violence," *American Sociological Review* 36, no. 3 (1971); and
Messner, "Regional and Racial Effects."

166 Davies article: Christie Davies, "Crime, Bureaucracy, and Equality," *Policy Review*, Winter 1983; quotations from pp. 98, 104.

167 "Widest spread of income inequality": Malcolm Sawyer, *Income Distribution in OECD Countries* (Paris: Organization for Economic Cooperation
and Development, 1978).

167 Archer data: Dane Archer, "Cities and Homicide: A New Look at an Old
Paradox," *Comparative Studies in Sociology* 1 (1978): 84.

168 Denmark homicides: U.S. Department of Commerce, Bureau of the Census, *Statistical Abstract of the United States, 1982–83*, p. 179; data are from
World Health Organization. Danish social spending figures from Anderson, "Persistence of Social and Health Problems," p. 555.

168 Reich figures: Robert B. Reich, *The Next American Frontier* (New York:
Random House, 1983), chap. 10.

PAGE

168 – 169   "Historical commitment": on the roots of these differences, see Norman Furniss and Timothy Tilton, *The Case for the Welfare State* (Bloomington: Indiana University Press, 1977); and Robert Kuttner, *The Economic Illusion* (Boston: Houghton Mifflin & Co., 1984), chap. 6.

169   International homicide rates: John Braithwaite and Valerie Braithwaite, "The Effect of Income Inequality and Social Democracy on Homicide," *British Journal of Criminology* 20, no.1 (January 1980); and Steven Messner, "Income Inequality and Murder Rates: Some Cross-National Findings," *Comparative Social Research* 3 (1980). The Braithwaites also find that homicide rates are inversely related to the strength of social-democratic political parties in various countries. See also John Braithwaite, *Inequality, Crime, and Public Policy* (London: Routledge & Kegan Paul, 1978).

169   Gilder quotation: George Gilder, *Wealth and Poverty* (New York: Basic Books, 1981), p. 139.

170   "Historians and Social Scientists": see especially Frances Fox Piven and Richard A. Cloward, *Regulating the Poor* (New York: Pantheon Books, 1971), chap. 8. Along with this migration and its accompanying institutional breakdown was a weakening of the norms enforcing racial subordination. As Piven and Cloward put it, "old patterns of servile conformity were shattered"; the "trauma and anger of an oppressed people" could now be turned outward as well as inward (p. 226). Though it's difficult to put precise figures on the effect this had on criminal violence, especially in the sixties, the connection seems too close to deny.

170   Texas-Wisconsin figures: calculated from *Statistical Abstract, 1982–83*, pp. 341–42, and *Uniform Crime Reports* (1980), pp. 57–58.

170 – 171   AFDC and homicide: James DeFronzo, "Economic Assistance to Impoverished Americans: Relationship to Incidence of Crime," *Criminology* 21, no. 1 (February 1983).

171   Titmuss quotation: Richard M. Titmuss, *Commitment to Welfare* (London: Allen & Unwin, 1968), p. 133.

172   Japan ethos: for a fine discussion, see Smith, *Japanese Society.*

172   "Prosperity causes crime": cf. James Q. Wilson, "Thinking About Crime" (1983), p. 83.

173   "When there is more to steal": see, for example, Louise Shelley, *Crime and Modernization* (Carbondale: Southern Illinois University Press, 1981), p. 33; and Preben Wolf, "Crime and Development: An International Analysis of Crime Rates," *Scandinavian Studies in Criminology* 3 (1971). Steven Stack, in "Social Structure and Swedish Crime Rates," uses such an "opportunity" theory of property crime to explain rising rates of theft in affluent post–World War II Sweden. Two anecdotes, widely separated in time and place, help illustrate the point. In a study of changes in

working-class life in England, Jeremy Seabrook quotes a woman reminiscing about life in the Depression: "there was no thieving because there wasn't owt to steal." *Unemployment* (London: Quartet Books 1982), p. 59. I'm reminded of the remark of a heroin addict–burglar I interviewed in the late seventies; he was thinking of moving from his industrially depressed city to southern California because "the stealin's better in L.A."

173   Third World homicide rates: calculated from Archer et al., "Cities and Homicide," p. 84.

173 – 174   Industrialization and violence: see, for example, Ted Robert Gurr, "Development and Decay: Their Impact on Public Order in Western History," and Roger Lane, "Urban Homicide in the Nineteenth Century: Some Lessons for the Twentieth," in *History and Crime*, ed. James Inciardi and Charles Faupel (Beverly Hills: Sage Publications, 1980); and John D. Hewitt and Dwight W. Hoover, "Local Modernization and Crime: The Effects of Modernization on Crime in Middletown, 1845–1910," *Law and Human Behavior* 6, no. 3–4 (1982). The reservations involve the effects of modernization on violent crime in the black community. As Roger Lane points out on the basis of his study of patterns of violence in Philadelphia, blacks were from a very early point "frozen out" of industrial and bureaucratic employment as industrialization proceeded; this "separate path of economic development" resulted in a unique pattern of violence "with a continually rising homicide rate." "Urban Homicide in the Nineteenth Century," p. 107.

174   Gurr quotation: Gurr, "Development and Decay," p. 43.

174   Messner study: Steven F. Messner, "Societal Development, Social Equality, and Homicide," *Social Forces* 61, no.1 (September 1982): 238.

175   India study: Clayton Hartjen, "Delinquency, Development, and Social Integration in India," *Social Problems* 29, no.5 (June 1982): 471. An interesting earlier study by Marshall Clinard of crime in two neighborhoods in Kampala, Uganda, in the 1960s affirms this point. Both neighborhoods were poor, but the one with more cohesiveness, greater participation in local organizations, less geographical mobility, and more frequent visiting among neighbors had considerably less crime—in spite of the fact that the other neighborhood had slightly *better* material living conditions. Marshall Clinard and Daniel Abbott, *Crime in Developing Countries: A Comparative Perspective* (New York: John Wiley & Sons, 1973), pp. 140–165.

177   "Less quantifiable aspects": compare the account of changes in a community in upstate New York related by anthropologist Janet M. Fitchen of Ithaca College. As traditional farming declined in rural New York, she argues, rural social institutions also declined: "In the 1920s, there were lots of other poor people. . . . There were functioning small communities, a church, a local schoolhouse, a general store, the local blacksmith—a social network that knit people together. You were somebody. You were part

of a community. People have lost that now. . . . You have to go to Watertown to go to the doctor, to go shopping, to get a job. The loss of the social community has had a real impact on poor people. They have not been integrated into the urban community, and they have been left without the support of the rural community." Quoted in Edward A. Gargan, "The Downside of Upstate," New York *Times,* September 16, 1984.

177 "Trapping the newcomers": on the devastating effects of rapid migration coupled with racial segregation on crime in Chicago's black neighborhoods after 1950, see Robert J. Bursik and Jim Webb, "Community Change and Patterns of Delinquency," *American Journal of Sociology* 88, no. 1 (July 1982); on the role of "proximity to the prosperous," see Richard Block, "Community, Environment, and Violent Crime," *Criminology* 17, no. 1 (May 1979), which finds that violent crime in Chicago in the mid-seventies was highest in neighborhoods where the very poor and the middle class lived in close proximity.

177 Switzerland and Japan: Clinard, *Cities with Little Crime;* Smith, *Japanese Society;* and Ronald P. Dore, *City Life in Japan* (Berkeley: University of California Press, 1958).

178 "Traditionally accepted brutalities": thus, while violent delinquency may be low in parts of India, several hundred women died in New Delhi alone in 1983 as victims of "bride burnings" carried out by their husbands and in-laws; see William Claiborne, "India's Bride Burnings," Washington *Post* National Weekly Edition, October 8, 1984.

CHAPTER 6: UNDERSTANDING CRIME: FAMILIES AND CHILDREN

182 – 183 Committee quotations: cited in A. M. Carr-Saunders, Hermann Mannheim, and E. C. Rhodes, *Young Offenders* (Cambridge: Cambridge University Press, 1944), pp. 1–2.

183 Burt quotation: cited in Carr-Saunders et al., *Young Offenders,* p. 23.

183 Glueck studies: for example, Sheldon and Eleanor Glueck, *Juvenile Delinquents Grown Up* (New York: Commonwealth Fund, 1940); and *Delinquents and Nondelinquents in Perspective* (Cambridge: Harvard University Press, 1968).

183 "Flaws": for a still-powerful critique, see Barbara Wootton, *Social Science and Social Pathology* (London: George Allen & Unwin, 1959), especially chap. 10.

184 Wilson quotation: "Thinking About Crime" (1983), p. 86.

186 Denton quotation: U.S. Congress, Senate Committee on Labor and Human Resources, *Work Ethic: Materialism and the American Family,*

Hearings, 97th Cong., 2nd sess. (Washington D.C.: U.S. Government Printing Office, 1982), p. 5.

187 – 188   Hirschi article: "Crime and Family Policy," pp. 6–10.

188   "Ghetto dropouts": the kernel of truth in this argument is that, as we shall see in the next chapter, simply holding down *any* job, no matter how poor or dead-end, has at least as many negative effects on youths' development as positive ones. The logical implication of this, however—that we ought to think in terms of upgrading employment opportunities for youth—is not one Hirschi considers.

188   Family size studies: Wadsworth, *Roots of Delinquency*, p. 43; and West, *Delinquency*, p. 37.

189 – 190   Hirschi quotations: "Crime and Family Policy," pp. 10–11.

190 – 191   Women's work: cf. Wadsworth, *Roots of Delinquency*, pp. 51–53.

191   UCLA study: Irla Lee Zimmerman and Maurine Bernstein, "Parental Work Patterns in Alternative Families: Influence on Child Development," *American Journal of Orthopsychiatry* 52, no.3 (July 1983).

191   Quality of work: see generally Jay Belsky, "The Determinants of Parenting: A Process Model," *Child Development* 55, no. 1 (February 1984); Urie Bronfenbrenner and A. C. Crouter, "Work and Family Through Time and Space," in *Families That Work*, ed. Cheryl Hayes and Sheila Kamerman (Washington, D.C.: National Academy of Sciences, 1982).

191   Effects of child care: see, for example, Rutter, *Changing Youth in a Changing Society*, pp. 249–250.

191   NAS review: Cheryl D. Hayes and Sheila Kamerman, eds., *Children of Working Parents: Experiences and Outcomes* (Washington, D.C.: National Academy of Sciences, 1983), p. vii.

192   Zigler quotation: Edward Zigler and Susan Muenchow, "Infant Day-Care and Infant Care Leaves," *American Psychologist*, January 1983, p. 91.

192   Kamerman quotation: Sheila Kamerman, *Parenting in an Unresponsive Society* (New York: Free Press, 1980).

192   Irish: Gilder, *Wealth and Poverty*, p. 138.

193   Shaw and McKay: Clifford R. Shaw and Henry McKay, "Are Broken Homes a Cause of Delinquency?" *Social Forces* 10 (May 1932): 514–524.

193 – 194   Inmates and broken homes: Petersilia et al., *Criminal Careers of Habitual Felons*, p. 74; and Murray and Cox, *Beyond Probation*, pp. 36–37.

PAGE

194 "Greater likelihood": Shaw and McKay, "Broken Homes," p. 522.

194 Court bias: Polk study, cited in Edwin H. Sutherland and Donald R. Cressey, *Criminology*, 10th ed. (Philadelphia: J. B. Lippincott, 1978), p. 215; F. Ivan Nye, *Family Relationships and Delinquent Behavior* (New York: John Wiley & Sons, 1958); John W. C. Johnstone, "Delinquency and the Changing American Family," in Shichor and Kelly, *Critical Issues in Juvenile Delinquency*, p. 88; and Wadsworth, *Roots of Delinquency*, p. 55.

195 "Overrepresentation": see, for example, Rachelle J. Canter, "Family Correlates of Male and Female Delinquency," *Criminology* 20, no. 2 (August 1982).

195 West quotation: *Delinquency*, p. 55. For early reviews on this issue, see Wootton, *Social Science and Social Pathology*, chap. 3; and Hyman Rodman and Paul Grams, "Juvenile Delinquency and the Family," in President's Commission on Law Enforcement and Administration of Justice, *Task Force Report: Juvenile Delinquency and Youth Crime* (Washington, D.C.: U.S. Government Printing Office, 1967), pp. 188–221.

195 – 196 Conflict in intact families: Nye, *Family Relationships*, p. 47; Joan McCord, "Alcoholism and Criminality," *Journal of Studies in Alcohol* 42, no. 2 (1981); Alexander Thomas and Stella Chess, "Genesis and Evolution of Behavioral Disorders," *American Journal of Psychiatry* 141, no. 1 (January 1984): 6; and Rutter, *Changing Youth*, pp. 149–150.

196 Pearce quotation: in Arthur I. Blaustein, ed., *The American Promise* (Rutgers, N.J.: Trans-Action Books, 1982), p. 12.

196 West quotation: *Delinquency*, pp. 55–56. Studying families surveyed in the University of Michigan's Panel Study of Income Dynamics, the sociologist Robert S. Weiss calculated that women who were divorced or separated lost between one-quarter and one-half of their married incomes; typically, they had not recovered anything close to their married incomes five years after the breakup. "The Impact of Marital Dissolution on Income and Consumption in Single-Parent Families," *Journal of Marriage and Family*, February 1984, pp. 117–126.

197 Hetherington quotation: cited in Urie Bronfenbrenner, *The Ecology of Human Development* (Cambridge, Mass.: Havard University Press, 1979), pp. 78–79.

197 Weinraub and Wolf study: Marsha Weinraub and Barbara M. Wolf, "Effects of Stress and Social Support on Mother-Child Interaction in Single- and Two-Parent Families," *Journal of Child Development* 54, no. 5 (October 1983).

198 Wilson study: Harriett Wilson, "Parental Supervision: A Neglected Aspect of Delinquency," *British Journal of Criminology* 20, no. 3 (July 1980).

PAGE

199   Wynne quotation: from letter in *Working Papers*, September–October 1982, p. 6.

199   Hirschi quotation: "Crime and Family Policy," p. 8.

199 – 200   U.S.-Sweden comparisons: Solheim, "Cross-Cultural Examination." Caribbean: Arnold, "Use of Corporal Punishment."

200   "Lower-class families": a classic study is Melvin Kohn, "Social Class and Parent-Child Relationships," *American Journal of Sociology* 68 (1963): 471–480.

200   "The kind of parenting": cf. Belsky, "Determinants of Parenting," p. 3.

201   "Classic studies": Albert Bandura and Richard Walters, "Dependency Conflicts in Aggressive Delinquents," *Journal of Social Issues* 14, no. 3 (1958); cf. Rutter, *Changing Youth*, pp. 153–155. In a recent confirmation of the same point, Leonard Eron and L. Rowell Huesman find, "The more critical the parent is of the child's behavior and accomplishments and the more the child is punished and shamed in public, the more likely he or she is to be aggressive as an adult. Similarly, the more authoritarian the parents' attitudes, the more aggressive the child will be when an adult and the less likely to achieve prosocial goals." "The Relation of Prosocial Behavior to the Development of Aggression and Psychopathology," *Aggressive Behavior* 10, no. 3 (1984): 207.

201   McCord and West studies: McCord, "Alcoholism and Criminality"; and West, *Delinquency*, p. 54.

201 – 202   Scheinfeld study: Daniel H. Scheinfeld, "Family Relationships and School Achievement Among Boys of Lower-Income Black Families," *American Journal of Orthopsychiatry* 53, no. 1 (January 1983).

202 – 203   "Exaggerated expectations": Yvonne Fraley, "The Family Support Center: Early Intervention for High-Risk Parents and Children," *Children Today*, January–February 1983, p. 14. James Garbarino, Janet Sebes, and Cynthia Schellenbach, "Families at Risk for Destructive Parent-Child Relations in Adolescence," *Child Development* 55, no. 1 (February 1984): 179–181; and Carolyn Newberger and Susan Cook, "Parental Awareness and Child Abuse," *American Journal of Orthopsychiatry* 53, no. 3 (July 1983): 516.

203 – 204   Lewis study: Dorothy Otnow Lewis, et al., "Violent Juvenile Delinquents: Psychiatric, Neurological, Psychological, and Abuse Factors," *American Journal of Psychiatry* 137 (1980): 1211–1216.

204   "Juan": Arthur H. Green, "Dimensions of Psychological Trauma in Abused Children," *Journal of the American Academy of Child Psychiatry* 22, no. 3 (May 1983): 234–235.

PAGE

205 – 206   Homicidal children: Dorothy O. Lewis et al., "Homicidally Aggressive Young Children: Neuropsychiatric and Experiential Correlates," *American Journal of Psychiatry* 140, no. 2 (February 1983).

206   North Carolina study: Jane H. Pfouts et al., "Deviant Behaviors of Child Victims and Bystanders in Violent Families," in *Exploring the Relationship Between Child Abuse and Juvenile Delinquency*, ed. Robert J. Hunner and Yvonne Elder Walker (Montclair, N.J.: Allanheld, Osmun, 1981). See also Debra Kalmuss, "The Intergenerational Transmission of Marital Aggression," *Journal of Marriage and Family* (February 1984).

206   McCord study: Joan McCord, "A Forty-Year Followup of Effects of Child Abuse and Neglect," *Child Abuse and Neglect* 7, no. 3 (1983). A careful treatment of the complexities of evaluating the impact of abuse on children's later behavior is Eli Newberger et al., "Child Abuse: The Current Theory Base and Future Research Needs," *Journal of the American Academy of Child Psychiatry* 22, no. 3 (1983).

207   Hirschi quotation: "Crime and Family Policy," p. 11.

208   Harvard study: Jessica Daniel, Robert Hampton, and Eli Newberger, "Child Abuse and Accidents in Black Families: A Controlled Comparative Study," *American Journal of Orthopsychiatry* 53, no. 4 (October 1983).

209   "Parents at risk": this portrait draws, inter alia, on the following research: Daniel et al., "Child Abuse and Accidents in Black Families"; Arthur H. Green, "Child Abusing Fathers," *Journal of the American Academy of Child Psychiatry* 18, no. 2 (Spring 1979); Janine Jason and Nathan Andereck, "Fatal Child Abuse in Georgia: The Epidemiology of Severe Physical Child Abuse," *Child Abuse and Neglect* 7, no. 1 (1983); James Garbarino, "A Preliminary Study of Some Ecological Correlates of Child Abuse," *Child Development* 47 (1976); James Garbarino and Deborah Sherman, "High Risk Neighborhoods and High Risk Families: The Human Ecology of Child Maltreatment," *Child Development* 51, no. 1 (1980); and Laurence D. Steinberg, Ralph Catalano, and David Dooley, "Economic Antecedents of Child Abuse and Neglect," *Child Development* 52, no. 4 (November 1981).

209 – 210   "An American child": Katherine Christoffel and Kiang Liu, "Homicide Death Rates in 23 Countries: U.S. Rates Atypically High," *Child Abuse and Neglect* 7, no. 3 (1983): 341. The U.S. homicide death rate for infants under one year was 5.3 per 100,000 births in the mid-seventies; in several countries, including Denmark, Norway, Ireland, and Sweden, the rate was so low that it was listed as 0 per 100,000.

210   Bronfenbrenner quotation: *Ecology of Human Development*, pp. 48–49.

210   Hirschi quotation: "Crime and Family Policy," p. 13. Wilson quotation: *Thinking About Crime* (1975), pp. 57–58.

PAGE

211 "Third-grade bullies": *USA Today*, August 26, 1983.

211 Robins quotation: Lee N. Robins and Kathryn S. Ratcliff, "Risk Factors in the Continuation of Childhood Antisocial Behavior into Adulthood," *International Journal of Mental Health* 7, no. 3–4 (Fall–Winter 1979): 97.

212 Shannon findings: *Assessing the Relationship*, p. 5.

212 – 213 Eron study: Leonard D. Eron, "The Consistency of Aggressive Behavior Across Time and Situations," paper presented at meetings of the American Psychological Association, August 27, 1983.

213 Chess findings: Thomas and Chess, "Genesis and Evolution of Behavioral Disorders," p. 7.

213 "No more than half": Lee N. Robins, "Childhood Conduct Disorders and Later Arrest," in Lee Robins, Paula Clayton, and John Wing, *The Social Consequences of Psychiatric Illness* (New York: Brunner-Mazel, 1980), p. 249.

214 "Within the person and his family": Robins and Ratcliff, "Risk Factors," p. 115.

214 – 215 Robins quotations: "Aetiological Implications in Studies of Childhood Histories Relating to Antisocial Personality," in *Psychopathic Behavior*, ed. R. D. Hare and D. Schalling (New York: John Wiley & Sons, 1978), pp. 263, 259.

216 Arrests for crimes of violence less common: Robins, "Childhood Conduct Disorders," p. 258.

216 "Not an important predictor": Robins and Ratcliff, "Risk Factors," pp. 114–115.

217 Poverty an "extreme measure": "Risk Factors," p. 111. Gluecks' technique: cf. Wootton, *Social Science and Social Pathology*, p. 329.

218 – 219 "Genetic factor" in school achievement: Lee N. Robins, Kathryn S. Ratcliff, and Patricia A. West, "School Achievement in Two Generations: A Study of 88 Urban Black Families," in *Children's Mental Health*, ed. S. J. Shamsie (New York: Spectrum Publications, 1978), p. 128.

219 "By serious geneticists and social scientists alike": see, for a rich discussion of this issue, R. C. Lewontin, Steven Rose, and Leon J. Kamin, *Not in Our Genes* (New York: Pantheon Books, 1984).

220 Thomas and Chess quotation: "Genesis and Evolution of Behavioral Disorders," p. 9.

220 "Rash of theories": see Elliott Currie, "Managing the Minds of Men: The Reformatory Movement in the United States" (Ph.D. diss., University of California, Berkeley, 1973).

CHAPTER 7: NEW DIRECTIONS

226 – 227 Comer metaphor: James P. Comer, "Black Violence and Public Policy," in *American Violence and Public Policy*, ed. Lynn A. Curtis (New Haven, Conn.: Yale University Press, 1985), p. 85.

229 "The hospital and the physician's office": for a lucid recent discussion of this view of medical care, see Richard L. Grossman, "The Public's Health: Toward a New Consensus," in *Rethinking Liberalism*, ed. Walter Truett Anderson (New York: Avon Books, 1983).

230 West quotation: West, *Delinquency*, p. 138.

230 Nonstranger violence study: cited in U.S. National Institute of Justice, *Justice Assistance News*, April 1983, p. 6.

231 Sherman-Berk study: cited in San Francisco *Chronicle*, May 29, 1984.

231 Berk and Loseke research: Sarah Fenstermaker Berk and Donileen R. Loseke, "Handling Family Violence: Situational Determinants of Police Arrest in Domestic Disturbances," *Law and Society Review* 15, no. 2 (1980–81).

231 Berk and associates research: Richard A. Berk et al., "Throwing the Cops Back Out: The Decline of a Local Program to Make the Criminal Justice System More Responsive to Incidents of Domestic Violence," *Social Science Research* 11, no. 3 (September 1982).

232 "Evidence is sparse": see, for example, Colin Loftin and David McDowall, "The Police, Crime, and Economic Theory," *American Sociological Review* 47, no. 3 (June 1982); and David Greenberg, Ronald Kessler, and Colin Loftin, "The Effect of Police Employment on Crime," *Criminology* 21, no. 3 (August 1983).

232 Foot patrol research: George Kelling, "Fighting Crime and the Fear of Crime: Police on Foot Patrol," *Christian Science Monitor*, April 21, 1983; Anthony Pate et al., *The Newark Foot Patrol Experiment* (Washington, D.C.: Police Foundation, 1981); and "Police Foot Patrols Reduced Crime, Says Flint, Michigan, Project," *Criminal Justice Newsletter*, September 27, 1982. See also the careful evaluation of a community "team" policing project in Hartford, Connecticut, in the late 1970s: Floyd J. Fowler and Thomas Mangione, *Neighborhood Crime, Fear, and Social Control: A Second Look at the Hartford Program* (Washington, D.C.: National Institute of Justice, 1982), which suggests that neighborhood-based police strategies led to increased arrests for robbery and burglary (until the experiment was largely dismantled, in part because of fiscal constraints).

232   Santa Ana police auxiliaries: cf. editorial, "Crime and Punishment," *New Republic,* December 6, 1982.

233   New York *Times* poll, Walinsky and Rubinstein proposal: New York *Times,* January 27, 1985, p. 20E.

233 – 234   Community service programs: see Kevin Krajick, "Community Service: The Work Ethic Approach to Punishment," *Corrections Magazine,* October 1982; and Edna McConnell Clark Foundation, *Overcrowded Time: Why Prisons Are So Crowded and What Can Be Done* (New York, 1982), pp. 30–31.

234   Rand probation research: cited in San Francisco *Examiner,* February 3, 1985.

234   Intensive probation: Jim Bencivenga, "Tough Probation Plan Eases Strain on Crowded Cellblocks," *Christian Science Monitor,* June 22, 1983; and Stephen Gettinger, "Intensive Supervision: Can It Rehabilitate Probation?" *Corrections Magazine,* March 1983.

236   Massachusetts study: see Robert Coates, Alden Miller, and Lloyd Ohlin, *Diversity in a Youth Correctional System: Handling Delinquents in Massachusetts* (Cambridge, Mass.: Ballinger, 1978); and William McCord and Jose Sanchez, "The Treatment of Deviant Children: A Twenty-Five Year Follow-Up Study," *Crime and Delinquency* 29, no. 2, (March 1983).

237   District of Columbia: President's Commission on Crime in the District of Columbia, *Report* (Washington, D.C.: U.S. Government Printing Office, 1966), pp. 701–702.

237   Martinson article: Robert Martinson, "What Works: Questions and Answers About Prison Reform," *Public Interest,* Spring 1974, p. 25.

237   "Similar conclusions": see, for example, William E. Wright and Michael C. Dixon, "Community Prevention and Treatment of Juvenile Delinquency," *Journal of Research in Crime and Delinquency* 14, no. 1 (January 1977).

238   West quotation: West, *Delinquency,* p. 138.

238   "Evidence for a more encouraging view": Paul Gendreau and Bob Ross, "Effective Correctional Treatment: Bibliotherapy for Cynics," *Crime and Delinquency,* October 1979; Lee Sechrest, et al., *The Rehabilitation of Criminal Offenders: Problems and Prospects* (Washington, D.C.: National Academy Press, 1979); Dale Mann, *Intervening with Convicted Serious Juvenile Offenders* (Washington, D.C.: U.S. Department of Justice, Office of Juvenile Justice and Delinquency Prevention, 1976); and Murray and Cox, *Beyond Probation.*

238 Martinson quotation: Robert Martinson, "New Findings, New Views: A Note of Caution Regarding Sentencing Reform," *Hofstra Law Review* 4, no. 2 (Winter 1979): 254. For another cautiously positive discussion, including an assessment of the British experience, see West, *Delinquency*, pp. 136–142.

239 "Therapeutic integrity": Gendreau and Ross, "Effective Correctional Treatment," p. 467; see also Delbert S. Elliott, "Recurring Issues in the Evaluation of Delinquency Prevention and Treatment Programs," in *Critical Issues in Juvenile Delinquency*, ed. David Shichor and Delos H. Kelly (Lexington, Mass.: Lexington Books, 1980).

239 NAS quotation: Sechrest et al., *Rehabilitation of Criminal Offenders*, p. 9.

239 Martinson quotation: Martinson, "New Findings, New Views," p. 254; NAS quotation: Sechrest et al., *Rehabilitation of Criminal Offenders*, p. 8.

240 UDIS camps: Murray and Cox, *Beyond Probation*, p. 111.

240 – 241 Coates quotation: Robert Coates, "Community-Based Services for Juvenile Delinquents: Concept and Implications for Practice," *Journal of Social Issues* 37, no. 3 (1981): 94–95.

241 Wiltwyck study: McCord and Sanchez, "Treatment of Deviant Children," pp. 239–251.

244 Coates quotation: Coates, "Community-Based Services," p. 91.

245 Wolfgang statement: U.S. Congress, Senate, Committee on the Judiciary, Subcommittee on Juvenile Justice, *Violent Juvenile Crime*, 97th Cong., 1st sess., July 9, 1981, p. 135.

245 Myrdal quotation: Alva Myrdal, *Nation and Family*, quoted in Daniel Patrick Moynihan, *The Politics of a Guaranteed Income: The Nixon Administration and the Family Assistance Plan* (New York: Random House, 1973), p. 42.

246 Kamerman and Kahn studies: see especially Kamerman, *Parenting in an Unresponsive Society*.

246 Ehrenreich and Piven: Barbara Ehrenreich and Frances Fox Piven, "Women and the Welfare State," in *Alternatives*, ed. Irving Howe (New York: Pantheon Books, 1984), p. 60.

246 – 247 Swedish legislation: Kamerman, *Parenting in an Unresponsive Society*, p. 131.

247 Unwanted pregnancies: data from Jacqueline Darroch Forrest, "The Impact of U.S. Family Planning Programs on Births, Abortions, and Miscarriages, 1970–1979," *Social Science and Medicine* 18, no. 6 (1984).

248   Project redirection: D. F. Polit, M. B. Tannien, and J. R. Kahn, *School, Work, and Family Planning: Interim Impacts in Project Redirection* (New York: Manpower Demonstration Research Corporation, 1983), cited in *Family Planning Perspectives* 16, no. 1 (January–February 1984): 38–40.

249   "Failures of parents": W. Norton Grubb and Marvin Lazerson, *Broken Promises: How Americans Fail Their Children* (New York: Basic Books, 1982), p. 229. Despite my disagreement with the authors on this issue, this is an often insightful discussion of the state of American policies toward children. For a more positive assessment of the results of parent programs, see Douglass R. Powell, "From Child to Parent: Changing Conceptions of Early Childhood Intervention," *Annals of the American Academy of Political and Social Science* 461 (May 1982).

249 – 250   CFRP evaluation: Abt Associates, *The Effects of a Social Program: Executive Summary of CFRP's Infant-Toddler Component* (Cambridge, Mass.: Abt Associates, 1982). For a more positive view of the programs' potential to enhance child development, see Dennis Affholter, David Connell, and Marrit Nauta, "Evaluation of the Child and Family Resource Program: Early Evidence of Parent-Child Interaction Effects," *Evaluation Review* 7, no. 1 (February 1983).

250 – 251   PCDC evaluation: Susan Ring Andrews et al., *The Skills of Mothering: A Study of Parent-Child Development Centers*, Child Development Monographs, vol. 7, no. 6 (Chicago: University of Chicago Press, 1982), pp. 7–77.

252   Danish family guidance: Marsden Wagner, *Denmark's National Family Guidance Program: A Preventive Mental Health Program for Children and Families* (Washington, D.C.: National Institute of Mental Health, 1978). In the mid-1970s, the family service ceased to be a separate agency, but was absorbed with its guiding principles intact into decentralized neighborhood "Social Centers" providing services to all families, including those without children. An overview of local family resource programs in America and of efforts to link them in a national coalition may be found in Linda Lipton, "Family Resource Programs," *Children Today*, September-October 1983, pp. 11–13.

253   Perry Project: cited New York *Times*, September 11, 1984; and San Francisco *Chronicle*, September 14, 1984. A comprehensive and encouraging recent assessment of the effects of early education programs is Irving Lazar, et al., *Lasting Effects of Early Education*, Child Development Monographs, vol. 47, nos. 2–3 (Chicago: University of Chicago Press, 1982). See also Jacqueline Royce, Irving Lazar, and Richard Darlington, "Minority Families, Early Education, and Later Life Chances," *American Journal of Orthopsychiatry* 53, no. 4 (October 1983): these authors conclude that evaluations of high-quality early-education programs in the 1960s and 1970s reveal "direct, positive effects on standardized tests, school competence, attitudes toward achievement, high school completion, and occupational attitudes" (p. 706).

PAGE

254   "Wider community ties": for an interesting discussion of the complexities
      of the idea of "community" in crime control, see Fred DuBow and David
      Emmons, "The Community Hypothesis," in *Reactions to Crime*, ed. Dan-
      iel A. Lewis (Beverly Hills: Sage Publications, 1981).

254   "Big Three": Judith Feins, *Partnerships for Neighborhood Crime Prevention*
      (Washington, D.C.: U.S. National Institute of Justice, January 1983), p.
      16.

255   "Solid evidence": on the research literature on neighborhood watch and
      other community crime-prevention programs, see Paul J. Lavrakis, "Citi-
      zen Self-Help and Neighborhood Crime Prevention Policy," in Curtis,
      American Violence and Public Policy; Feins, *Partnerships for Neighborhood
      Crime Prevention*, especially pp. 55–57; and Anne Newton, "Prevention
      of Crime and Delinquency," *Criminal Justice Abstracts* 10, no. 2 (June
      1978). The evidence gap is illustrated in the National Institute of Justice
      report's discussion of the effects of neighborhood watch programs estab-
      lished in Detroit during the late 1970s. According to the report, "citywide,
      there was a 30 percent reduction" in "all major crimes against persons and
      property" from 1979 to 1981, which the report attributes to neighborhood
      watch and regards as a major aspect of the "city's sense of rebirth" (Feins,
      p. 6). The FBI's *Uniform Crime Reports*, however, show that index crimes
      went *up* in Detroit by a whopping 36 percent between 1979 and 1981;
      murder was up 17 percent and robbery 37 percent. If there was indeed a
      "sense of rebirth" in that beleaguered city in the late seventies and early
      eighties, it could hardly have been due to a declining crime rate (calculated
      from Federal Bureau of Investigation, *Uniform Crime Reports*, 1980, 1981,
      and 1983).

255   NIJ quotation; Feins, p. 17.

255   "Displacement": see Feins, pp. 55–57; and Thomas Gabor, "The Crime
      Displacement Hypothesis," *Crime and Delinquency* 27, no. 3 (July 1981).

256   "Environmental design": Lavrakis, "Citizen Self-Help"; and Sally Engle
      Merry, *Urban Danger: Life in a Neighborhood of Strangers* (Philadelphia:
      Temple University Press, 1981), chap. 8.

256 – 257   Chicago Area Project: Steven Schlossman et al., *Delinquency Pre-
      vention in South Chicago: A Fifty-Year Assessment of the Chicago Area Project*
      (Santa Monica, Calif.: Rand Corporation, 1984).

258   Dispute resolution: Elizabeth Vorenberg, *A State of the Art Survey of
      Dispute Resolution Programs Involving Juveniles* (Washington, D.C.:
      American Bar Association, 1982). For a critical view, see Feeley, *Courts on
      Trial*, pp. 110–111.

259   Shelter programs: a good overview of domestic violence programs is
      Albert R. Roberts, ed., *Battered Women and Their Families* (New York:
      Springer, 1984).

259 – 260   "Mediating structures": Robert Woodson, "Helping the Poor Help Themselves," *Policy Review*, Summer 1982; and *A Summons to Life: Mediating Structures and the Prevention of Youth Crime* (Boston: Ballinger, 1981).

260   House of Umoja: Woodson, "Helping the Poor Help Themselves"; and Lynn A. Curtis, "Neighborhood, Family, and Employment: Toward a New Public Policy Against Violence," in *American Violence and Public Policy*.

260 – 261   Reagan praise: Howell Raines, "Reagan Boosts Volunteers to Replace Program Cuts," New York *Times*, October 5, 1981.

261 – 262   AEI Conference: Robert Woodson, ed., *Youth Crime and Social Policy* (Washington, D.C.: American Enterprise Institute, 1981), pp. 113–128.

265   Job training in other countries: figures from Reich, *The Next American Frontier*, p. 220.

265 – 266   Greenberger study: Ellen Greenberger, "A Researcher in the Policy Arena: The Case of Child Labor," *American Psychologist*, January 1983, p. 108; see also Laurence D. Steinberg et al., "Effects of Working on Adolescent Development," *Developmental Psychology* 18, no. 3 (1982).

266   "Much research": for example, Paul Osterman, "Youth, Work, and Unemployment," *Challenge*, May–June, 1978.

267   "Community full employment": Gar Alperovitz and Jeff Faux, *Rebuilding America* (New York: Pantheon Books, 1984), chap. 8.

267   Attali quotation: Jacques Attali, "Towards Socialist Planning," in *Beyond Capitalist Planning*, ed. Stuart Holland (New York: St. Martin's Press, 1979).

269   "Concrete suggestions": see, for example, Alperovitz and Faux, *Rebuilding America*, especially chap. 15; and Michael Harrington, "A Case for Democratic Planning," in Howe, *Alternatives*, especially pp. 115–137.

270   Curtis quotation: Lynn A. Curtis, *A National Neighborhood Crime Prevention Policy for the Nineteen Eighties* (Washington, D.C.: Eisenhower Foundation, 1983), p. 5. See also Curtis, "Neighborhood, Family, and Employment," pp. 216–219.

272   Kuttner quotation: "Jobs," p. 33. On the principles of European welfare policies generally, see his *Economic Illusion*, chap. 6; and Norman Furniss and Timothy Tilton, *In Defense of the Welfare State* (Bloomington: Indiana University Press, 1977).

273   Wilson quotation: "Thinking About Crime" (1983), p. 80.

NOTES

PAGE

273   Civil Works Administration: see Bonnie Schwartz, *The Civil Works Administration, 1933–34* (Princeton, N.J.: Princeton University Press, 1984).

273   Lekachman quotation: *Greed Is Not Enough*, p. 202.

274   Poll results: Field Institute and National Council on Crime and Delinquency Research Center, "Attitudes of Californians Toward Crime, Prison and Jail Construction, Bail System and Criminal Justice Agency Performance" (San Francisco: NCCD, 1981); New York *Times*, January 27, 1985; and *Public Opinion*, August–September 1981, p. 34.

275   Galbraith quotation: *The New Industrial State* (Boston: Houghton Mifflin Co., 1967), p. 52.

277   Bonger quotation: Willem Bonger, *Criminality and Economic Conditions*, ed. Austin T. Turk (Bloomington: Indiana University Press, 1969), p. 41.

277   Tawney quotation: R. H. Tawney, *The Acquisitive Society* (New York: Harcourt, Brace & World, 1948), p. 5. The point is not lost on serious conservatives today: "A society that seeks a steady expansion of desires and a simultaneous satisfaction of them may be, at least in the short run, a great place for advertising account executives and manufacturers of small appliances. But over time, it must be unstable domestically and vulnerable internationally." George Will, *Statecraft as Soulcraft: What Government Does* (New York: Simon & Schuster, 1984), p. 137.

INDEX

Abrahamse, Allan, 71
adolescent parents, 248
Aid to Families of Dependent
    Children (AFDC), 126, 170–71
Alperovitz, Gar, 267, 269
American Enterprise Institute, 259,
    261
Anderson, Tavs Folmer, 151
Andrews, Susan Ring, 251
Anne Arundel County, Md., 258
anthropology, cultural, 36
anticrime strategy, 225–26, 228–29
    community crime-prevention
        programs, 254–63, 276
    criminal-justice system, revision
        of, 229–34, 275
    delinquency prevention, 256–58
    early-education programs, 252–54
    employment policy, 263–75, 276
    family-assistance programs, 244–52,
        275
    rehabilitation, 235–44, 275
antisocial personality syndrome,
    213–14
    ability to conform, 218–19
    environmental circumstances,
        216–17
    fallacies of, 217–18
    immediate situation, irrelevance
        of, 215–16
    personality deficiencies, 214–15
    racism of, 218–19
apprehension of criminals, 68–69,
    87–88, 231–32
Archer, Dane, 167

Attali, Jacques, 267
Australia, 5, 59
Austria, 119

Ball, John C., 70
Baltimore, 70
Bandura, Albert, 201
Bayley, David, 46, 47
Becker, Gary, 26
Bell, Daniel, 49
Berecochea, John, 71
Berger, Peter, 261
Berk, Richard, 126, 127, 231
Berk, Sarah Fenstermaker, 231
Bethe, Hans, 94
Biles, David, 59
Birmingham, Ala., 251
blacks
    incarceration of, 155
    personal crimes by, 154
    subculture of violence, 163–65
    violent crimes by, 147, 148, 153–54
    See also racial aspects of crime
Blau, Judith and Peter, 149, 162
Blumstein, Alfred, 86–87, 155
Bonger, Willem, 277
Boston, 63
Bowker, Lee, 58–59
Braithwaite, John, 157, 169
Braithwaite, Valerie, 169
Brazil, 176, 278
Brenner, M. Harvey, 107–8
Bronfenbrenner, Urie, 210
Bruck, David, 41
Burt, Cyril, 183, 184

California, 5, 31, 66–67
California Youth Authority (CYA), 86, 95–97, 148–49, 193
Canada, 5
CAP. See Chicago Area Project
Carlson, Kenneth, 62, 63
Castellano, Thomas, 110, 159
CFRP. See Child and Family Resource Programs
Chaiken, Jan and Marcia, 71
Chess, Stella, 196, 213, 220
Chicago Area Project (CAP), 256–57
"Chicago school," 26, 59
child abuse, 199, 202–7, 209–10, 247, 248
Child and Family Resource Programs (CFRP), 249–50
child care outside the home, 189, 191, 192, 246, 270
child-rearing
  assistance programs for, 246–51
  behavior problems and, 200–2
  comparative studies, 41–42, 199–200
  conservative viewpoint, 41–42, 197–99
  corporal punishment, 42, 207–8
  courts, influence of, 42–43
  income and, 200
  "metaphysic of the age," 41–42
  moral decline and, 37–38, 41–42
  nonemployment and, 271–72
  nurturant orientation, 200, 201
  social situation and, 198n
  See also child abuse
Chiricos, Theodore, 56
Civilian Conservation Corps (CCC), 127–28
Clinard, Marshall, 177
Cloward, Richard, 161
Coates, Robert, 240–41, 244
Cohen, Lawrence, 109
Columbus, Ohio, 78, 87
Comer, James P., 226
Committee for Investigating the Causes of the Alarming Increase in Juvenile Delinquency in the Metropolis (1816), 182

community, influence of, 56–58, 174–75
community crime-prevention programs, 276
  block watches, 254–55
  conservative viewpoint, 262–63
  delinquency prevention, 256–58
  dispute resolution, 258–59
  self-help nature of, 255–56
  shelters for victims of family violence, 258–59
  voluntarism and, 259–62
  youth-based organizations, 259–62
community-service sentencing, 233–34
comparable worth, 266–67
Compton, Calif., 144, 145
Conrad, John, 78, 79, 81, 87, 88
conservative criminology, 10–12
  causes of crime, 22–23
  child abuse, 207
  child-rearing, 41–42, 197–99
  community crime-prevention programs, 262–63
  comparative crime rates, 24–25
  control, emphasis of, 45–47
  courts, influence of, 42–43
  cultural perspective on crime, 47–49, 163–65
  economic model of crime, 26–28, 82
  egalitarianism, 166–71
  employment policy, 273
  family-assistance programs, 245
  family life and crime, 183, 184–90, 210–211
  family planning, 247–48
  genetic factors of crime, 40n, 211–12, 220–21
  human nature and crime, 23–24, 25, 187
  incarceration, 29–32, 34, 59–60
  inequality and crime, 145–46, 151–53, 156, 157
  job programs, 130–31
  moral decline, 35–40
  punishment as deterrent, 26–28
  school discipline, 42–45
  single-parent families, 192–93
  unemployment, causes of, 121–23

unemployment and crime, 106, 108, 120–21, 140–41
voluntarism, 259–62
women, violence against, 208
constitutional factors. *See* genetic factors of crime
conviction rates, 65–67
Cook, Susan, 203
corporal punishment, 42, 199, 207–8
Cox, Louis A., 72–75, 78, 79, 194, 238, 240
Crime and Human Nature (Wilson and Herrnstein), 40*n*, 210*n*
crime fantasies, 115
criminal-justice system
  child-rearing and, 42–43
  class bias in, 156, 159
  deterrence and, 60–61
  family violence and, 230–31
  mandatory sentences, 62, 63
  mid-range sanctions, 233–34
  policing innovations, 231–33
  racial bias in, 152–53, 154–55
  revision of, 229–34, 275
  single-parent families, bias re, 194
  targeting of resources, 229–30
criminal research, 18
Cuba, 24
Cultural Contradictions of Capitalism (Bell), 49
cultural perspective on crime, 47–49
  absolute deprivation, 161
  conservative viewpoint, 47–49, 163–65
  hard version, 163–65
  liberal viewpoint, 47–48
  relative deprivation, 161, 162
  soft version, 160–62, 165
culture of poverty, 132
Curtis, Lynn, 270
CYA. *See* California Youth Authority

Daniel, Jessica, 208
Danziger, Sandra, 137
Davies, Christie, 166
death penalty, 41
death rates, 153–54
deFronzo, James, 126, 170–71

delinquency, 13–14
  backgrounds common to, 97
  child abuse and, 202–6
  class differences and, 158
  disadvantaged position and, 147
  distribution of criminal behavior, 84–86
  early identification of, 97
  economic inequality and, 150–51, 158
  employment as cause of, 187–88
  family size and, 188–89
  family violence and, 195–96, 203–4, 205–6
  gang violence, 55
  genetic factors of, 211–19
  historical studies re, 182–83
  incarceration, criminal activity fostered by, 80
  job programs and, 138–39
  prediction of, 95–97
  prevention programs, 72–75, 256–58
  punishment and, 77–79, 198–202
  racial aspects of, 148
  recidivism and, 73–74, 147
  school violence, 44–45
  self-report studies re, 156–59
  single-parent families and, 193–97
  subculture values of, 161–62
  underemployment and, 115–16
  unemployment and, 109, 110–11
  working mothers and, 189–92
Delinquency and Opportunity (Cloward and Ohlin), 161
Denmark, 6, 24, 29, 150–51, 167, 252
Denton, Jeremiah, 186
deterrence
  apprehension, problems re, 68–69
  conviction rates and, 65–67
  criminal-justice system and, 60–61
  delinquency and, 72–75, 77–79
  of drunken driving, 68
  formal punishment as, 57
  general, 53, 56–69
  incarceration, opposite effects of, 75–81
  incarceration as, 58–61, 69–72
  informal sanctions, 56–58
  mandatory sentences, effect of, 61–65

research re, 56
sentence length, effect of, 71–72
special, 53, 69–81
deterrence doctrine, 53, 55–56
Detroit, 7, 64
Dickinson, Katherine, 137
Dinitz, Simon, 78, 79, 81, 87
District of Columbia, 145, 237
drug addicts, 70, 136–37
drug dealing, 114
drug laws, 61–63
drunken driving, 68

early-education programs, 252–54
East St. Louis, Ill., 7, 144, 145
economic inequality and crime,
    149–50
  bias in accounting for
    relationship, 155–56
  comparative studies, 167–68
  delinquency and, 150–51, 158
  homicide rates, 169
  prosperity as cause of crime,
    172–78
  self-report studies re, 156–59
  social consequences of, 160
economic model of crime, 26–28,
    82
Ehrenreich, Barbara, 246
Eisenhower Foundation for the
    Prevention of Violence, 269–70
Ekland-Olson, Sheldon, 57
Elder, Glen, 128
Elliot, Delbert, 158
Employment Act of 1946, 273
employment as cause of crime,
    187–88
employment policy, 276
  community full employment, 267
  comparable worth, 266–67
  conservative viewpoint, 273
  Depression-era, 127–29
  local economic development and,
    269–71
  nonemployment, support of,
    271–72
  opposition to, 273
  planning mechanisms, 269
  private economy and, 267–69
  public opinion re, 274
  quality of work, 265–66, 270–71

for rural poor, 118
successes of, 119
U.S. lack of, effects of, 119–20
work roles for youths, 266
See also job programs
England, 6, 41, 119, 130
  child-rearing in, 198n
  delinquency in, 80, 182–83, 188,
    190–91, 195
  incarceration rates, 29, 30, 31, 59
  inequality and crime, 150
environmental design, 256
Eron, Leonard, 212, 213
exclusionary rule, 66–67

family-assistance programs, 275
  adolescent parents, 248
  child-rearing assistance, 246–51
  conservative viewpoint, 245
  family planning, 247–48
  governmental involvement,
    necessity of, 245–46
  liberal viewpoint, 244–45
  working mothers, assistance for,
    246–47
family life and crime
  conservative viewpoint, 183,
    184–90, 210–11
  decline of the family, 186–87
  early intervention, effectiveness of,
    219–20
  failure of incarceration, as
    explanation for, 185–86
  fallacy of autonomy, 185, 214
  fallacy of intractability, 185, 211
  family discord, 195–96
  family size, 188–89
  family violence, 203–4, 205–6,
    230–31, 258–59
  government actions re, 210–11
  liberal viewpoint, 183–84
  parental authority, 187–88
  women, violence against, 208
  working mothers, 189–92, 246–47
  youth employment, 187–88
  See also child-rearing; genetic
    factors of crime; single-parent
    families
family planning, 247–48
Family Relationships and Delinquent
    Behavior (Nye), 194

family-support programs, 248–52
family violence, 203–4, 205–6, 230–31
  shelters for victims of, 258–59
Fattah, David, 261
Fattah, Falaka, 260–61
Faux, Jeff, 267, 269
Federation of New York Judges,
  11
Felson, Marcus, 109
female-headed families. *See*
  single-parent families
Figlio, Robert, 77
Finland, 5, 42
Flint, Mich., 232
France, 29, 130, 168
Freudian psychology, 36
full-employment policy. *See*
  employment policy

Galbraith, John Kenneth, 275
Garbarino, James, 202
Gendreau, Paul, 238, 239
General Accounting Office, U.S., 66
genetic factors of crime
  ability to conform, 218–19
  antisocial personality syndrome,
    213–19
  childhood-aggression–criminality
    link, 212–13
  conservative viewpoint, 40n,
    211–12, 220–21
  racist implications of, 212, 218–19
Germany, Federal Republic of
  (West Germany), 5, 28, 119, 130,
    168, 191, 265
Georgia, 126, 234
Gibbs, Jack P., 56
Gilder, George, 169, 192
Gillespie, Robert, 108
Glaser, Daniel, 109
Glueck, Sheldon and Eleanor,
    183, 184, 189, 190, 197, 217,
    245
Gore, Susan, 129
Graddy, Elizabeth, 86–87
Great Britain. *See* England
Great Depression, 38, 123–26, 127–29,
    257
Great Society programs, 12, 15, 248
Green, Arthur H., 204
Greenberger, Ellen, 265

Greenwood, Peter, 71, 92
Guinses, V. G., 261
gun-control laws, 63, 234n–235n
gun-related felony laws, 63–65
Gurr, Ted Robert, 174

Hakluyt, Richard, 104
Hampton, Robert, 208
Hartjen, Clayton, 175
Head Start, 249, 252
Health and Human Services, U.S.
    Department of, 249–50
Herrnstein, Richard, 40n
Hetherington, E. Mavis, 196–97
Heuman, Milton, 64
Highland Park, Ill., 144, 145
Highland Park, Mich., 144, 145
High-rate offenders, 70–71
    prediction of, 91–93, 105
Hindelang, Michael, 154
Hirschi, Travis, 41, 156, 157, 187–88,
    189, 190, 192, 199, 200, 207, 210
Hispanics, violent crimes by, 148
Holt, John, 43
homicide, 5, 6, 7, 25, 119, 124, 126, 144,
    153–54, 169
Houston, 34, 170
Huizinga, David, 158
human ecology, 225
human nature as cause of crime,
    23–24, 25, 187
Humphrey-Hawkins Full
    Employment and Balanced
    Growth Act, 273

Illinois, 7
immediate gratification, ethos of,
    48–49
imprisonment. *See* incarceration
incapacitation
    cost-benefit ratio, 99–100
    costs of, 88–90
    crime prevention through, 81–82
    distribution of criminal behavior,
      83–87
    ineffectiveness of, 87–88
    replacement effect of, 82–83
    social consequences of, 91
    See also selective incapacitation
incarceration
    of blacks, 155

comparative rates, 28–29
conservative viewpoint, 29–32, 34, 59–60
costs of, 88–90
crime prevention through, 52
crime rate and, 11, 32–34, 58–60
criminal activity during, 81
criminal activity fostered by, 77–81
as deterrent, 58–61, 69–72
high-rate offenders and, 70–71
inmate subcultures, 75–76
liberal viewpoint, 53, 55, 76–77
limitations of, 100
negative effects on prisoners, 75–77
prison overcrowding, 62
recidivism, 70–72
for robbery, 30–31
sentence length, 71–72
U.S. rates of, 7, 28–29, 30, 32
See also deterrence; incapacitation
incidence of crime, 86
India, 175
inequality and crime, 144–45
ascribed inequalities, 162
class v. race inequalities, 149–50
comparative studies, 150–51
conservative viewpoint, 145–46, 151–53, 156, 157
efforts to combat, 166–71
implications of, 178–79
liberal viewpoint, 156, 157, 159
socioeconomic status, 146–49
See also cultural perspective on crime; economic inequality and crime; racial aspects of crime
inmates
income prior to arrest, 145
unemployment prior to arrest, 105
Italy, 119

Jaman, Dorothy, 71
Japan, 5, 119, 130, 168, 265
crime rate, 24, 45–46, 129
incarceration rate, 28, 31
supportive society of, 46–47, 177
Jensen, Arthur, 218, 249
Job Corps, 134–35, 139, 264
job programs
community-based, 133
conservative viewpoint, 130–31

delinquency, effect on, 138–39
drug addicts, effect on, 136–37
exit from program, 139–40
ex-offenders, effect on, 138–39
failures of, 134
intensive programs, 134–35
job creation, 131, 132, 264
pretrial diversion projects, 133–34
in prisons, 132–33
resources of, 133
skill and attitude improvement, 131–32, 264
supported-work programs, 135–37, 139
welfare mothers, effect on, 137–38
work satisfaction, provision of, 137–38
Johnstone, John, 194

Kahn, Alfred, 245
Kamerman, Sheila, 192, 246
Kozol, Jonathan, 43
Krohn, Marvin, 119
Kulka, Richard A., 45
Kuttner, Robert, 272

Land, Kenneth, 109
Lane, Roger, 174
Lekachman, Robert, 273
Lenihan, Kenneth, 126
Lewis, Dorothy, 203–4, 205
liberal criminology, 12–16
cultural perspective on crime, 47–48
deterrence doctrine, 55–56
early-education programs, 252
family-assistance programs, 244–45
family life and crime, 183–84
incarceration, 53, 55, 76–77
inequality and crime, 156, 157, 159
limitations of, 13–14, 227–28, 236
rehabilitation, 16, 236
selective incapacitation, 99
Loftin, Colin, 64, 65
Logan, Charles, 56
Lombroso, Cesare, 120–21
London, 182, 195
Loseke, Donilee, 231
Lyman School, 241–43
Lynd, Robert and Helen, 125

McCord, Joan, 196, 201, 206
McCord, William, 241
McDermott, Joan, 45
McDowell, David, 64
McKay, Henry, 193, 194
mandatory sentences
  courts, effect on, 62, 63
  drug laws, 61–63
  gun-control laws, 63
  gun-related felony laws, 63–65
Manhattan Court Employment
  Project, 133–34
Manpower Demonstration Research
  Corporation (MDRC), 136–37,
  138–39, 248
Martinson, Robert, 237, 238, 239
Massachusetts, 63, 196, 236, 240–41
MDRC. *See* Manpower
  Development Research
  Corporation
Mead, Margaret, 36
mediating structures, 259–60, 262
Merry, Sally Engle, 256
Merton, Robert K., 161
Messner, Stephen, 169, 174
Mexico, 176, 278
Michigan, 7, 63–65
Middletown (Lynd), 125
Mill, James, 182
Milwaukee, 170
minimum wage, 120–21
Minneapolis, 231
Monahan, John, 99
moral aspects of crime, 19
moral decline, 35–36
  beginnings of, 36
  child-rearing and, 37–38, 41–42
  comparative studies, 40–41
  elitist nature of, 38–40
Moynihan, Daniel Patrick, 119
Muenchow, Susan, 192
Mullen, Joan, 90
Muncie, Ind., 125
murder. *See* homicide
Murphy, Francis T., Jr., 8, 11–12
Murray, Charles A., 72–75, 78, 79,
  194, 238, 240
Myers, Samuel, 71
Myrdal, Alva, 245
Myrdal, Gunnar, 118

National Academy of Sciences, 56,
  82, 191, 238, 239
National Commission on Law
  Observance and Enforcement
  (1931), 107
National Commission on the Causes
  and Prevention of Violence
  (1969), 7–8, 14, 71
National Council on Crime and
  Delinquency, 274
National Institute of Justice (NIJ),
  66, 90, 230, 254
National Institute of Mental Health
  (NIMH), 252
Neoconservatives (Steinfels), 48
Netherlands, 6, 28, 29, 41, 167,
  168
Newark, N.J., 232
Newberger, Carolyn, 202
Newberger, Eli, 208
Newsweek, 10
New York City, 67, 233–34
New York State, 234
  incarceration policies, 32–34
  mandatory sentencing in, 61–63
New York Times, 232, 260, 274
NIJ. *See* National Institute of
  Justice
nonemployment, 271–72
nonstranger crimes, 230, 255
Norway, 6, 24, 28, 119, 122
Nye, F. Ivan, 194, 195

Oakland, Calif., 7, 116
Oak Lawn, Ill., 144–45
Ohlin, Lloyd, 161
Orsagh, Thomas, 108

Pandiani, John A., 124, 127–28
Parent-Child Development Centers
  (PCDC), 250–51
parole, 33
Paternoster, Raymond, 56
pathology, social and personal, 227,
  228, 236
Patterson, James T., 131
PCDC. *See* Parent-Child
  Development Centers
Pearce, Diana, 196
Petersilia, Joan, 154

Philadelphia, 77–78, 84–85, 146–48, 260
Philippines, 176, 278
Phillips, Llad, 110–11
Piven, Frances Fox, 246
police
    apprehensions by, 69, 231–32
    armories for, 8
    foot patrols, 232
    young people involved with, 232–33
political aspects of crime, 19
political economy, 227–28
Polk, Kenneth, 194
prediction of criminality. See selective incapacitation
President's Commission on Crime in the District of Columbia (1966), 145, 237
President's Commission on Law Enforcement and the Administration of Justice (1967), 15, 55, 76
prevalence of crime, 86
preventive conflict reduction, 258–59
prisons
    costs of, 89
    job programs in, 132–33
    overcrowding in, 62
probation, intensive, 234
Project Redirection, 248
prosperity and crime, 172–78
public response to crime, 4–5
punishment, 9–10
    administration of, 54
    as deterrent, 26–28, 53
    effectiveness of, 54
    formal, 54–55, 57
    See also deterrence; incapacitation; incarceration

racial aspects of crime, 39–40, 147–50, 153–55, 163–65, 212, 218–19
Racine, Wis., 57, 77, 84, 212
Raines, Howell, 260
Rand Corporation, 66, 68, 70, 92–94, 105, 154, 193, 234, 238
rape, 5, 6, 7, 126
Rauma, David, 126
Reagan, Ronald, 23, 44, 260–61

Reagan administration, 10, 48–49, 66
recidivism, 70–72
    ethnic background and, 243
    in juvenile delinquents, 73–74, 147
rehabilitation, 14, 235–36, 275
    community conditions and, 241–44
    community resources and, 240–41
    failures of, 237–39
    ideological attacks on, 236, 237–38
    liberal viewpoint, 16, 236
    past programs, 236–37
    residential camps, 74, 240
    successes of, 238, 239–41
    therapeutic integrity of, 239
    therapeutic v. punitive programs, 241–44
Reich, Robert B., 168
repeat offenders, 87
Ricardo, David, 182
Rice, Kent, 109
robbery, 5, 6, 25, 30–31, 60, 93
Robins, Lee, 211, 213–19
Roosevelt, Franklin D., 127
Ross, Bob, 238, 239
Rossi, Peter, 126
Rubinstein, Jonathan, 233
Rutter, Michael, 45

Sacramento, Calif., 86
Saltzman, Linda, 56
Sampson, Robert, 110, 159
Sanchez, Jose, 241
San Francisco, 258
Santa Ana, Calif., 232
Santa Barbara, Calif. 231
Scheinfeld, Daniel, 201–2
Schlossman, Steven, 256, 257
school discipline, 42–45, 199
school violence, 44–45
secondary labor market, 113
selective incapacitation, 91–93
    criteria for selection, 94
    early identification, 95–97
    liberal viewpoint, 99
    limitations of, 93–95
    politics of, 98–99
self-expression, ethos of, 37–38
self-report studies, 156–59
Sellin, Thorsten, 77, 107

Shannon, Lyle, 57, 77, 84, 212
Shaw, Clifford, 193, 194, 256
Sherman, Lawrence, 231
Short, James F., 125
single-parent families
  conservative viewpoint, 192–93
  criminal-justice system bias re, 194
  delinquency and, 193–97
  parental-absence factor, 195
  support systems for, 196–97
Smith, Douglas, 156
Smith, Robert J., 46
"Social Aspects of the Business
  Cycle" (Thomas), 107
Social Darwinism, 274, 277
social policies and crime, 18–19
social service programs. See welfare
South Carolina, 32
Specter, Arlen, 245
Steinberg, Lawrence, 265
Steinfels, Peter, 48
"stranger" crimes, 255
Strasburg, Paul, 148
subculture of violence, 163–65
subemployment, 118
suppression effect, 73–74
Supreme Court, U.S., 42, 43, 199
Sweden, 6, 28, 119, 130, 168, 265
  corporal punishment, outlawing
    of, 42, 199
  drunken-driving laws, 68
  family-assistance programs,
    246–47, 272
  wage policies, 122
  working mothers in, 191–92
Switzerland, 6, 24, 177

Taggart, Robert, 132
Task Force on Violent Crime
  (Reagan administration), 10, 48
Tawney, R. H., 19, 277
Texas, 34, 93, 126, 170, 234
Thinking About Crime (Wilson), 22,
  23, 24, 35, 184, 210
Third World countries, 6, 173,
  174–76
Thomas, Alexander, 220
Thomas, Dorothy S., 107
Thousand Oaks, Calif., 144
time-series analysis, 58

Titmuss, Richard, 171
Tittle, Charles, 56, 57, 156
Toby, Jackson, 43–44, 45
Tullock, Gordon, 26

UDIS. See Unified Delinquency
  Intervention Services
Umoja, House of, 260–61
underemployment and crime, 112–13,
  116–17
  delinquency, 115–16
  illicit work, 116
  nonviolent crime, 113–15
  violent crime, 115–16
unemployment, 104
  conservative viewpoint, 121–23
  of inmates, 105
  jobless and not in search of work,
    110–11
  long-term, 138
  measurement of, 109–10
  minimum wage and, 120–21
  welfare and, 122–23
unemployment and crime
  compound interest effect, 107–8
  conservative viewpoint, 106, 108,
    120–21, 140–41
  contradictory effects, 108–9
  delinquency, 109, 110–11
  economic fluctuations, effects of,
    106–7
  homicide, 119
  jobless and not in search of work,
    110–11
  local unemployment, 110
  public policies re, 118–30
Unified Delinquency Intervention
  Services (UDIS), 72–75, 79, 194,
    238, 240
United States
  child abuse in, 209–10
  comparative crime rates, 5–7, 24–25
  consumer society of, 225
  economic inequality in, 167–68
  incarceration rates, 7, 28–29, 30,
    32
  pro-crime policies of, 226–27
  upward trend of crime, 6–7
  welfare in, 168–71
URSA Institute, 116

van den Haag, Ernest, 26, 27, 82, 145
van Dine, Stephen, 87, 88
velocity of criminal career, 78
Vera Institute of Justice, 27, 67, 68,
    113–15, 120, 133–34, 135–36, 148,
    233
"vicimization" studies, 6, 154, 159
Villemez, Wayne, 156
voluntarism, 259–62
voluntary cessation of crime, 57
Votey, Harold, 110–11

Wadsworth, Michael, 150, 188, 190,
    194
Waldo, Gordon, 56
Walinsky, Adam, 233
Wall Street Journal, 28
Walters, Richard, 201
Wealth and Poverty (Gilder), 192
Weinraub, Marsha, 197
welfare
    comparative studies, 168–69
    crime, effect on, 124–27, 129–30,
        169–71
    for ex-offenders, 126–27
    unemployment caused by, 122–23
    See also family-assistance programs
West, Donald, 80, 150, 151, 188, 190,
    195, 196, 201, 230, 238
West Germany. See Germany,
    Federal Republic of
"What Are the Courts Doing to
    Our Children?" (Wynne), 42–43
Wildcat Service Corporation, 135–36
Wilson, Harriet, 198n
Wilson, James Q., 232
    causes of crime, 22–23
    comparative crime rates, 24
    Crime and Human Nature, 40n,
        210n
    employment policy, 273
    family life and crime, 184–85, 200,
        210

genetic causes of crime, 40n
incarceration, importance of,
    29–30
inequality and crime, 145
job programs, 131
moral decline, 35–36, 37–38, 39
Thinking About Crime, 22, 23, 24,
    35, 184, 210
unemployment and crime, 106, 140
Wiltwyck School, 241–44
Winslow, Emma, 107
Wisconson, 7, 170
Witte, Ann Dryden, 108, 112
Wolf, Barbara M., 197
Wolfgang, Marvin, 77, 84–85, 146–48,
    245
Wolpin, Kenneth I., 30, 31
women
    violence against, 208
    See also single-parent families;
        working mothers
Woodson, Robert, 260, 261–62
work
    as bond to society, 263–64
    character-shaping qualities, 112
    criminality and, 114–15
    illicit, 116
    See also employment policy; job
        programs
working mothers, 189–92, 246–47
work satisfaction, 137–38, 265–66,
    270–71
Wright, Carroll D., 104, 112–13, 120
Wynne, Edward A., 42–43, 199

youth crime. See delinquency
youth culture, 38–39
youth employment, 187–88
youth population, 9
Ypsilanti, Mich., 253

Zigler, Edward, 192
Zimring, Franklin, 83

Elliott Currie is a visiting scholar at the Center for the Study of Law and Society at the University of California, Berkeley, and has taught criminology and sociology both at Berkeley and at Yale University. Currie has also served as a consultant to the California Governor's Task Force on Civil Rights and to the National Advisory Council on Economic Opportunity, and as a staff member of the National Commission on Causes and Prevention of Violence. His publications include two books—*Crisis in American Institutions* and *America's Problems*, both with Jerome Skolnick—and numerous articles and reports on poverty, welfare, umemployment, and crime.